TRANSATLANTIC WOMEN'S LITERATURE

EDINBURGH STUDIES IN TRANSATLANTIC LITERATURES
Series Editors: Susan Manning and Andrew Taylor

With the end of the Cold War and the burgeoning of a global culture, the premises upon which Area Studies were based have come into question. Starting from the assumption that the study of American literatures can no longer operate on a nation-based or exceptionalist paradigm, the books in this new series work within a comparative framework to interrogate place-based identities and monocular visions. The authors attempt instead to develop new paradigms for literary criticism in historical and contemporary contexts of exchange, circulation, and transformation. Edinburgh Studies in Transatlantic Literatures seeks uniquely to further the critical, theoretical and ideational work of the developing field of transatlantic literary studies.

Titles in the series include:

TRANSATLANTIC WOMEN'S LITERATURE

◆ ◆ ◆

HEIDI SLETTEDAHL MACPHERSON

EDINBURGH UNIVERSITY PRESS

For Allan

© Heidi Slettedahl Macpherson, 2008

Edinburgh University Press Ltd
22 George Square, Edinburgh

Typeset in 11/13 Sabon
by Servis Filmsetting Ltd, Stockport, Cheshire, and
printed and bound in Great Britain by
Biddles Ltd, King's Lynn, Norfolk

A CIP record for this book is available from the British Library

ISBN 978 0 7486 2445 4 (hardback)

The right of Heidi Slettedahl Macpherson
to be identified as author of this work
has been asserted in accordance with
the Copyright, Designs and Patents Act 1988.

CONTENTS

ACKNOWLEDGEMENTS

This project developed out of an early teaching interest in study abroad opportunities and transatlantic literature, which was bolstered by my participation in the Maastricht Center for Transatlantic Studies as a member of the Board of Directors from 1997 to 2007 for the University of Central Lancashire. Fellow directors have offered me a great deal of creative and academic support, and I particularly want to thank Terry Rodenberg, Neil Wynn and Tim Schorn for their friendship, good humour and annual trips to the Bombardon in Maastricht.

I have benefited from presenting my work-in-progress in the following places: the Tourism and Histories Conference, at the University of Central Lancashire (2003); the University of Lodz, Poland (2004) on a British Council funded trip; the Americanisation and the Teaching of American Studies (AMATAS) Conference at the University of the West of England (2004); the London Conference for Canadian Studies (2005); the Maastricht Center for Transatlantic Studies biennial conferences (2002, 2004, 2006); the Transatlantic Studies Association Conference (2002); the British Association for American Studies Conferences (2006, 2007); the American Literature Association Conference (2007); and the STAR seminar in Edinburgh (2007). Thanks are extended to all of the organisers for these events as well as the British Academy for funding my travel to the ALA conference in Boston. Thanks are also extended to my former institution, the University of Central Lancashire, which offered me a sabbatical to help complete this book, to Andrew Taylor and Susan Manning for first commissioning and then editing the book, and to Nicola Wood for her sympathetic and careful copy-editing of it.

Aspects of this book have been developed from previous publications, including articles in *Literature Compass, Ariel: A Review of International English Literature* and *Prospects*; and book chapters in *Issues in Americanisation*, edited by Neil Campbell, Jude Davies and George McKay (EUP, 2004), and *Gender, Genre and Identity in Women's Travel Writing*, edited by Kristi Siegel (Peter Lang, 2004).

Thanks go to my frequent writing partner, Will Kaufman, who has co-edited three major projects on Transatlantic Studies with me as well as a number of articles. His advice, guidance and generous support whilst I was at Central Lancashire were second to none, and his willingness to read drafts of my work – often at short notice – has not gone unnoticed. Our many discussions over what Transatlantic Studies actually *is* inform this work at many levels (with any errors or omissions remaining my own).

For encouragement and support, I thank my good friends in BAAS, particularly Janet Beer, Susan Castillo, Jude Davies, Martin Halliwell, Catherine Morley, Carol Smith, Helen Taylor and Jenel Virden; my former colleagues at Central Lancashire, particularly David Bagley, Vikki Cook, John Joughin, Daniel Lamont, Alan Rice, Theresa Saxon and Janice Wardle; and my current colleagues at De Montfort University, particularly David Alder, whose friendship and humour have made my transition between universities so much easier than it could have been, and Rachael Walters, whose invaluable assistance has ensured that I have the time and space to write.

Finally, thanks go to my family, especially Allan Macpherson, for whom I made that second, and lasting, transatlantic move.

INTRODUCTION: 'NO REGION FOR TOURISTS AND WOMEN'

As a woman I have no country. As a woman I want no country.

Virginia Woolf, *Three Guineas* (1938)[1]

The feminizing of the land is both a *poetics* of ambivalence and a *politics* of violence.

Anne McClintock, *Imperial Leather* (1995)[2]

Taken out of context, Woolf's famous pronouncement seems to suggest an ahistorical misalliance between women and nations. It also suggests that a woman's desire is disassociated from the land of her birth (or her adoption). Yet at the same time, as the second epigraph conversely suggests, women and nation have been frequently conflated, from how desirable land is described (virginal), to the feminine pronoun 'she' used to describe a country, to words that evoke a familial connection (mother country). After all, as Anne McClintock argues, 'All nations depend upon powerful constructions of gender. Despite many nationalists' ideological investment in the idea of popular *unity*, nations have historically amounted to the sanctioned institutionalization of gender *difference*.'[3] Taken together, these contested viewpoints provide a starting point for discussions of transatlantic women's literature, since both reveal the impact that gender has upon the writing on/of nations.

Of course, Woolf was, in fact, protesting the way in which women were disenfranchised, rather than suggesting that women's desire didn't extend to the nation; if anything, she wished to extinguish a woman's unthinking patriotism. However, the frequency with which

Woolf's famous lines are quoted out of context suggests that her words have resonance beyond their historical moment. But what of other women writers? The twentieth century has seen a number of women's texts that engage with seeing nations from the outside, either explicitly, where writers comment on the ways in which nationality is constructed (particularly in travel books or memoirs), or implicitly, in texts where nations are seen through the actions of their inhabitants or their visitors. Of course, every travel writer implicitly or explicitly contrasts worlds. What is significant about the twentieth century, though, is the increasing freedom experienced by many (though not all) European and American women travellers, with fewer overt pressures to dress or act in particular ways;[4] such loosening of cultural constraints might lead to a suggestion that gender becomes less important for these women travellers and writers. Yet it appears that the opposite is true; gender remains a key concern throughout the twentieth century in relation to nationhood, nationality, identity and travel, as I will explore in the chapters that follow.

It is no coincidence that women's fictional narratives of discovery use and re-use the metaphors of travel against stasis. Consider the titles of well-known feminist novels: *Fear of Flying, Heading West, Anywhere But Here*. While women have been cast as the ones left behind in male narratives of adventure and quest, assuming the role of patient Penelopes awaiting their heroes' returns rather than questing themselves, they have leading roles in women's narratives of discovery, travel and escape.

It has become a cultural commonplace that women's journeys are circular, not linear; determined, like their lives, by seasons and cycles, not destinations or goals. Such a reconceptualisation of women's 'essential nature' can either be liberating or constricting, depending on motive. For example, some aspects of women's lives are revalued as a result of feminist interrogations of psychoanalytic or cultural structures, since the focus on a circular structure validates a form of journey which does not conform to the Oedipal Complex (a pathway which equates progress and maturation with linearity), but instead exists in a pre-Oedipal state, linked to the maternal and the feminine. At the same time, however, such essentialising *places* women as firmly as have other totalising narratives. As Mary Morris reflects, 'I find it revealing that the bindings in women's corsets were called *stays*. Someone who wore stays wouldn't be going very far.'[5] If women's clothing has historically acted as a metaphor for women's bounded behaviour, it is not surprising that, as Lindsey Tucker notes, 'to conceive of women and mobility in the same space has been difficult in historical as well as literary terms.'[6]

To fill this gap, *Transatlantic Women's Literature* examines culturally resonant literature that imagines 'views from both sides' and analyses the imaginary, 'in-between' space of the Atlantic. The transatlantic narrative, which necessarily explores unequal encounters between people (the contact zone extending beyond its colonial roots) and the explicit construction of national identities, is a fundamental part of twentieth- and twenty-first-century literature. Moreover, women's interventions into this Atlantic space are important in both historical and literary terms. In *Transatlantic Insurrections*, Paul Giles argues that 'to read national literatures in a transnational way is . . . to suggest the various forms of contingency that have entered into the formation of each naturalized inheritance.'[7] But contingency is not related just to national literatures; it relates, too, to literature in which gender is a key component. Thus, *Transatlantic Women's Literature* emphasises 'contingency' as much as radical rupture in its exploration of a variety of (primarily) twentieth-century women's transatlantic texts. In what follows, I will offer a considered exploration of the ways in which the space of the Atlantic and women's space work together in the construction of meaning in twentieth-century transatlantic texts. I will also explore how the paradigm of Transatlantic Studies is shifting, as it becomes a more established way of viewing literary studies.

Although the transatlantic has long been an implicit part of the exploration of literature and culture(s), it has only fairly recently become subject to sustained critical analysis in its own right, particularly since the rise of postcolonial theory as a critical paradigm. In 1987, Marcus Rediker published *Between the Devil and the Deep Blue Sea*, examining the role of eighteenth-century Atlantic seafarers and pirates in questions about nation-states. Six years later, Paul Gilroy published his now seminal (though controversial) text, *The Black Atlantic: Modernity and Double Consciousness*. In it he argues that scholars 'should take the Atlantic as one single, complex unit of analysis in their discussions of the modern world and use it to produce an explicitly transnational and intercultural perspective'.[8] Although there are obvious critiques of his work – Fionnghuala Sweeney has recently argued that 'there is arguably little difference in delineating an Atlantic rather than a national border, when the Atlantic only serves to reprivilege western discursive practice as a thing in itself'[9] – Gilroy's text has institutionalised the term 'Black Atlantic', and the significance of this new viewpoint cannot be underestimated. His emphasis on texts which 'operate at other levels than those marked by national boundaries'[10] implicitly suggests that to be marked by national identities is not to be confined by them.

Other notable texts include Joseph Roach's *Cities of the Dead* (1996) and his exploration of 'Circum-Atlantic Performance' in London and New Orleans; Peter Linebaugh and Marcus Rediker's *The Many Headed Hydra: Sailors, Slaves, Commoners, and the History of the Revolutionary Atlantic* (2000); and the various contributions made by Paul Giles to this area, including *Transatlantic Insurrections: British Culture and the Formation of American Literature, 1730–1860* (2001), *Virtual Americas: Transnational Fictions and the Transatlantic Imaginary* (2002), which also ranges widely, exploring the work of a variety of authors from Frederick Douglass to Thomas Pynchon, and *Atlantic Republic: The American Tradition in English Literature* (2006). Alongside these texts are other explorations of nationhood, which inform discussions of the transatlantic, including Benedict Anderson's oft-quoted *Imagined Communities* (1983), Edward Said's *Reflections on Exile and Other Literary and Cultural Essays* (2000), Salman Rushdie's *Imaginary Homelands: Essays and Criticism 1981–1991* (1992), Homi Bhabha's *The Location of Culture* (1994) and James Clifford's *Routes: Travel and Translation in the Late Twentieth Century* (1997), texts I will discuss further below, in relation to the contested terminology employed by critics of the transatlantic.

Feminist critics such as Inderpal Grewal and Caren Kaplan argue that critics must situate their explorations of travel within a post-colonial framework, suggesting, for example, that tourism cannot be divorced from the history of imperialism.[11] They have urged critics to think in transnational terms and to recall the links between gender, nation and travel. Anne McClintock has similarly registered the gaps and silences of theories of travel that disregard women, particularly in the tenth chapter of *Imperial Leather*, 'No Longer in a Future Heaven', where she offers a careful rendition of male critical failings. Sara Mills explores women's travel writing and suggests that 'most travel writers portray members of other nations through a conceptual and textual grid constituted by travel books,'[12] revealing how reading impacts upon writing (and vice versa). Indeed, Heather Henderson suggests that 'the literate traveler cannot escape the literature that preconditions his [*sic*] experience of travel.'[13] Such realisations bolster my contention, delineated throughout *Transatlantic Women's Literature*, that many transatlantic narratives reveal or concentrate on the process of *misreading*, both by their own narrators and by those around them, and this appears to be true whether the narrative is travel literature, memoir or indeed fiction. This sense of misreading operates on a generic level, a conceptual level, and at the level of plot, and will be explored further throughout this book.

Other texts that offer examples of the current interest in earlier transatlantic sojourns and their critical importance include the Longman anthology *Transatlantic Romanticism* (2006, ed. Newman et al.), which covers American, Canadian and British literature during the one-hundred-year period from 1767 to 1867 and Anna Brickhouse's *Transamerican Literary Relations and the Nineteenth-Century Public Sphere* (2004). Books such as *Transatlantic Modernism*, *Transatlantic Crossings* and *Transatlantic Manners* make explicit through their titles their interest in this oceanic space.[14] Moreover, new journals, including *Atlantic Studies*, *Comparative American Studies* and the *Journal of Transatlantic Studies*, offer evidence that however it is conceptualised (socially, politically, historically, aesthetically), the transatlantic has become an area of ongoing critical investigation.[15] As such, these texts lay the theoretical and historical groundwork for a work such as *Transatlantic Women's Literature*, which focuses primarily on literature from the last century.

Many texts in the larger field of Transatlantic Studies focus on colonial or early modern transatlantic encounters. Transatlantic *literary* criticism explores a number of canonical transatlantic literary relations, often focusing either on pre-twentieth-century literature or on 'modernist exiles'; what *Transatlantic Women's Literature* does is explore how the diffuse ideas circulating around such contested terms as 'the transatlantic' interact with feminist analysis of gender in later twentieth-century literature, both in the form of memoirs and travel literature and in the fictional texts that use transatlantic travel as an important motif.

Critical discussions of displacement, travel, movement and change are not new. Critics as varied as Homi Bhabha, James Clifford, Edward Said, Mary Louise Pratt, Graham Huggan, Inderpal Grewal, Caren Kaplan and others have debated the roles and definitions of the exile, the expatriate, the traveller and the tourist. They have contested each other's definitions and evoked a series of critical frameworks for exploring unhousement, rehousement, movement and change. This book, therefore, builds upon and reconfigures a number of ideas in circulation. My focus is on the intersection of gender and travel, however that is defined, in relation to Transatlantic Studies, a term that also calls for additional critical intervention.

The Transatlantic Paradigm

As an evolving critical position, Transatlantic Studies needs further definition, especially since, like any other evolving subject, its proponents sometimes make exaggerated claims in relation to the new knowledge that this viewpoint offers, or of reasons why this viewpoint and not another, similar one, is best. In one sense, Transatlantic Studies is similar to American Studies, in that it is formed around a sense of geographical borders. But also like American Studies, it is not wholly explained through (or away) by such boundaries. Sheila Hones and Julia Leyda suggest that a 'critical geography' of American Studies is required, and their words, I argue, are equally applicable to Transatlantic Studies:

> Because geography is as much performed as it is found or described, it also includes the routine discursive *production* of the what, the where, and the why. In other words, while American Studies conventionally takes its identity from large, apparently stable, commonsense geographical frameworks, those frameworks themselves are always at the same time actively being generated, reinscribed or reinvented through the very mundane disciplinary practices and discourses to which they appear to lend order.[16]

Similarly, though the Atlantic space is one that appears to be easily definable (if continually in flux), the practice of Transatlantic Studies cannot be sufficiently defined or perhaps more accurately, *fixed* by reference to this geography alone, since this space is also subject to constant reconstruction. In defining itself, Transatlantic Studies must engage with similar though not equivalent terms, such as 'circum-Atlanticism', 'globalisation', 'transnationalism' and 'worlding'.

Whilst Reingard Nethersole argues that prefixes like 'trans' represent the 'homogenizing tendencies' of globalisation,[17] I prefer the prefix 'trans' because of the way that it implies two related, though not equal ideas: 'beyond' and 'across'. Thus distance and connection are simultaneously suggested, and it is this dual force that merits sustained critical attention, particularly in relation to women's texts. 'Trans' also implies 'through' and therefore offers a richer mix of ideas than, for example, circum-Atlantic studies. It is not that such texts travel *around* the Atlantic space that interests me; rather, it is the ways in which transatlantic texts offer opportunities to view disparate places within the same critical framework that is of interest. This requires a recognition that such critical placing involves contestation and misapprehension. In this way, *Trans*atlantic Studies suggests the multiple connections between continents divided by oceanic spaces; such localities can be both linked and separate, an idea that becomes vital to any reading of women's transatlantic narratives, which routinely engage with space and reconstruction: of place and location (both figurative and real), of identity and of genre. Similarly, transatlanticity evokes a sense of connection which is not suspended above the continents connected by the Atlantic, but rather is dynamically enacted upon by both, whether that means Africa and North America, or Europe and South America, as well as the individual countries contained within these boundaries and borders.

Globalisation and transnationalism are terms that literary studies have adopted from the social sciences; they have particular resonance and application in economics, ethnography, anthropology and politics. Globalisation now almost inevitably ensures a negative viewpoint, since it is too closely linked in the critical imagination to Americanisation. As R. Radhakrishnan argues, 'globality shores up dominance and continues the anthropological fantasy of maintaining the other in intimate and yet exotic followership.'[18] In this way, globality (or globalisation) reflects a repackaging of Americanisation or Westernisation rather than an egalitarian process of exchange. Radhakrishnan suggests that globalisation is seen as 'a utopian resolution to the problems of the world: a utopia sans politics, ethics, or ideological content', but this utopia is one of a 'seductive immanence, of the here-and-now' which 'bracket[s] away once and for all questions of representation and ideological perspectivism'.[19] It is no surprise, then, that critics who want to explore global issues resist the term, with its connotations of either dominance or naïveté (if not, in some cases, both).

Unlike globalisation, transnationalism is sometimes associated with positive or at least less harmful interactions between countries. Like globalisation, though, there are many perspectives on what such a viewpoint might mean or be, and given its connections to Transatlantic Studies, it is worth spending some time reviewing critical stances on the subject. In the special issue of the *Journal of American History* entitled 'The Nation and Beyond: Transnational Perspectives on United States History', David Thelen suggests three ways of looking at transnationality:

We might imagine from afar how the phenomenon passed *over* the nation, observing the nation as a whole; or how it passed *across* the nation, seeing how it bumped over natural and manmade [*sic*] features; or how it passed *through* the nation, transforming and being transformed.[20]

This view of transnationality seems to see it as an inner or inward perspective on a nation, whereas for Paul Giles, transnationalism 'positions itself at a point of intersection . . . where the coercive aspects of imagined communities are turned back on themselves, reversed or mirrored, so that their covert presuppositions and ideological inflections become apparent'.[21] This sense of reflecting back is equally important for Transatlantic Studies, which looks not just across the nation, but over the ocean as well, to transform and reform the view along the way.

In its most frequently articulated terms, transnationalism is overtly political. In her essay on The Body Shop, 'A World Without Boundaries', Caren Kaplan explores the ways in which the links imagined and assumed by transnationalism 'deconstruct[] the long-standing marxist cultural hegemony model by demonstrating the impossibility of finding a pure position of a site of subjectivity outside the economic and cultural dynamics that structure modernity'.[22] Furthermore, she suggests that feminist interventions into transnationality offer the opportunity to 'resist the practices of modernity – i.e., nationalism, modernism, Imperialism, etc. – that have been so repressive to women'.[23] Where other critics talk approvingly of global feminism, Kaplan is clear that such a term covers over the inequalities of power, in that Euro-American feminists offer their Western perspectives as somehow global and applicable across spaces, a presumption that needs to be resisted. In *Scattered Hegemonies*, Grewal and Kaplan define transnationalism through gender:

> We use the term 'transnational' to problematize a purely locational politics of global-local or center-periphery in favor of . . . the lines cutting across them. As feminists who note the absence of gender issues in all of these world-system theories, we have no choice but to challenge what we see as inadequate and inaccurate binary divisions. Transnational linkages influence every level of social existence.[24]

Transnationality, like Transatlantic Studies, offers several opportunities for examining how nations and the ideas around nations impact upon each other, or as Grewal puts it, have 'exceeded the bounds of the nation'.[25] Thus, I will be using both terms in my discussions of women's narratives. Rather than suggesting homo-geneity, transnationalism implies the flow of ideas and things across spaces, which, as James Clifford points out, 'do not point in a single historical direction'.[26] Transnationalism does not, however, suggest that nationhood or nationalism have gone away, especially since such flows are always uneven:

> Nationalisms articulate their purportedly homogeneous times and spaces selectively, in relation to new transnational flows and cultural forms, both dominant and subaltern. The diasporic and hybrid identities produced by these movements can be both restrictive and liberating. They stitch together language, traditions, and places in coercive and creative ways, articulating embattled homelands, powers of memory, styles of aggres-sion, in ambiguous relation to national and transnational structures.[27]

Indeed, the very inclusion of the term 'nation' within transnational-ism offers the opportunity to reflect on its ongoing critical pull, some-thing that the term 'globalisation' covers over. I find it significant that Clifford's words above also evoke disparate *gendered* images – stitch-ing, battles, aggression – which suggests that hybrid identities are coerced or created in gendered ways. Indeed, Clifford is clear in his acknowledgement that both nationalism and travel are different for women as opposed to men, giving examples such as US female sol-diers driving cars in Saudi Arabia, or female migrant domestic workers whose unofficial duties sometimes include non-consensual sex. As a result, it is clear to Clifford that 'specific histories of freedom and danger in movement need to be articulated along gender lines'.[28]

Alongside transnationalism lies worlding, which has been vari-ously defined by its proponents, who trace the word back to Gayatri Chakravorty Spivak. She, in turn, claims that her use of the word is a 'vulgarization of Martin Heidegger's idea'.[29] Spivak argues that world-ing is a way of creating or shaping a historical narrative in imperial or colonialist terms which simultaneously deny those historical processes and make them appear natural or naturalised, so that the world can be seen only through these lenses. John Muthyala argues that

> worlding the world is a kind of double movement: while it draws the world into the realm of the cognizable by establishing zones of possibil-ity, relation, and encounter within which the world can become 'worldly,' it relegates to the margins of social existence those elements that seem to threaten this process.[30]

Like globalisation, then, worlding has the potential effect of eliding its true processes and power differentials. Taking another perspective, Susan Gillman, Kirsten Silva Greusz and Rob Wilson suggest that worlding is a 'trans-disciplinary critical tactic' which reveals 'how modes and texts of contemporary being and worldly dwelling can become a historical process of taking care and setting limits, making the world-horizon come near and become local and informed, instantiated as an uneven/incomplete material process of world-becoming'.[31] This version of worlding is a conscious one, which 'produces a concept of comparability attuned to the crucial spatio-temporal relation'.[32] To a certain extent, then, worlding will be important to the exploration of women's transatlantic texts which either deny or explore the power bases linked to individual countries, whilst keeping in mind Woolf's sentiments above, that women's partial disenfranchisement may (perhaps even should) affect their views of all nations.

Exploring how worlding works in relation to 'America', Muthyala suggests the need to *re*world America (which has come to stand in for the specific nation of the United States):

> [R]eworlding America reconfigures spatial displacement as marking not just a redrawing of territorial boundaries and a contesting of the sometimes atavistic, sometimes creolized visions that have controlled them, but as making visible the processes by which the dissonances of the socio-cultural morphologies of 'America' are produced and managed.[33]

The relevance of these overlapping concepts for an exploration of literary practice is, I hope, readily apparent. Transatlantic literature self-consciously explores how identity is created and read through images of nationhood, travel and change; furthermore, questions of insider- and outsidership are explicitly addressed, particularly in relation to desire. Mary Layoun suggests that such narratives are 'attempts to negotiate dominant narratives of nationalism in which they participate and the boundaries which those dominant narratives draw and seek to maintain. Such narrative negotiation is contestatory and acquiescent, often simultaneously.'[34]

Clearly, transatlantic narratives do not offer a simple reading experience (hence the claim above that they rely on a series of mis-readings), nor can they be said to maintain the boundaries of inside and out, even as they may attempt to do so. Leakages and slippage are almost generically inscribed into such texts, and in this way, they have some connections to the larger question of how nations and nationalism is maintained. For Wai Chee Dimock, 'Induction into a nation comes at a price; it disciplines the inducted by the very logic by which it purports to be universal,'[35] and this is certainly one way to erect boundaries and borders, even whilst suggesting otherwise. As the narrators of these texts negotiate their relationships to new or different countries, they contrast the myths of universality with the realities (or, again, myths) of specificity, locating themselves within or against such frameworks. Giles argues that 'national identity must be brought explicitly into the frame as an object of scrutiny in itself rather than being accepted uncritically,'[36] and the texts under analysis here do just that, working through and around national myths and blindnesses.

Travelling Gender and the Politics of Location

In relation specifically to literature, the transatlantic exchange has been figured in multiple ways, depending on motive, agency and experience: crossing the ocean has very different meanings for the immigrant, the migrant, the exile, the slave, the traveller, the tourist and the expatriate, though of course, for some, these designations overlap. Contrasting just two of these terms – traveller and migrant – Iain Chambers suggests that the difference lies in the end point, home:

> To travel implies movement between fixed positions, a site of departure, a point of arrival, the knowledge of an itinerary. It also intimates an eventual return, a potential homecoming. Migrancy, on the contrary, involves a movement in which neither the points of departure nor those of arrival are immutable or certain. It calls for a dwelling in language, in histories, in identities that are constantly subject to mutation. Always in transit, the promise of a homecoming – completing the story, domesticating the detour – becomes an impossibility.[37]

These ideas exert their force in the chapters that follow, which explore what home and homecoming mean for various travelling women, both those who undertake short journeys and those whose leave-taking is more permanent.

Whilst Chambers makes a good argument for the difference between travel and migrancy, other critics suggest that such critical boundaries are themselves subject to slippage. Separating these strands may mark an impossible task, particularly since agency seems a key aspect of these various definitions. Chelva Kanaganayakam, for example, sets out to explore and contrast 'exile' and 'expatriate' and argues for a splicing of the two terms, yet ends up suggesting that each is poised on a 'cusp', making any such distinction slippery at best.[38] Edward Said argues that exile is 'fundamentally a discontinuous state of being'[39] but that to celebrate the figure of the literary exile is to deny the reality of the experience of exile, especially for the unlettered many as opposed to the privileged few who write movingly about their experiences. Yet, as Kaplan suggests in *Questions of Travel*, Euro-American modernism valorises the lone individual traveller, whether exile *or* expatriate, and privileges a detached sensibility:

> The conflation of exile and expatriation by modern writers and critics can be read in the way that distance has come to be privileged as the best perspective on a subject under scrutiny and in the related discourse of aesthetic gain through exile. When detachment is the precondition for creativity, then disaffection or alienation as states of mind becomes a rite of passage for the 'serious' modern artist or writer.[40]

It is certainly the case that many texts in the field of Transatlantic Studies focus on modernist literary relations and canonical texts; *Transatlantic Women's Literature* engages briefly these ideas, particularly in relation to Nella Larsen's *Quicksand*, which includes the figure of the artist in a modernist framework, and Eva Hoffman's *Lost in Translation*, in which the narrator explicitly adopts a New Critical viewpoint in order to aid her understanding of her adopted country and its literature. However, my exploration of exiles and expatriates extends beyond the modernist moment and takes issue with detachment as a precondition or goal. Indeed, it is precisely affiliation that affects many women's narratives of travel and movement, given concerns over the 'proper' behaviour for wives, mothers and daughters.

Salman Rushdie conflates the terms of exile and expatriate, arguing that writers in this position, like himself,

> are haunted by some sense of loss, some urge to reclaim, to look back, even at the risk of being mutated into pillars of salt. But if we do look back, we must also do so in the knowledge – which gives rise to profound uncertainties – that our physical alienation . . . almost inevitably means that we will not be capable of reclaiming precisely the thing that was lost; that we will, in short, create fictions, not actual cities or villages, but invisible ones, imaginary homelands.[41]

Rushdie's viewpoint is not detached as in the modernist narrative, but wholly engaged with place and distance, though nostalgia such as his is, indeed, a staple of transatlantic literature from whatever era. (It is intriguing, though, that he links the expatriate with the feminine image of pillars of salt, most commonly associated with Lot's wife.) Eva Hoffman suggests that questions of home and away have more acute resonance now than in the past, though it is certainly possible to argue that such a present-tense viewpoint suggests an inability to move beyond a contemporary frame. Nevertheless, her point remains valid: 'the notion of "home" may have been, in recent times, peculiarly overcharged, as the concepts of "country" and "nation" have been superimposed on each other with a seeming inevitability.'[42]

The list of contested terms does not, however, end here. Even the terms 'tourist' and 'traveller' resist final definition and have been subject to sustained scrutiny. In 1976, Dean MacCannell made the bold claim, 'we are all tourists' in his groundbreaking work, *The Tourist: A New Theory of the Leisure Class*.[43] Thirteen years later, in discussing the changes he could have made to the text for the 1989 edition, MacCannell noted the rise in feminist criticism and the ways in which this would have had an impact on the language choices he would have made had he chosen to rewrite (rather than just reissue) the text. Yet at the same time, he dismissed the importance of such refashioning: he considered the 'tourist' 'the most frivolous of these putatively genderless but masculine figures [like the president or the surgeon], so beside the point of gender politics that I doubt feminists would think it worthwhile to attack him'.[44] Despite his gender blindness here, which both acknowledges but then dismisses the importance of inclusivity, his discussion of the normative male tourist still offers important insights into how tourists are defined and perceived.[45] MacCannell argues against the way in which the tourist is dismissed by critics as seeking only the inauthentic experience, yet this perception remains entrenched in some critics' minds. For Barry Curtis and Claire Pajaczkowska, for example, travel is about transformation, whereas tourism focuses only on 'a circular confirmation of self-identity'.[46]

Yet to claim the tourist is an inferior version of the traveller, as Paul Fussell does repeatedly in *Abroad* (1980), for example, invites other critics to argue that such designations are faulty at best and rest on a nostalgic imperialism; indeed, Kaplan goes so far as to link the tourist and the exile in the same imagined space, suggesting that each attempts to construct authenticity as 'elsewhere'.[47] Conversely, Curtis and Pajaczkowska *contrast* the tourist and the exile (who is also linked to the traveller), suggesting that the difference between them lies in their relationship to time and home.[48] In his seminal text, *The Tourist Gaze*, John Urry argues that the tourist experience is marked by the division between the ordinary and the extraordinary, and he further argues that 'tourists are semioticians, reading the landscape for signifiers of certain pre-established notions or signs derived from various discourses of travel and tourism,'[49] thus giving them more credit than other critics do regarding motivation and ability.

Perhaps the difficulty in consolidating the competing definitions around which critics explore transatlantic issues lies in what Rob Wilson and Wimal Dissanayake call the 'transnational imaginary,' or the

> *as-yet-unfigured* horizon of contemporary cultural production by which national spaces/identities of political allegiance and economic regulation are being undone and imagined communities of modernity are being reshaped at the macropolitical (global) and micropolitical (cultural) levels of everyday existence.[50]

The sense that the transatlantic offers *unfinished*, continuously evolving cultural encounters is paramount for our understanding of the journey; there is no *one kind* of transatlantic travel, and the basis on which the individual travels – whether it is compulsory or chosen, for leisure or immigration – impacts directly on the experience.

It is not my task in this book, therefore, to argue that there are stable definitions of exile, expatriate, refugee or immigrant; as I have shown, critics who attempt such definitions are subject to further readings of their work which disprove their set agendas (as is, for example, Said; Kaplan suggests that despite his demarcation of exile and refugee, he ends up collapsing such distinctions or moving away from his own insights, reinforcing the modernist – and, in Kaplan's eyes, therefore 'bad' – view of the solitary exile). Yet it is patently clear that women writers invoke such definitions and self-definitions, and it is on this basis that I will use the terms outlined above. Nella Larsen's Helga Crane is a happy expatriate, until she discovers that expatriation, in her case, becomes synonymous with exoticism. Bharati Mukherjee constructs an illegal immigrant who wishes for assimilation and exoticisation in equal measures, even if such protean desires ensure critical disapproval. Jenny Diski takes the stance of an anti-tourist in her memoir and travel narratives. Eva Hoffman is in exile in Canada (indeed, the second part of her book insists this is the case, taking 'Exile' as its title). Anne Tyler constructs American characters who define themselves as the norm against the encroaching foreignness of others, or who attempt not to 'see' the foreign in the assumption that to note difference is to fall prey to its negative seductiveness; and Isabel Allende offers up a cross-dressing migrancy with no logical endpoint. For all of these writers, the gendered traveller marks a point of enquiry, a space for further discussion, and an opportunity to explore how she defines herself, or is defined.

Since the 1990s, discourses of travel have become more frequently articulated, and the intersections of gender, race and class with mobility have become more pronounced, with critics exploring what it means to move in space, to travel in ways that reconfigure identity relations and power. As mentioned above, McClintock, Grewal and Kaplan read against the grain of male theorists, particularly noting their inattention to gender. In turn, many male critics have now taken up the challenge that gender studies present; in his book *Routes: Travel and Translation in the Late Twentieth Century*, for example, James Clifford conscientiously notes the importance of gender in relation to travel narratives, and Said is careful to include both male and female pronouns in his later work on travel and exile. While Ulf Hannerz rather resolutely refers to the generic 'he' throughout *Transnational Connections*, particularly in relation to the figure of 'the cosmopolitan', his elision of the female is unusual in contemporary texts.

This is not to suggest, however, that the battles Kaplan and other feminist critics have been waging on gender blindness have been entirely won (indeed, in the case study on Isabella Bird below, we shall see how gender awareness gets turned back on itself by critics who wish to ignore gender politics). Specifically in relation to women's exploration of travel and gender, issues to do with the politics of location take on varied and deep resonance, and the whole question of the gendering of the nation – and the traveller – remain central to understanding such texts.

The term 'politics of location' has been variously used since the 1980s, and, as Kaplan argues, is 'a particularly North American feminist articulation of difference' as well as 'a method of interrogating and deconstructing the position, identity, and privilege of whiteness'.[51] In *Questions of Travel*, Kaplan recapitulates an argument about the politics of location which was also published in her co-edited collection, *Scattered Hegemonies*. Extending her work in her monograph,

Kaplan also changes terminology. Instead of the 'Western' women of the earlier texts, such women become 'Euro-American' in *Questions of Travel*, more closely signalling their location, perhaps. The transition from Western (which implicitly signals the 'otherness' of the East) indicates Kaplan's own growing sense of the importance of particularity and a resistance to suspect uses of such terms. Situating women travellers within the boundaries or frameworks that mark their identification politics is key to understanding both what they see when they are abroad and how they are received and viewed themselves. Although, as Clifford suggests, no one is unalterably and forever 'fixed' by identity, at the same time, individuals cannot ignore or entirely leave aside the 'specific structures of race and culture, class and caste, gender and sexuality, environment and history'[52] that shape them. Clifford's argument, closely linked to his exploration of identity, is that location 'is an itinerary rather than a bounded site – a series of encounters and translations'.[53] In this sense, then, it equates somewhat with discussions of Transatlantic Studies itself.

For Kaplan, an awareness of the politics of location can help us to understand why, for example, the ability to travel has been seen as a sign of 'liberation' (primarily for white, class privileged women) as well as why the idea of a 'global sisterhood' becomes utterly untenable in such a dynamic.[54] Whilst travel as liberation is a powerful symbol, and one used by many of the women writers whose work is being analysed here, one needs to treat its symbolism cautiously, noting what this symbolism elides as well as what it reproduces. Liberation for whom and at what cost are perhaps the questions of travel that need the most attention. How one travels (and performs one's gender whilst doing so) become other issues of note. For if women no longer wear stays, there is certainly, to some extent, still a focus on their appearance as travellers. Inderpal Grewal makes a convincing argument when she suggests that the nineteenth-century English abhorrence of the veil, or of harems, was a way of deflecting attention away from the real inequalities felt by English women at home, suggesting similarities rather than differences across cultures; this reaction against what appears to be foreign (and elevation of one's own cultural practices as not only the norm, but that which should be aspired to and admired) remains a fairly consistent part of twentieth-century transatlantic texts as well, though at the same time, there is less apparent certainty in these positions.

Hannerz rightfully argues that 'there were always interactions, and a diffusion of ideas, habits, and things, even if at times we have been habituated to theories of culture and society which have not emphasized such truths.'[55] Now that cultural theories do emphasise such points, as this exploration of transnationalism and Transatlantic Studies makes clear, it is somewhat easier to see these effects in a range of texts. In order to set the discussion of twentieth-century women's travelling narratives in context, and to explore further the idea of abhorrence and cultural contrasts, I turn now to a well-known nineteenth-century text, *A Lady's Life in the Rocky Mountains*, to offer some contrasts but also continuities with the twentieth-century texts that follow.

'No Region for Tourists and Women': Isabella Bird's Travel and Travail

This case study analyses how Isabella Bird's nineteenth-century collection of letters home, *A Lady's Life in the Rocky Mountains* (1879), offers a complex, transatlantic exploration of gender.[56] The text depicts an idealised freedom from constraint, but it also provides evidence of the ways in which the gendered self cannot be fully or easily abandoned. For example, in her sojourn across the Rockies, Bird rides her horse as a man would, but reverts to side-saddle when she encounters settlements, despite finding such a riding position painful. She discovers that her hosts often want her help with (feminine) chores, and learns to make herself 'agreeable', yet manages to mistake, in one instance, cayenne pepper for cinnamon, thus (intentionally?) rendering her cake inedible. Moreover, her more generalised freedom from constraint – her trying out of various gender positions – is still circumscribed by her culture and its mores. In discussions of a man called Mountain Jim, who alternately arouses and repulses her, she maintains a distanced voice of piety and Christian charity, but there is a long gap in the text surrounding time spent in his company, alone.

However, Bird also perpetuates the prejudices of her times. For example, her discussions of the Native American population are bigoted, disrupting any sort of canonisation of the female hero that a naïve reader might wish to set up. As Anne McClintock reminds us, white women 'were not hapless onlookers of empire but were ambiguously complicit both as colonizers and colonized, privileged and restricted, acted upon and acting',[57] and Bird's discussion (and hierarchism) of various races and nationalities reveals this clearly. In these ways and others, Bird is unable to step fully out of her own cultural inheritance even while exploring a different set of identities whilst abroad (and this recognition is also important for each of the other texts discussed throughout). Rockwell Gray contends that to travel is 'to move through differing geographical and cultural realms of multi-determined meaning', whereas Karen Lawrence argues that 'home is, of course, never totally left behind.'[58] These opposing (but connected) viewpoints are both crucial for a discussion of this text.

Isabella Bird makes a useful first case study to consider, not because I want to set her up as distinctive or iconic, but because in many respects she is representative of a particular kind of lady traveller of the nineteenth century; a British woman who, assured of her class, ethnic and national superiority, nevertheless finds that travel affords her freedom from the very things that make her (in her eyes and others) superior. Moreover, she cannot fully articulate this freedom, which nevertheless leaks out of her gentile narrative of crossing the Rocky Mountains, particularly in relation to the fact that her claims of frailty alternate with extensive articulations of feats of strength. If at one point, she claims that a mountaineering feat is too much for her – 'had I known that the ascent was a real mountaineering feat I should not have felt the slightest ambition to perform it. As it is, I am only humiliated by my success, for "Jim" dragged me up, like a bale of goods, by sheer force of muscle' (88) – at other points her skills are much in evidence. Indeed, she brags that she drives cattle as well as the men do, so much so that she is called a ' "good cattle-man" ' in Estes Park (116). In addition, she details extensive injuries from a fall almost as if they are a badge of honour:

> The flesh of my arm looks crushed into a jelly, but cold-water dressings will soon bring it right; and a cut on my back bled profusely; and the bleeding, the many bruises and general shake, have made me feel weak, but circumstances do not admit of 'making a fuss,' and I really think that the rents in my riding-dress will prove the most important part of the accident. (62)

Here, if Bird's female *body* is temporarily disabled, it is her costume that is most problematic, for Bird has a clear need to maintain respectability, even as she is fascinated by those, such as Mountain Jim, who give up such claims. Indeed, the regularity with which Bird declaims on costume is surely not accidental, whether she is comparing herself to San Francisco woman 'much "got up" in paint, emerald green velvet, Brussels lace, and diamonds' next to whom Bird 'sustained the reputation which our countrywomen bear in America by looking a "perfect guy" ' (24), or whether she is identifying the ways in which her dress has been affected by her travels. Indeed, subsequent editions of her book included a drawing of her Hawaiian riding dress, precisely to 'visually demonstrate the wholly feminine nature of the costume in question'.[59] Evelyn Bach suggests that Bird's freedom to travel is 'facilitated by her care to maintain every appearance of feminine propriety'.[60]

As Clifford argues, '[W]omen travelers were forced to conform, masquerade, or rebel discreetly within a set of normative male definitions and experiences.'[61] Thus, whilst her tales of adventure, risk and making-do rival those of her male counterparts, one is always made aware of her gender and her sex, not least by Bird herself. Indeed, compressing class and gender in one instance, Bird reveals that she has been asked to stay on in her lodgings in the mountains over the winter when the other women (less able, less robust) move away:

> Evans offers me six dollars a week if I will stay into the winter and do the cooking after Mrs. Edwards leaves! I think I should like playing at being a 'hired girl' if it were not for the bread-making! But it would suit me better to ride after cattle. The men don't like 'baching,' as it is called in the wilds – *i.e.* 'doing for themselves.' They washed and ironed their clothes yesterday, and there was an incongruity about the last performance. I really think (though for the fifteenth time) that I shall leave tomorrow. (120)

Leave, of course, she does, because part of her (largely unacknowledged) reason for travel is to move outside this very domesticity, and to ensure that her gender does not equate with the jobs she is required to do. Instead, she heads out into nature, observes and catalogues sights and sites, and stakes her own claims to space. Indeed, she even suggests that her favourite area, Estes Park, belongs to her:

> It is unsurveyed, 'no man's land,' and mine by right of love, appropriation, and appreciation; by the seizure of its peerless sunrises and sunsets, its glorious afterglow, its blazing noons, its hurricanes sharp and furious, its wild auroras, its glories of mountain and forest, of canyon, lake, and river, and the stereotyping them all in my memory. (95–7)

Unlike a typical travel writer, though, Bird claims she would not tell others how to follow her; she would keep the space pristine and undisturbed, yet she does not have this in her power. By the time her book is published, others have already seduced tourists to the area.

Mills suggests that it is the very 'factual' nature of women's travelling narratives that makes them 'potentially extremely subversive', especially when set alongside the literature of the time which represented women as frail.[62] Yet Mills also notes that this potential for subversion is easily undermined by the fact that such characters were seen as exceptional, or eccentric – not like other women. Certainly Isabella Bird's freedom to travel depends upon the confinement of others (including, in a sense, her female audience), and on their lower rank and status. She strategically becomes in this dynamic an *exceptional* woman; as indeed she was. She was a founding member of the Royal Scottish Geographical Society and refused to speak to the British Geographical Society until they made her a member.[63] She stands outside her gender, or both within and outside it; constantly checking how she is assessed, and performing above expectation at crucial moments, whilst strategically underperforming at others.

Mills rightly notes that 'it is not necessary to read travel writing as expressing the truth of the author's life, but rather, it is the result of a configuration of discursive structures with which the author negotiates.'[64] These negotiations are apparent from the very first lines of the book. Bird, disclaiming any intention of publishing her work, is nevertheless persuaded first to publish her letters home in *Leisure Hour* 'at the request of its editor' (11). Thus, the volume that becomes *A Lady's Life in the Rocky Mountains* goes through a series of iterations before it becomes this 'factual' account, and as noted above, there are many elements missing from Bird's narrative.

What is very apparent in her text, though, is a constant assessment of transatlantic travel, and of transatlantic travellers themselves (including herself). She pronounces easily on other nationalities, finding the Irish unlikeable, for example, and she is both drawn to and repulsed by her own countrymen. Proclaiming definitively that 'an American is nationally assumptive, an Englishman personally so' (154), Bird limns an encounter with a fellow Briton, who ignores her until he recognises their shared nationality, at which point he proclaims 'a profound contempt for everything American' (154–5), as if assuming she will share his feelings. She also mentions, somewhat mockingly, 'The Earl', a man whose 'insular peculiarities' occasioned his moniker (103).

In her guise as a travelling lady, she is often mistaken for a Dane or a Swede, and therefore she hears quite outspoken criticism of her countrymen and women. The English, she is told, are greedy and travel ' "only to gratify their palates" ' (144); at another point, she is party to a conversation where her hosts, the Chalmerses, suggest that their English neighbours, the Hugheses, are repugnant and unrefined, so much so that Mrs Chalmers claims, ' "Those English talked just like savages, I couldn't understand a word they said" ' (51). Displaced and unaccustomed to the hardships of the West, the Hugheses stand in for the displaced original inhabitants of the region, whose customs and mores are unreadable and whose language impedes rather than aids meaning. Of course, Bird's inclusion of this vignette is not without an ulterior motive; she finds the Chalmerses repugnant and her depiction of them is far from flattering. To Bird, the Hugheses' home is an 'oasis' where she can converse with an 'educated lady' for a change, something that she values highly (51). To a certain extent, then, Bird divides people by status as much as by nationality.

Yet it is the very fact of status that also nonplusses her. She comments on the 'respectful courtesy to women' in the West (25) and is amazed that the men whom she encounters do not try to take advantage of the fact that she travels alone. Moreover, whereas she acknowledges a general lawlessness – or, 'manifest indifference to the higher obligations of the law' (67) – she contrasts this with the fact that property is less at risk in the Wild West than in Great Britain. Finally, though, Bird acknowledges, as is expected of her, that it is women's calming influence that will make the American West a more civilised place. If she fails a little in her own duty in this area (despite her attempts to reform Mountain Jim, he dies the desperado that he is, unrepentant and unforgiven), she nevertheless reinforces the message that a woman exerts the most power when she is quiet and refined, not when she exercises 'noisy self-assertion, masculinity, or fastness' (208). Having driven cattle, ridden on her own through the mountains, and conquered areas unfit for 'women and tourists' (53), Bird nevertheless conforms to her expected denouement, quoting Oliver Goldsmith's 'The Traveler' on one's heart remaining with one's own people, and William Cowper's famous line 'England, with all thy faults, I love thee still!' (199) in the penultimate letter of the book. Bird herself suggests that 'surely one advantage of travelling is that, while it removes much prejudice against foreigners and their customs, it intensifies tenfold one's appreciation of the good at home, and, above all, of the quietness and purity of English domestic life' (199). As such, Bird returns to England – only, of course, to leave it once again, for other travels, on other continents.

In January 1905, the *Journal of the Royal African Society* ran an obituary of Mrs J. F. Bishop – Isabella Bird – who had died in October 1904. The journal comments that the society had 'lost a generous supporter and member' in the person of Mrs Bishop, whose 'travels are too well known to need more than a brief recapitulation'. Finally, the paragraph-long obituary notes, 'She was meditating an extensive exploration of North Africa before her health (never very robust) gave way a year ago.'[65] Thus this intrepid explorer, who is nevertheless far from 'robust', is named as a married (though in fact widowed) woman rather than called by the name she is known to us today, and her frailty, so important for her gender, remains intact despite her obvious health whilst abroad.

Perhaps even more fascinatingly, she became the figure of academic debate in the early 1990s in the pages of the *Transactions of the Institute of British Geographers*. In an article entitled 'Toward a Feminist Historiography of Geography', Mona Domosh argues for a reconsideration of Victorian women travellers and their contributions to science. In particular, she contends that

> the 'pre-scientific' experiences of women travellers at the turn of the century, therefore, are in one sense more relevant today for what they can tell us about the role of the outsider and the methods of observation than for any information about 'new' places.[66]

She further suggests that a feminist historiography could therefore be not only appropriate, but fundamental to current understandings of their role. Suggesting that the experience of women like Isabella Bird 'lay outside the realm of acceptable discourse', Domosh seeks to claim this experience and rename it.[67]

Such an intellectual project clearly has its detractors, including David R. Stoddart, who wrote a stinging reply, which, if anything, confirms Domosh's view of critical disregard: 'I am not aware, for example, that Isabella Bird ever made a measurement, a map or a collection, or indeed ever wrote other than impressionistically about the areas she visited.'[68] Moreover, Stoddart suggests that women like Bird do not need special consideration: 'No feminist historiography is required to analyse their contributions: they looked after themselves, their careers and their scholarship perfectly well without such assistance.'[69] If Bird was 'never robust' in life, she seems fairly sturdy – if Stoddart is to be believed – in death. Yet what makes her fascinating is that in both cases, her gender is the most important issue of concern. She is either a lady who did no useful scientific work (what lady does?), and can therefore be dismissed, or she was a female pioneer whose successes rivalled those of men and is therefore worthy of further exploration herself. Certainly Bird herself exhibited some ambivalence towards her role, a fact that is not uncommon for nineteenth-century women travel writers, who could not shake off a consideration of their gender.[70]

Nor, it seems, can twentieth-century women travellers, both fictional and real, fully step outside consideration of their gender (nor do they uniformly want to). In what follows, I will explore how gender and travel interact across the transatlantic space that offers connections and distances in equal measures. For all travellers, according to Chambers:

> To come from elsewhere, from 'there' and not 'here', and hence to be simultaneously 'inside' and 'outside' the situation at hand, is to live at the intersections of histories and memories, experiencing both their preliminary dispersal and their subsequent translation into new, more extensive, arrangements along emerging routes.[71]

Yet for women, the paradox of what such inside and outside boundaries suggest is rarely resolved. Victorian women travellers were both inside and outside the colonial identifications of their male counterparts, with the result that 'the clash of feminine and colonial discourses construct texts which are at one and the same time presenting a self which transgresses and which conforms both to patriarchal and imperial discourses.'[72] If this dilemma is clearly played out for earlier women writers, it is less visible in the latter part of the twentieth century, yet questions over propriety, status and privilege remain key to understanding the texts that transatlantic women produce.

Chambers suggests that living abroad entails '*a conversation in which different identities are recognised, exchanged and mixed, but do not vanish*',[73] and this recognition of multiple, irresolvable identity performances is at the heart of women's transatlantic travel. For women writers, the transatlantic encounter almost insistently marks either a rejection or a continuation of 'home' and their texts engage with the concepts of movement and stasis in deceptively simple or overtly complex ways. Literary tourists and travellers seek or resist identification with the new cultures that they encounter. However, this phenomenon is more complex than a simple mapping of masculinity and femininity, ethnicity or nationality onto the transatlantic space, and an interrogation of all these concepts is central to this book.

Women writers have created a body of fictional and non-fictional narratives that appear to illuminate or mythologise aspects of national character, as well as to problematise the politics of tourism and travel in their negotiations of gendered identity. The texts analysed here project and define a highly unstable cultural geography, as they place their narrators in the position of tourists and travellers encountering the familiar in the 'foreign' or vice versa. It is no surprise that travel texts perform the dual role of illumination and fictionalisation, given that tourists and travellers themselves participate in a similar process of construction – of identity and nationality, self and other.

Transatlantic Women's Literature is divided into three parts, each with its own short introduction, followed by two closely-read case studies that explore the transatlantic narrative in depth. It analyses both fictional and factual narratives, for as Karen Lawrence argues, 'Travel writing reveals a set of alternative myths or models for women's place in society.'[74] The juxtaposition of fiction and fact allows for an interrogation into the myriad ways in which female movement is depicted, defined and negotiated.

In Part One, I explore the construction of racial identities across the transatlantic space and the lure of the exotic 'other'. After a short introduction in which I show how this exotic other is problematised through reference to two late twentieth-century texts – Paule Marshall's *Praisesong for the Widow* (1983), which imagines an idealised transatlantic ethnic heritage that a middle class African-American learns to access through the cultural memory of chant and dance, and Jamaica Kincaid's scathing essay attacking Caribbean tourism, *A Small Place* (1988) – I go on to offer sustained analysis of Nella Larsen's early twentieth-century novella *Quicksand* (1928) and Bharati Mukherjee's critically contested late twentieth-century novel *Jasmine* (1989). In *Quicksand*, the Danish-African-American Helga Crane attempts to leave questions of race and allegiance behind in moving to her (white) mother's native land, but finds that her black skin is accentuated and capitalised upon by her relatives for social gain. Helga is visibly othered by those she is closest to, and questions over who has the power to define are paramount. In *Jasmine* Mukherjee offers an Indian woman narrator who, arriving in the US in order to commit *sati*, almost accidentally embarks upon a quixotic adventure instead. This adventure relies on familiar American myths and images, but Mukherjee alters them strategically to acknowledge the impact of gender and ethnicity on transatlantic travel. As a result, Jasmine's encounters with 'America' – both mythic and real – affect her negotiations of her transatlantic, gendered identity. In both texts, an exploration of the mythic appeal of the exotic is closely linked to gender and performance.

In Part Two, I explore the role of identity selection and national performance in memoirs of travel. To travel is to invent not only the destination, but also the traveller, as identity becomes a performance which tailors itself to whatever audience it encounters. Eva Hoffman 'performs' her complicated national allegiances in her move from Poland to North America in her first memoir, *Lost in Translation* (1989) as well as subsequent texts, whereas Jenny Diski 'performs' the role of the anti-tourist in her travel books, *Skating to Antarctica* (1997) and *Stranger on a Train: Daydreaming and Smoking around America with Interruptions* (2002). What is clear for both texts, though, as well as other travel memoirs, is that 'shifts of identity are highly complex, sometimes unstable, and often have reversible elements built into them.'[75]

In Part Three, I return to fiction, examining the pull of home and the reinvention of foreignness both within and outside the family, first in relation to Anne Tyler's *The Accidental Tourist* (1985) and *Digging to America* (2006), and then in relation to Isabel Allende's *Daughter of Fortune* (1999). According to Charles Vandersee, 'America is a site where people appear by accident and meet by accident rather than by ancestry and assignment.'[76] The texts in this section explore the accidental nature of foreignness. Tyler's families have permeable boundaries that admit outsiders who do not belong to genetic families but whose presence alters such families in dynamic and unstable ways, and she articulates overtly the concerns over foreignness in both texts. Isabel Allende's *Daughter of Fortune* extends the analysis of transatlantic (as well as transpacific) encounters as both restricting and transformative. In particular, the novel explores how racial and gender identities become blurred in the process of crossing the ocean. Like Mukherjee's text above, *Daughter of Fortune* acknowledges the mythic practices of Americanness, and reconfigures the ocean as the origin of a fairytale adventure for a female picaro, complete with identity shifts, cross dressing and the sloughing off of inherited culture.

Karen Lawrence maintains that 'the trope of travel – whether in its incarnations as exile or adventure, tourism or exploration – provides a particularly fertile imaginative field for narrative representations of women's historical and personal agency.'[77] It is precisely for this reason that women's narratives of transatlantic travel are such rich sources for explorations of identity and representation. Fictional travel narratives, like their 'real' counterparts, provide accounts of *difference* by exploring the politics of location while simultaneously examining localities. As cultural outsiders, these fictional travellers comment upon the society from which they spring and the societies to which they now belong.

What all these fictional travel narratives have in common is a sense that gender is a condition which impinges upon – even determines – the travel experience. Each displays a postmodern sensibility, where identity is a performance which is fluid, not fixed. This is, of course, intimately bound up in travel itself. As Trinh T. Minh-ha suggests, 'If travelling perpetuates a discontinuous state of being, it also satisfies, despite the existential difficulties it entails, one's insatiable need for detours and displacements in postmodern culture.'[78] The conclusion argues that these texts contribute to the evolving definitions of transatlantic literature, with important implications for the future development of Transatlantic Studies as a theorised space.

NOTES

1. Virginia Woolf, *Three Guineas* (New York: Harcourt, Brace and Company, 1938), p. 166.
2. Anne McClintock, *Imperial Leather: Race, Gender and Sexuality in the Colonial Contest* (Routledge: New York, 1995), p. 28, italics in original.
3. Ibid. p. 353, italics in original.
4. Of course, for some women, religious and cultural regulations and mores require or enforce restrictions on dress, and when visiting some sacred sites, both men and women are required to cover up. Nonetheless, it is clear that for many women, there is greater freedom in relation to appearance now than there has been in the immediate past.
5. Mary Morris, 'Women and Journeys: Inner and Outer', in Michael Kowalewsi (ed.), *Temperamental Journeys: Essays on the Modern Literature of Travel* (Athens, GA: University of Georgia Press, 1992), p. 25, italics in original.
6. Lindsey Tucker, *Textual Escap(e)ades: Mobility, Maternity, and Textuality in Contemporary Fiction by Women* (Westport, CT: Greenwood, 1994), p. 1.

7. Paul Giles, *Transatlantic Insurrections: British Culture and the Formation of American Literature, 1730–1860* (Philadelphia, PA: University of Pennsylvania, 2001), p. 1.
8. Paul Gilroy, *The Black Atlantic: Modernity and Double Consciousness* (London: Verso, 1993), p. 15.
9. Fionnghuala Sweeney, 'The Black Atlantic, American Studies and the Politics of the Postcolonial', *Comparative American Studies* 4 (2) (2006): 125.
10. Gilroy, *Black Atlantic*, p. 218.
11. See, in particular, *Scattered Hegemonies: Postmodernity and Transnational Feminist Practices*; *Questions of Travel: Postmodern Discourses of Displacement*; and *Transnational America: Feminisms, Disaporas, Neoliberalisms*.
12. Sara Mills, *Discourses of Difference: An Analysis of Women's Travel Writing and Colonialism* (London: Routledge, 1993), p. 73. Originally published in 1991.
13. Heather Henderson, 'The Travel Writer and the Text: "My Giant Goes with Me Wherever I Go," ' in Michael Kowalewsi (ed.), *Temperamental Journeys: Essays on the Modern Literature of Travel* (Athens, GA: University of Georgia Press, 1992), p. 239.
14. Full bibliographic details for these texts are as follows: Martin Halliwell, *Transatlantic Modernism: Moral Dilemmas in Modern Fiction* (Edinburgh: Edinburgh University Press, 2005); Sarah Street, *Transatlantic Crossings: British Feature Films in the United States* (London: Continuum, 2002); and Christopher Mulvey, *Transatlantic Manners: Social Patterns in Nineteenth-Century Anglo-American Travel Literature* (Cambridge: Cambridge University Press, 1990).
15. See also the edited collections, Will Kaufman and Heidi Slettedahl Macpherson (eds), *Transatlantic Studies* (Lanham, MD: University Press of America, 2000), and Heidi Slettedahl Macpherson and Will Kaufman (eds), *New Perspectives in Transatlantic Studies* (Lanham, MD: University Press of America, 2002), the ABC-Clio *Transatlantic Relations* encyclopaedia series, as well as academic organisations and associations, such as the Maastricht Center for Transatlantic Studies (www.cmsu.edu/mcts) and the STAR project on Scotland's Transatlantic Relations at Edinburgh (www.star.ac.uk). The Duke University project, 'Oceans Connect: Maritime Perspectives in and Beyond the Classroom', which ran from 1997 until 2002 and was supported by the Ford Foundation, is another example of such a cross-disciplinary project, and though it ranged beyond the transatlantic space, and therefore is partially outside of boundaries of my own critique, it offered a challenge to traditional conceptions of area studies paradigms.

16. Sheila Hones and Julia Leyda, 'Towards a Critical Geography of American Studies', *Comparative American Studies* 2 (2) (2004): 186, italics in original.
17. Reingard Nethersole, 'Models of Globalization', *PMLA* 116 (3) (2001): 643.
18. R. Radhakrishnan, 'Globalization, Desire, and the Politics of Representation', *Comparative Literature* 53 (4) (2001): 318.
19. Ibid. p. 324.
20. David Thelen, 'The Nation and Beyond: Transnational Perspectives on United States History', *The Journal of American History* 86 (3) (1999): 968, italics in original.
21. Giles, *Virtual Americas*, p. 17.
22. Caren Kaplan, ' "A World Without Boundaries:" The Body Shop's Trans/National Geographics', *Social Text* 43 (1995): 48.
23. Ibid.
24. Inderpal Grewal and Caren Kaplan (eds), *Scattered Hegemonies: Postmodernity and Transnational Feminist Practices* (Minneapolis, MN: University of Minnesota Press, 1994), p. 11.
25. Inderpal Grewal, *Transnational America: Feminisms, Disaporas, Neoliberalisms* (Durham, NC: Duke University Press, 2005), p. 8.
26. James Clifford, *Routes: Travel and Translation in the Late Twentieth Century* (Cambridge, MA: Harvard University Press, 1999), p. 9. Originally published in 1997.
27. Ibid. p. 10.
28. Ibid. p. 6.
29. Gayatri Chakravorty Spivak, 'Three Women's Texts and a Critique of Imperialism', *Critical Inquiry* 12 (1985): 260 n. 1.
30. John Muthyala, *Reworlding America: Myth, History, and Narrative* (Athens, OH: Ohio University Press, 2006), p. 3.
31. Susan Gillman, Kirsten Silva Greusz and Rob Wilson, 'Worlding American Studies', *Comparative American Studies* 2 (3) (2004): 262.
32. Ibid.
33. Muthyala, *Reworlding*, p. 15.
34. Mary Layoun, 'The Female Body and "Transnational" Reproduction; or, Rape by Any Other Name?', in Grewal and Kaplan, *Scattered Hegemonies*, p. 65.
35. Wai Chee Dimock, 'Scales of Aggregration: Prenational, Subnational, Transnational', *American Literary History* 18 (2) (2006): 220.
36. Giles, *Virtual Americas*, p. 256.
37. Iain Chambers, *Migrancy, Culture, Identity* (London: Routledge, 1994), p. 5.
38. Chelva Kanaganayakam, 'Exiles and Expatriates', in Bruce King (ed.), *New National and Post-Colonial Literatures* (Oxford: Oxford University Press, 1996), pp. 201–13.

39. Edward Said, *Reflections on Exile and Other Literary and Cultural Essays* (London: Granta, 2000), p. 177.
40. Caren Kaplan, *Questions of Travel: Postmodern Discourses of Displacement* (Durham, NC: Duke University Press, 1996), p. 36.
41. Salman Rushdie, *Imaginary Homelands: Essays and Criticism 1981–1991* (London: Granta, 1992), p. 10.
42. Eva Hoffman, 'The New Nomads', in André Aciman (ed.), *Letters of Transit: Reflections on Exile, Identity, Language, and Loss* (New York: The New Press, 1999a), p. 58.
43. Dean MacCannell, *The Tourist: A New Theory of the Leisure Class* (Berkeley, CA: University of California Press, 1999), p. 191. Originally published in 1976. In an epilogue to the 1999 edition, which marked the second printing of the second edition, MacCannell argued that this claim still stood, as long as it was augmented by the understanding that sometimes, we take on the mantle of tour guide, too.
44. MacCannell, *Tourist*, p. xxiv.
45. It is also true, as Kaplan points out, the tourist

    is not a postmodern cosmopolitan subject who articulates hybridity for anxious moderns but a specifically Euro-American construct who marks shifting peripheries through travel in a world of structured economic asymmetries. Thus we cannot transform the tourist into the primary figure of our era because the tourist is as time bound and historically constructed as any other trope and cannot be made to stand for what it does not signify. (Kaplan, *Questions*, p. 63)

46. MacCannell, *Tourist*, p. 94; Barry Curtis and Claire Pajaczkowska, ' "Getting There": Travel, Time and Narrative', in George Robertson et al. (eds), *Travellers' Tales: Narratives of Home and Displacement* (London: Routledge, 1994), p. 206.
47. Kaplan, *Questions*, p. 64.
48. Curtis and Pajaczkowska, ' "Getting There" ', pp. 202–3.
49. John Urry, *The Tourist Gaze* (London: Sage, 2002), pp. 12–13. Originally published in 1990.
50. Rob Wilson and Wimal Dissanayake, 'Introduction: Tracking the Global/Local', in Rob Wilson and Wimal Dissanayake (eds), *Global/Local: Cultural Production and the Transnational Imaginary* (Durham, NC: Duke University Press, 1996), p. 6, italics in original.
51. Kaplan, *Questions*, p. 163.
52. Clifford, *Routes*, p. 12.
53. Ibid. p. 11.
54. Kaplan, 'World', p. 47.
55. Ulf Hannerz, *Transnational Connections: Culture, People, Places* (London: Routledge, 1996), p. 18.

56. Isabella Bird, *A Lady's Life in the Rocky Mountains* (London: Penguin, 1997). Originally published in 1873, the text that Penguin uses is the 1879 version. All references to this text will be cited parenthetically.

57. McClintock, *Imperial Leather*, p. 6.

58. Rockwell Gray, 'Travel', in Kowalewski, *Temperamental Journeys*, pp. 36–7; Karen Lawrence, *Penelope Voyages: Women and Travel in the British Literary Tradition* (Ithaca, NY: Cornell University Press, 1994), p. 19.

59. Evelyn Bach, 'A Traveller in Skirts: Quest and Conquest in the Travel Narratives of Isabella Bird', *Canadian Review of Comparative Literature/Revue Canadienne de Littérature Comparée* 22 (3–4) (1995): 590.

60. Ibid.

61. Clifford, *Routes*, p. 32.

62. Mills, *Discourses*, p. 119.

63. Morag Bell and Cheryl McEwan, 'The Admission of Women Fellows to the Royal Geographical Society, 1892–1914; the Controversy and the Outcome', *The Geographical Journal* 162 (3) (1996): 296–7.

64. Mills, *Discourses*, p. 9.

65. 'Obituary Note', *Journal of the Royal African Society* 4 (14) (1905): 261.

66. Mona Domosh, 'Toward a Feminist Historiography of Geography', *Transactions of the Institute of British Geographers* 16 (1) (1991): 99.

67. Ibid. p. 100.

68. David R. Stoddart, 'Do We Need a Feminist Historiography of Geography, And If We Do, What Should It Be?', *Transactions of the Institute of British Geographers* 16 (4) (1991): 484.

69. Ibid. p. 485.

70. Mills, *Discourses*, p. 103.

71. Chambers, *Migrancy*, p. 6.

72. Mills, *Discourses*, p. 106.

73. Chambers, *Migrancy*, p. 18, italics in original.

74. Lawrence, *Penelope*, p. xi.

75. Paul White, 'Geography, Literature and Migration', in Russell King et al. (eds), *Writing across Worlds: Literature and Migration* (London: Routledge, 1995), p. 3.

76. Charles Vandersee, 'Intertextual, International, Industrial Strength', *American Literary History* 6 (3) (1994): 419.

77. Lawrence, *Penelope*, p. 20.

78. Trinh T. Minh-ha, 'Other Than Myself/My Other Self', in Robertson et al., p. 21.

PART 1
THE EXOTICISED OTHER

INTRODUCTION

The construction of racial and ethnic identities across the transatlantic space almost inevitably leads to an investigation into the lure of the exotic 'other'. The enforced othering of those from different social, ethnic and religious backgrounds is a well-known phenomenon, one that a range of critics has ably examined, from Edward Said's exploration of Orientalism to Mary Louise Pratt's analysis of the 'contact zone' as well as other postcolonial examinations of identity and identity makers. Indeed, European and American travel literature, particularly from the nineteenth century, frequently rested on a notion of otherness against which the authors measured themselves and 'home'. Yet the concept of home is not entirely without its difficulties. Alasdair Pettinger's important anthology, *Always Elsewhere: Travels of the Black Atlantic*, explores how diasporic writers negotiate a sense of shifting identity, acknowledging that for these writers,

> it is not always clear where 'home' is. And for that reason it is the subject of a much wider range of emotions – nostalgia, indifference, exasperation, perplexity, embarrassment. In any case, the expected contrast between the familiarity of home and the strangeness of abroad that underpins so much travel literature is often absent.[1]

Moreover, many writers of the Black Atlantic encounter racist assumptions about who can travel, and why. Inderpal Grewal thus argues that the framework of travel as a 'universal form of mobility' is seriously flawed; it is, rather, a Eurocentric construction that aestheticises travel as choice and denies its other manifestations, such as slavery, deportation, im/migration, and indentured servitude.[2] At the same time, travel for travel's sake by diasporic writers seems to sit uneasily in the minds of some commentators. Pettinger reveals: '[T]he very *idea* that Black people might actually travel for the sake of it is hard for some to accept: "Are you visiting relatives?" "Do you work here?"'[3]

One of the disturbing implications here, of course, is that writers of the Black Atlantic will have conceptions of 'foreignness' thrust upon them wherever they go, including the domain of the casual tourist. The privilege of conferring foreignness upon others is not theirs, such an argument seems to suggest. It is in this framework, then, that I want to explore two short examples of transatlantic objectification by Caribbean writers, in order to unsettle notions of power and privilege, and to pave the way for the two chapters that follow, on Nella Larsen's *Quicksand* and Bharati Mukherjee's *Jasmine* respectively. Paule Marshall's *Praisesong for the Widow* (1983), which imagines an idealised transatlantic ethnic heritage, can be profitably read alongside Jamaica Kincaid's scathing essay attacking Caribbean tourism, *A Small Place* (1988).[4] Here, the Caribbean – an Atlantic location that is neither American nor European but impacted upon by both – becomes a site of renewal (*Praisesong*) or disease (*A Small Place*), with the tourist implicated in both constructions.

Before examining these texts and their construction of exoticism, however, I want to unpick the image of the Caribbean as a tourist destination, one that is even (especially?) promulgated by its authorised tourist websites. That the tagline of the official tourist website to Antigua was, until recently, 'The Caribbean you've always imagined', should give us pause, in that it both acknowledges the artificial construction of an actual geographic site and somehow covers over this understanding.[5] You – the tourist – are both subject and object of the advertising, which effectively erases the Antiguan resident.

'Come savour the many flavours of peaceful Antigua!' the Antigua online tourist guide demands. 'Immerse yourself in an exotic, amiable world at the heart of the Caribbean geographically, socially, culturally and spiritually.' In this reading, Antigua becomes 'a beach with an island in the middle': a tourist site *par excellence*. The brochure language continues: 'Its famed countless, silky beaches lapped by iridescent azure seas are cooled by lyric breezes.' Antigua is 'unspoilt', 'naturally charming', with a 'tradition of service' for 'selective visitors'. In short, it is paradise. At this point, it will come as no surprise that the visual sign of Antigua is a white woman lounging in a red bikini. *This* Antigua is a tourist's paradise: safe, clean, beautiful – white.[6] It is an image begging to be deconstructed. Linked into the desire for elsewhere, it is nevertheless an elsewhere of replication, and one that asserts the primacy of economic advantage and normative whiteness. It is an image that Kincaid's essay seeks to disrupt, if not destroy.

In Alain de Botton's lyrical paean to travel, *The Art of Travel*, he offers a clear reading of the European desire for an 'exotic' island as he deconstructs a tourist brochure of Barbados, yet (unlike Kincaid below), he suggests, albeit comically, that those who are at risk are the tourists themselves:

> Those responsible for the brochure had darkly intuited how easily their readers might be turned into prey by photographs whose power insulted the intelligence and contravened any notions of free will: over-exposed photographs of palm trees, clear skies and white beaches. Readers who would have been capable of scepticism and prudence in other areas of their lives reverted in contact with these elements to a primordial innocence and optimism. The longing provoked by the brochure was an example, at once touching and bathetic, of how projects (and even whole lives) might be influenced by the simplest and most unexamined images of happiness, of how a lengthy and ruinously expensive journey might be set in motion by nothing more than the sight of a photograph of a palm tree gently inclining in a tropical breeze.
>
> I resolved to travel to the island of Barbados.[7]

The final, one line paragraph wittily sums up the seduction of travel: its promise of another way of being, its sense of freedom and abandonment. Indeed, this is its very pull – though as de Botton later notes, discovering ennui in Barbados, 'A momentous but until then overlooked fact was making its first appearance: that I had inadvertently brought myself with me to the island.'[8] There is, therefore, no such thing as complete abandonment, and even a philosopher holds no claims to reading the transatlantic with objective eyes. De Botton's encounter with ennui is forcibly countered by Kincaid, who argues that the luxury of white ennui is responsible for destroying paradise. It is significant that de Botton's exploration of the Caribbean takes place not in his chapter 'On the Exotic' but in an earlier chapter, 'On Anticipation'. For the exotic, he explores Schiphol Airport in Amsterdam, a site not often associated with the adjective. This very unexpected use of the exotic offers an important counterpoint to the assumed location of the exotic, and what qualifies as such, and indeed, throughout the rest of this book, the exotic (linked to the foreign) continues to be explored in ways that unsettle and disrupt the alignment of the term with a specific kind of ethnicity.

Is this experience, as Pettinger and others above suggest, somehow different for diasporic writers? Paule Marshall's answer in *Praisesong for the Widow* suggests an unequivocal yes. Avey Johnson, the African-American widow of the title, experiences a similar ennui to de Botton while she is still on a Caribbean cruise ship named Bianca Pride, a cruise that is figured immediately as a retreat into whiteness. Avey's ennui has a different source from de Botton's: on board the ship (the sign of 'tourism with a vengeance' which, Paul Fussell argues, now stands in the place of real travel vessels),[9] she actually misrecognises herself and sees herself as – she thinks – the white passengers see her. This view is so disturbing that she elects to leave the ship early.

Here, the Caribbean is a site that the Caribbean-American tourist first circles around, and then tries to leave. Indeed, Avey's tourist journey signifies, in Carole Boyce Davies's eyes:

> a journey into the heart of whiteness, alienation, and separation. It is a frivolous journey which conveys only tourist status to Avey and symbolizes her middle class detachment and her immersion, achieved through her [late] husband's financial success, into Western, capitalist values and ethics.[10]

Davies's viewpoint seems, ironically, to accord with the potentially racist assumptions above, suggesting that travel for leisure is an inherently inappropriate pursuit for women like Avey, particularly within a Caribbean location. Yet *Praisesong for the Widow* is a call to home, to the country of origin, with the acknowledgement that for the Caribbean-American protagonist, this call is multiple and shifting. Avey is 'hailed' as Caribbean, an identity she at first refuses to recognise when approached by the islanders: ' "I'm afraid you've mistaken me for someone from around here, or from one of the other islands . . . who might know what you're talking about . . . I'm from the States. New York . . ." and she repeated it, "New York" ' (168, ellipses in original). Yet when she is asked by a Caribbean acquaintance to 'call her nation', she is not asked to identify with the US, but with her Caribbean and African ancestors. Avey's attempt to place herself, to relocate herself geographically, is complicated and incomplete.

As a tourist, Avey must insist upon and maintain distance; she is even faintly repulsed by the familiarity of the islanders, and recoils from their assumption of intimacy: '[F]rom the way they were acting she could have been simply one of them there on the wharf' (69). Avey's tourist persona is *shipped* from one island to another, but most of her vacation is spent inside; when Avey travels (off itinerary) on an excursion to Carriacou, in contrast, she does so upon a rickety sail-boat which moves with and against the waves rather than cutting through them as the cruise ship did. Unsurprisingly, she is violently ill, but even this purging is metaphorically part of her journey: she must let go of what she has become (what she has incorporated into her being), in order to reclaim an earlier self.

Davies argues that for Avey to recover, she must 'make the reverse journey back into the heart of blackness',[11] and thus here, the transatlantic journey is an imaginary one. Her journey is not so much circular as spiral, in that she moves back into a recognition of her historical and ethnic past, one that embraces her African as well as her Caribbean heritage. This reverse journey, as many critics have commented, mimics the Middle Passage as well as, more optimistically, the flight of the Ibos.[12] According to legend, the Ibos simply walked away from South Carolina and slavery by treading across water to their homeland. The spiral nature of Avey's journey is apparent when she resolves to return to the site of the Ibo Landing, in Tatem, South Carolina, where she spent her youth. Avey thus moves, initially, from the US on a cruise ship which is trapped in a circular and regulated pattern; she detours to Grenada, hoping for a non-stop flight back home. But stop she does; and soon she is taking her second detour: to Carriacou. From here she moves into her past and reconnects with it, so that her proposed journey back home will lead, eventually, to a new home in the old ancestral spot of Tatem. Perhaps the most important lesson that she learns comes to her early: ' "Just because we live over this side don' mean we's from this place, you know" ' (163). In learning to 'call her nation', Avey learns to reconnect.

Lindsey Tucker argues that for African-American women writers, 'mobility remains potent as a metaphor that is always more collective than individual.'[13] While Avey's journey is individual, it does resonate with the larger migrations – both enforced and chosen – that her Caribbean heritage implies. In this manifestation, the Caribbean is a *centrally* located transatlantic space, and one that offers renewal, rejuvenation and connection. Here, the gendered tourist misreads her situation (she considers herself separate from the islanders) but is never, herself, misread. Rather, she comes to understand that readings of her as Caribbean are accurate readings, and her tourism therefore rejuvenates her not in the way that those critical of tourists suggest (rich, naïve people getting away from it all to a 'simpler' space) but in ways that connect her transnationally to others.

The site of this renewal, however real, is somewhat indistinct, Carriacou remaining 'more a mirage rather than an actual place. Something conjured up perhaps to satisfy a longing and need' (254). This formulation of mirage is important. In *Praisesong for the Widow*, Marshall uses real locations but sites them within the realm of the mythic and imaginary. Marshall's exploration of the Caribbean is thus a complex one, in that she both recognises and manipulates the images attached both to the land itself and to those who visit or live there.

As has already been noted, John Urry has famously argued that 'tourists are semioticians, reading the landscape for signifiers of certain pre-established notions or signs derived from various discourses of travel and tourism.'[14] The discourse of travel, then, is marked by signs which are meant to be recognisable, which are meant to be read in ways that conform to and confirm the tourists' imagined location(s) – as indeed the tourist brochures above capitalise on with clear financial returns. Jamaica Kincaid turns this idea on its head in *A Small Place*, reading not the tourist location so much as the tourists themselves, as she attacks the tourist's leisured desire for the other and the exotic. If Marshall suggests an overarching beneficial connection between transatlantic spaces, Kincaid argues for the opposite. Her scathing attack on tourists offers a 'you people' address that forcibly others her imagined reading public: 'There must have been some good people among you, but they stayed home. And that is the point. That is why they are good. They stayed home' (35). Kincaid's extended essay – an angry memoir of resistance that links contemporary American tourism to British colonial rule – rereads paradise (Antigua) as a location of violent, historical encounters with lasting damage to this island space. If tourists, in escaping temporarily from their own lives, simply reflect back on themselves, they do not see this other location, which Kincaid's essay brings to the fore: a poor island, with no money to restore damaged buildings or build good quality schools and hospitals; an island with little rainfall.

Kincaid begins her attack with an innocuous line: 'If you go to Antigua as a tourist, this is what you will see' (3), yet alongside this list of sights, she offers other sights, another reading, which reveal the exploitation of the tourist's stay. Most importantly, though, according to Kincaid, the tourist sees one thing:

> You see yourself taking a walk on that beach, you see yourself meeting new people (only they are new in a very limited way, for they are people just like you). You see yourself eating some delicious, locally grown food. You see yourself, you see yourself . . . (13, ellipses in original)

Yet even in this seeing of yourself, you are mistaken, for, as Kincaid goes on to point out, 'A tourist is an ugly human being' (14). Kincaid's tourist is sometimes European, more likely American, and white (always white): the latest in a long line of people with colonial desires and misplaced superiority whose engagement with the contact zone leads to subjugation and destruction. *A Small Place* reveals the suspect political dimensions of an apparently innocent package tour, through which the tourist is both the logical extension of British colonial rule and American economic might. In this apparently innocent realm, the local 'tradition of service' is the logical extension of slavery. Native and tourist stand in entrenched opposition to each other; what defines them is power, or the lack of it.

Kincaid's strategy is the explicit othering of the descendants of those who have othered the Antiguan residents. She dismisses the tourist whilst recognising the tourist's damaging impact, and tries to prick the tourist's conscience at the same time: 'You needn't let that slightly funny feeling you have from time to time about exploitation, oppression, domination develop into full-fledged unease, discomfort; you could ruin your holiday' (10). Alison Donnell argues that the essay is 'a consummate work of ventriloquism which deploys a whole series of voices in order to debate the value and limitations of the cultural discourses and positions available to those interested in this small place and its people'.[15]

For Kincaid, the injunction against transatlantic encounters is absolute.[16] Her readings of Antigua strategically alter its 'exotic' appeal. The essay refuses – whilst strategically using – the very desire for the exotic. After all, Kincaid herself employs the language of a glossy tourist brochure in the final chapter of the small book (though, to be sure, to different ends):

> Antigua is beautiful. Antigua is too beautiful. Sometimes the beauty of it seems unreal. Sometimes the beauty of it seems as if it were stage sets for

a play, for no real sunset could look like that; no real seawater could strike that many shades of blue at once . . . no real day could be that sort of sunny and bright, making everything seem transparent and shallow; and no real night could be that sort of black, making everything seem thick and deep and bottomless. (77)

Yet Kincaid goes further than this; she doesn't allow the exotic beauty to speak for itself, but rather she reads over the beauty and acknowledges that

It is as if, then, the beauty – the beauty of the sea, the land, the air, the trees, the market, the people, the sounds they make – were a prison, and as if everything and everybody inside it were locked in and everything and everybody that was not inside it were locked out. (79)

The exotic here is an unacknowledged prison, the island's beauty used against itself, and (some of) the island's residents are complicit in this. It is this very complicity with exoticism that will be explored in the next two chapters, which move beyond the tourist to the traveller, that character who attempts a longer sojourn or indeed complete relocation. The 'exotic' is thus relocated to Denmark and to the heartland of the USA in these chapters, and exoticism becomes detached from place and associated with individuals.

NOTES

1. Alasdair Pettinger, 'Introduction', in *Always Elsewhere: Travels of the Black Atlantic* (London: Cassell, 1998), p. xvii.
2. Inderpal Grewal, *Home and Harem: Nation, Gender, Empire, and the Cultures of Travel* (London: Leicester University Press, 1996), p. 2.
3. Pettinger, *Always*, p. xiii, italics in original.
4. Paule Marshall, *Praisesong for the Widow* (London: Virago, 1989). Originally published in 1983. Jamaica Kincaid, *A Small Place* (London: Vintage, 1997). Originally published in 1988. These texts will be cited parenthetically.
5. See http://www.geographia.com/ANTIGUA-BARBUDA/press4.htm; the website has been updated with a new 'brand': 'The beach is just the beginning.' See http://www.antigua-barbuda.org/index.htm (accessed 27 July 2007)
6. See http://www.turq.com/antigua/ (accessed 27 July 2007); the original image of the white woman has subsequently been replaced by a photograph of a palm tree and one of a tourist looking out onto the waves;

this tourist is in shadow, which does not highlight skin colour or ethnicity, but the figure is still 'read' as white.

7. Alain de Botton, *The Art of Travel* (London: Hamish Hamilton, 2002),
   pp. 8–9.
8. de Botton, *Art*, p. 20.
9. Paul Fussell, *Abroad* (Oxford: Oxford University Press, 1982), p. 41.
   Originally published in 1980.
10. Carole Boyce Davies, 'Black Woman's Journey into Self: A Womanist
    Reading of Paule Marshall's *Praisesong for the Widow*', *Matatu:
    Journal for African Culture and Society* 1 (1)(1987): 22.
11. Davies, 'Black Woman', p. 23.
12. See, for example, G. Thomas Couser, 'Personal and Collective Memory
    in Paule Marshall's *Praisesong for the Widow* and Leslie Marmon
    Silko's *Ceremony*', in Amritjit Singh et al. (eds), *Memory and Cultural
    Politics: New Approaches to American Ethnic Literatures* (Boston, MA:
    Northeastern University Press, 1996), pp. 106–20, especially p. 111.
13. Lindsey Tucker, *Textual Escap(e)ades: Mobility, Maternity, and
    Textuality in Contemporary Fiction by Women* (Westport, CT:
    Greenwood, 1994), p. 11.
14. John Urry, *The Tourist Gaze* (London: Sage, 2002), pp. 12–13.
    Originally published in 1990.
15. Alison Donnell, 'Writing for Resistance: Nationalism and Narratives of
    Liberation', in Joan Anim-Addo (ed.), *Framing the Word: Gender and
    Genre in Caribbean Women's Writing* (London: Whiting and Birch,
    1996), p. 33.
16. Of course, Jamaica Kincaid herself famously lives outside of Antigua,
    having emigrated to the United States. She is thus here in the position of
    'returning stranger' though the text doesn't explicitly comment on this,
    or on the fact that her own biography shows that she, too, left home.

CHAPTER 1

CONSTRUCTING RACE ACROSS THE ATLANTIC: NELLA LARSEN'S *QUICKSAND*

Nella Larsen's *Quicksand* (1928) is an early twentieth-century novella that offers a contested reading of racial otherness and transatlantic exoticism.[1] Although it is a flawed text which relies on a series of coincidental encounters and more than a touch of melodrama, it is nevertheless a significant one in relation to questions of transnationalism and identity. Published originally on its own, it is now available only in a volume with a second novella, *Passing. Passing* receives substantially more critical interest than *Quicksand*, perhaps because of its subject matter, which, through its title, overtly signals its interest in issues of occluded identity, or perhaps because *Quicksand*'s conclusion points so resolutely to the negative, an ironic closure to a text that explores the problematics of racial uplift.

Quicksand's narrative encourages a bleeding between spaces and identities as it limns the peripatetic life of Helga Crane. Helga believes that she was born out of wedlock, and this early uncertainty over identity markers is repeated in a variety of ways throughout the plot. Helga's white Danish mother raised her in the US, after her black American father abandoned the family. Her mother marries a white man when Helga is a child and bears more children, the result of which is Helga's exclusion from family life. She is temporarily 'rescued' by a white uncle who sends her to school, and she eventually secures a job teaching in the prestigious, but to her stifling black school, Naxos, which is dedicated to racial uplift. Abandoning this post and the man she was to marry, James Vayle, Helga travels to Chicago, only to be renounced by her uncle's new wife, before moving on to New York.

Helga is disowned by her American-based wealthy white family because they are ashamed of her mother's liaison with a black man, and this is a betrayal that Helga feels keenly. At the same time, precisely because of her mother's ethnicity, Helga is unsure of her own position within the African-American community in Harlem and is complicit with a hiding of this identity, almost colluding, therefore, with a reverse passing into blackness. Such conflicts inevitably unsettle Helga, who moves frequently between locations in a search for a place to belong.

Helga is, the text tells us, 'in love with the piquancy of leaving' (15), and this is something she does with regularity throughout the short novel. Midway through the text, Helga makes what she thinks is a lasting move to Denmark, to be embraced by her white European (as opposed to white American) relatives, an embrace that is at first comforting and welcomed, though later experienced with some unease, as familial-racial alliances are set in opposition to each other. After her two year sojourn in Copenhagen, she returns – temporarily, she thinks – to New York. Although she plans to cross the ocean again, she never does. Instead, in despair one night over her thwarted plans to seduce Dr Anderson, a man who has shown up in several key moments of her life, she finds herself in a Pentecostal church, branded a jezebel. Helga, still a virgin, decides to make this label stick (as others have not) and seduces the visiting minister, the Reverend Mr Pleasant Green, before swiftly marrying him, moving to rural poverty in Alabama, and bearing four children in quick succession. As this summary reveals, this is a novella that incorporates a variety of identity markers and allegiances – both national and racial – as well as a series of spaces within a mere 135 pages.

Helga is, in a sense, caught up in beginnings, which is why, perhaps, her ending is so unsatisfactory for the reader. With each new move to another space, Helga feels that the new beginning is going to lead to better things, and this is as true of Alabama as it is of other locations: 'As always, at first the novelty of the thing, the change, fascinated her. There was a recurrence of the feeling that now, at last, she had found a place for herself, that she was really living' (118). However, by the conclusion of the book, fewer than twenty pages later, the once-vibrant Helga is overcome by monstrous maternity and is possibly facing – if not welcoming – death.

Almost all criticisms of Larsen's short novel explore Helga's love of colour and the ways in which Larsen frames her heroine as an artistic object; many trace resonances between Helga's life story and Larsen's (contested) biography; most explore the disappointing con-

clusion to the text.[2] Few, however, explore the transatlantic resonances of the novel in any depth, beyond suggesting that Helga's
journey to Denmark is another step on her quest for stable identity,
a quest that is ultimately (and perhaps inevitably) unfulfilled. Yet
Helga's transatlantic crossing offers the most important space for critique of this novella. After all, Larsen (presumably deliberately) suggests a resonance with some infamous African Americans travelling
in Europe between the wars. The response they received parallels, in
part, the responses that Helga produces in the Europeans she encounters, and it is Helga's process of accepting – and later rejecting – these
transatlantic responses that is the key to situating the text within a
contested framework of identity and exoticism.

As Toni Morrison records in her novel *Beloved*, 'Definitions
belonged to the definers – not the defined.'[3] In Morrison's novel this
sentiment evokes the power differential between the enslaved and
those who abuse their labour, and portrays a hierarchy that is seemingly fixed on racial lines. Yet the very need to articulate the fixity of
this position belies its transitory nature, as Morrison's novel and
others have shown. Who has the power to define shifts, a factor that
is implicitly and explicitly explored in transatlantic texts. In such
texts, space itself is in flux, demarcated only in the abstract.
Quicksand explores what it means to be defined, and how through,
among other things, a transatlantic sojourn, constant role reversals
are imposed on the 'definers' and the 'defined'. It is my intention in
what follows to explore how Larsen's text focuses on the impact of
race and gender in a transatlantic framework and sets up uncomfortable questions about who is in control of transatlantic image making
and identity.

It is significant that it is almost exactly half way through
Quicksand that Larsen's heroine – if such she is – travels to Denmark
to visit her Danish relatives, imagining that such a movement will
allow her the space to become a newer, better, more authentic
version of herself, and it is this part of the text on which I plan to
dwell, not least because it is her very transatlantic identity that
causes Helga anxiety, whilst also offering her (admittedly limited)
opportunities. On the ship taking her to Copenhagen, she has 'that
blessed sense of belonging to herself alone and not to a race' (64).
Her fantasies of difference, despite troubling her in the US, are
reconfigured here as positive, and as opportunities to explore: 'With
rapture almost, she let herself drop into the blissful sensation of visu-
alizing herself in different, strange places, among approving and

admiring people, where she would be appreciated, and understood'
(57). This adolescent desire for approval and understanding is at
odds with strangeness, but she remains unaware of the tension in her
desire.

Although critics label the novella semi-autobiographical (not
withstanding the very different ending that Helga Crane endures),
they disagree about whether Larsen herself ever made a transatlantic
journey. In recounting her own life, Larsen spoke of a trip to Denmark
to visit family as a child (a memory that is also recounted in
Quicksand) and a longer visit as a young adult, where she claimed to
have studied at the University of Copenhagen. These facts were taken
as read by scholars until two texts in the early 1990s cast doubt on
Larsen's claims. Charles R. Larson's *Invisible Darkness* and Thadious
M. Davis's biography *Nella Larsen: Novelist of the Harlem
Renaissance: A Woman's Life Unveiled* both suggest that Larsen
fictionalised her life, in order to appear 'different' herself: thus Helga's
adolescent desire becomes, in these readings, Larsen's own. Here, too,
the transatlantic sojourn is figured as exotic, unusual, and therefore
something that casts doubt over authenticity.

Larson's contention that Nella Larsen never visited Copenhagen is
based upon his own suppositions and a lack of evidence about such
travel. Larson claims: 'I have come to the conclusion that her
Denmark years are a total fabrication, a fancy embroidery upon the
tragedy of her early life.'[4] Yet as a biographer, Larson admits to
having to grapple with the lack of documentary evidence for many
aspects of Larsen's biography. He claims that on her application for a
passport in 1930, she writes that she had never had a previous passport, and argues that this invalidates her claim to earlier transatlantic
travel. However, US passports were not compulsory until as late as
1941,[5] which means that the lack of an earlier passport cannot be
read as definitive proof that previous transatlantic travel did not
occur.

Claudia Tate follows Larson and Davis in seeing the Copenhagen
sections of *Quicksand* as completely fabricated, as does Cheryl A.
Wall, whereas other critics – notably George Hutchinson – argue that
Larsen did indeed visit and live in Copenhagen as she claims.[6]
Hutchinson's painstaking reconstruction is convincing, though
perhaps the truth of Larsen's visits will never be fully established.
Certainly it is the case that African-American writers, artists and
scholars visited Europe in the early part of the twentieth century as,
critics point out, had many in centuries past, with a variety of

receptions. Most famously they include Frederick Douglass, who toured Ireland and Great Britain; Ida B. Wells who visited England at the end of the nineteenth century, Philiss Wheatley who did so a century earlier; W.E.B. Du Bois who travelled extensively in Europe; Richard Wright, who emigrated to France; and James Baldwin, who spent considerable time in France and elsewhere in Europe. Larsen's contemporary Jessie Faucet also travelled extensively in Europe.

Thus Helga's focus on difference, whether or not it has a biographical connection to Larsen, certainly has antecedents. Josephine Baker famously traded on her reputation for exoticism in the Revue Negre performances in Paris, her body displayed as a text to be misread, a point to which I will return later. A less well-known misread exoticism is recounted in Langston Hughes's 1956 autobiography, *I Wonder as I Wander*. Hughes, exploring the opportunities and artifice available to African Americans abroad, recalls an encounter with a woman in Paris who claimed to have Javanese and Dutch heritage and who 'spoke hesitant English and broken French with a Georgia drawl'. Although Hughes's companion suggests that the woman is 'colored, from somewhere in Dixie, passing for Javanese in Paris', Hughes notes:

> The girl was so exotic-looking that I doubted she was American, and disputed his insistence on it. I was wrong. Later I ran into the girl in New York talking perfectly good Harlemese, and not passing for anything on Lenox Avenue where she was quite at home.[7]

Here, it appears, the tag 'exotic' cannot be associated with the tag 'American', and yet such markers do exist simultaneously, though disruptively. Clearly, both the viewer and the location are implicated in this assertion of exoticism, almost more so than the individual to whom the tag is attached, and questions of who defines whom are raised again.

If Helga's self-creation in Europe is not as dramatic as this, it is true that she deliberately defines herself as a transatlantic 'other' in order to attract and maintain the gaze and attention of the Danes: 'Intentionally, she kept to the slow, faltering Danish. It was, she decided, more attractive than a nearer perfection' (74). Helga's desire for attractiveness is paramount, and her decision to embrace 'otherness' and to foreground the distinctions between herself and those around her is another step in her ongoing self-betrayal. Always a capable woman who is shown in several earlier instances to react against confinement – even to the point of abandoning a successful teaching career because it does not allow her to give full reign to her abilities – Helga here codes her behaviour as *chosen*, resisting (or refusing to see) another reading which links faltering to incompetence, with implications attached both to her race and to her gender. Helga's masquerade is, however, linked to both identity markers.

Judith Butler argues that one aspect of performativity (in *Gender Trouble*, linked solely to gender though equally applicable to race performativity) is that it obscures its genesis: 'If the "cause" of desire, gesture, and act can be localized within the "self" of the actor, then the political regulations and disciplinary practices which produce that ostensibly coherent gender are effectively displaced from view.'[8] Thus, Helga believes she *chooses* to perform faultily, but her choice is circumscribed by the culture that she interacts with and against. She is 'choosing' to fulfil a role that has been explicitly set out for her.

Helga's express aim in moving to Denmark is to leave questions of race and race allegiance behind. Yet it is clear that Helga's desire for release from an explicit awareness of race is a naïve one; moreover, her decision to move to northern Europe almost necessarily ensures that she will be marked by race even more visibly than before. In the US South and in Chicago and Harlem, she is read as African-American, her skin colour virtually unremarked upon. Indeed, the first long description of her, upon which many critics focus, shows Helga bathed in light and darkness, costumed in a rich green and gold negligee, but this lengthy passage does not explicitly highlight Helga's own skin colour or ethnicity. As Linda Dittmar acknowledges:

> What Larsen refrains from telling us in this opening passage is that Helga is black. Skin, lips, nose, and hair – Larsen's treatment has them elude (though never quite negate) racial coding, just as the description of Helga's taste for orientalist exoticism positions her outside of both Western and African aesthetics.[9]

Yet throughout the text, as if to highlight the importance of visual markers, Larsen deliberately focuses on a variety of colours, as the following passage on Helga's US departure demonstrates:

> The liner drew out from churning slate-colored waters of the river into the open sea. The small seething ripples on the water's surface became little waves. It was evening. In the western sky was a pink and mauve light, which faded gradually into a soft gray-blue obscurity. (63)

Larsen's use of colour here is not accidental; as Wall has remarked, grey is coded in Larsen's work as a marker of racial indeterminacy.[10] It is therefore significant that Helga's would-be lover, Dr Anderson, has grey eyes, whereas her friend in New York, Anne Grey, is ironically named such, because she finds the intermingling of races repugnant. In exploring Larsen's use of colour, critics most often focus on passages relating to a jazz club in Harlem, where Helga is confronted with a kaleidoscope of different skin tones:

> [T]he crowd became a swirling mass. For the hundredth time she marvelled at the gradations within this oppressed race of hers. A dozen shades slid by. There was sooty black, shiny black, taupe, mahogany, bronze, copper, gold, orange, yellow, peach, ivory, pinky white, pastry white. There was yellow hair, brown hair, black hair; straight hair, straightened hair, curly hair, crinkly hair, woolly hair. She saw black eyes in white faces, brown eyes in yellow faces, gray eyes in brown faces, blue eyes in tan faces. Africa, Europe, perhaps with a pinch of Asia, in a fantastic motley of ugliness and beauty, semi-barbaric, sophisticated, exotic, were here. But she was blind to its charm, purposely aloof and a little contemptuous, and soon her interest in the moving mosaic waned. (59–60)

This is indeed a significant passage, offering, as it does, transatlantic convergence, particularly as the entire jazz scene is infused with contradictory narratives about race and race allegiance. For example, near the end of the night, Helga berates herself for being taken in by the 'jungle' and this strengthens her resolve to leave the US. Thus, this medley of colours is directly linked to Helga's transatlantic push and her choice to depart from the 'mosaic of Harlem to become an isolated exotic'.[11]

Important as these textual moments are, particularly the last one, where Helga is the gazer and not the gazed upon, it is just as important to highlight less obvious passages focusing on colour and movement, such as the one above that makes the Atlantic – the in-between – a grey space. The water closer to shore, closer to the US, is 'seething', only to become 'little waves' in the open sea. Such a description does more than illustrate the movement of water; it is a metaphor for Helga's view of racial politics, and it is significant that the further from shore she gets, the happier Helga feels.

For all her awareness of others looking at her, indeed her own encouragement to do so, Helga remains stubbornly blind to the implications of her desire. Yet even on the ship taking her from the US, she is subject to the transatlantic gaze that constructs her in particular ways: by the ship's purser, who remembers her as a 'little dark girl' who travelled with her mother, a woman clearly not so emphatically marked by colour (63), and by her fellow passengers, all Danes, whose 'politely curious glances . . . soon slid from her' (64). To them, again, Helga is a spectacle, though of limited interest and appeal. On arrival in Copenhagen, the morning sky turns from 'purply gray' to 'opal' and 'gold' before righting itself as blue (64), as if to suggest the riches that await Helga on these new shores. Certainly it is the case that she will soon be adorned with wealth she had not previously imagined, all for the purpose of putting her on display, making her subject to the gaze and accentuating her ethnically African ties.

One of the first examples of the transatlantic gaze comes on the afternoon of her arrival in Copenhagen. (After all, her transatlantic origins are obscured when she lives in the US, since there she is simply viewed as a light-skinned African-American; thus in the country of her birth, her colour could be read as deriving from historical rape and capture rather than more recent 'miscegenation'.) The transatlantic gaze is revealed when the maid wakes Helga after a nap. Larsen inserts several passages of Helga's awakenings in the text, yet they rarely stand up to the freight of symbolism attached; Helga almost never really awakens, and those times that she does – as at the end of the novel, when she recognises what a mistake she has made in marrying the Reverend Pleasant Green – she does not have the strength to put in motion her plans to rectify the error.

In Copenhagen, however, she wakes refreshed, and is both the spectator – watching the maid go about her duties – and the spectacle herself, the object of the gaze: 'In New York, America, Helga would have resented this sly watching. Now, here, she was only amused. Marie, she reflected, had probably never seen a Negro outside the pictured pages of her geography book' (68). Helga's response is intriguing: in an othered space, she doesn't mind being othered, yet she also understands that most representations of – in her terms – a 'Negro' would be set at a remove, and possibly, if not probably, stressing exoticism, perhaps even barbarity.

It is because Helga sees herself at the opposite end of this construction (she is, after all, a *cultured* African-American woman who has distanced herself from the 'jungle') that she grants the maid the opportunity to look. Of course, the maid is a woman not of her Danish family's social standing, and thus Helga's assumed class position in Denmark (as opposed to the US) allows her to feel superior. Indeed, Helga believes that Marie views her thus as well. Of course, it is not long before Helga encounters constructions of barbarity again, but this time from her own family.

In convincing Helga to wear something more colourful (something that the established women of Naxos disliked as showy and improper but that Helga has always craved), Aunt Katrina says, ' "And you're a foreigner, and different. You must have bright things to set off the color of your lovely brown skin. Striking things, exotic things. You must make an impression" ' (68). Thus on a shopping trip, Helga is presented with a range of new adornments, from bracelets with their (unacknowledged) iconography of slavery to long earrings and buckles for her shoes, so much so that 'Helga felt like a veritable savage as they made their leisurely way across the pavement from the shop to the waiting motor. This feeling was intensified by the many pedestrians who stopped to stare at the queer dark creature, strange to their city' (69). 'Savage', 'queer', 'creature' – the words themselves signify that Helga's assumed superiority is in question and that at some level, though not yet at a conscious one, she recognises this.

Helga's discomfiture with this scene is replicated in other situations: a tea later that day and an evening event at which she is again quite visibly on display. She remains virtually silent throughout these encounters, not only because her grasp of Danish is incomplete, but because she cannot articulate even in English how this display makes her feel – or rather, because this display evokes competing and contradictory desires within her. At first:

> Helga herself felt like nothing so much as some new and strange species of pet dog being proudly exhibited. Everyone was polite and very friendly, but she felt the massed curiosity and interest, so discreetly hidden under the polite greetings. The very atmosphere was tense with it. 'As if I had horns, or three legs,' she thought . . . . (70)

Later, however, when she is dressed in ' "practically nothing but a skirt" ' (70), she becomes 'thankful for the barbaric bracelets, for the dangling ear-rings, for the beads about her neck. She was even thankful for the rouge on her burning cheeks and the very powder on her back. No other woman in the stately pale-blue room was so greatly exposed' (70). The colour of the room is linked to northern European good taste; she is the opposite, decked out in green velvet, 'cut down' to offer maximum exposure of her skin for the delight and viewing of the audience of Danes. The parallels with the European display of Josephine Baker's body are surely not accidental. Moreover, there is also an implicit link between this space and the other space in which black bodies had historically been displayed for white audiences: in Harlem. Kimberley Roberts argues that during the Harlem Renaissance, 'the black body became an economic quantity for consumption by white audiences in various venues',[12] but Helga fled Harlem because she did not want to be part of this display, never recognising that it would be recapitulated elsewhere.

Despite her misgivings, Helga 'liked the small murmur of wonder and admiration which rose when Uncle Poul brought her in. She liked the compliments in the men's eyes as they bent over her hand. She liked the subtle half-understood flattery of her dinner partners' (70), and it is this part of the bargain that she accepts: she will tolerate being treated as other so long as that is accompanied by admiration. When it is not, she resists the position offered to her.

It is her very 'foreignness' (in ethnic rather than national terms) that constitutes her value for her Danish relatives, and this is a sea-change from her childhood, where her black skin provoked resentment and unease, and eventually led to exile from her family. Helga comes to understand that her Aunt Katrina means to accent Helga's difference, and while she is unsure of the propriety of this stance – 'Hitherto all her efforts had been toward similarity to those about her' (72) – she allows it to proceed, so long as it offers her a place, of some kind, in Danish society. In fact, in a wonderfully condensed if not confused passage, Helga is appraised as worthy of being painted by the famous Axel Olsen, though the business of deciding this is kept between her aunt, her uncle and the painter: 'Here she was, a curiosity, a stunt, at which people came and gazed. And was she to be treated like a secluded young miss, a Danish *frøkken*, not to be consulted personally even on matters affecting her personally?' (71–2). The answer is yes – and no. Helga's recognition and slight misrecognition of her place signify her unwillingness to confront fully her own status in Denmark. It is not so much her position as a Danish miss that means she is not consulted; it is her position as an exotic other, a position that she both colludes with and resents. She knows that she is a 'decoration. A curio. A peacock' (73); she understands that her role is to 'incite': 'She was incited to inflame attention and admiration. She was dressed for it, subtly schooled for it. And after a little while she gave herself up wholly to the fascinating business of been seen, gaped at, desired' (74). *Gave herself up*. The language says it all.

As Wall notes, 'to succeed on the terms she is given, she must play herself false. While Helga . . . never considers passing for white, she is keenly aware that the image she projects is fraudulent.'[13]

Kimberly Monda is less forgiving, arguing that Helga has been 'seduced into playing the role of "primitive" other through the false experience of subjectivity granted by consumeristic purchasing and self-display'.[14] Helga's desire for approval, for the admiring gaze, blinds her to the downside of this position. She argues: 'She had to admit that the Danes had the right idea. To each his own milieu. Enhance what was already in one's possession' (74). Yet Helga's milieu is exactly that which is in doubt – where does she belong? Does Europe extend to her that which the US did not? Jeffrey Gray posits the possibility that it may:

> For the African-American artist, Europe functions as a way of altering positionality, and thus as a means of finding one's way out of notions of 'essence' . . . because the geographical/cultural movement itself allows the Subject the possibility of uncovering the constructedness of representations, on either side of the Atlantic.[15]

If Helga is, as Wall suggests, 'an artist without an art form', then perhaps this altering of her position helps.[16] But Gray isn't so sure after all: 'all that Helga finally "has" in Europe is her alterity, which, though impossible for her to bring into focus, becomes her obsession and her treasure.'[17]

To be different, she must resist the US, and she claims not to think of it often, 'excepting in unfavourable contrast to Denmark' (75). Yet she contradicts her own position by acknowledging that this is a willed gesture, not an unconscious one: 'So she turned her back on painful America, resolutely shutting out the griefs, the humiliations, the frustrations, which she had endured there. Her mind was occupied with other and nearer things' (75). In fact, she resists thinking of the US because 'it was too humiliating, too disturbing. And she wanted to be left to the peace which had come to her. Her mental difficulties and questionings had become simplified' (75). They are simplified, perhaps, but not banished. Her own problems with identity and position become exacerbated after the first of what turns out to be many visits to a local vaudeville house, the Circus. The evening's entertainment is dull, but it is remarkably enlivened by the entrance of two black men, whom Helga supposes to be American. Her description of their antics focuses on the exaggeration of their movements: they 'pranced', 'cavorted' and 'danced, pounding their thighs, slapping their hands together, twisting their legs, waving their abnormally long arms, throwing their bodies about with a loose ease' (82–3). It is in seeing this performance – so wildly applauded by her companions – that Helga reviews her own performance.

For contemporary audiences, this performance also draws forth comparisons with Josephine Baker's shows in Paris. Debra Silverman explores the way in which the Revue Negre was considered insufficiently 'black' in its original form, and in need of further elaborations from a Parisian producer, Jacques Charles:

> The 'blackening' of the Revue Negre was a move to domesticate and homogenize the black American performers in the show – to create 'authentic' blackness as already figured in stereotypes of blackness. It can be read as a move to sensationalize and dramatize blackness – the move to personify and embody stereotypical performances of blackness for the pleasure of an audience.[18]

As audience, Helga is unable to feel pleasure, yet she compulsively returns to the show, 'an ironical and silently speculative spectator' (83). Yves Clemmen suggests that this is because Helga understands that her 'uniqueness is denounced as artificial: all along she has been seen by others as a generic Negro woman'.[19] Indeed, Helga's own confused thoughts suggest as much: 'For she knew that into her plan for her life had thrust itself a suspensive conflict in which were fused doubts, rebellion, expediency, and urgent longings' (83). Yet at the same time, this is too easy an answer, as an encounter with an old countrywoman betrays:

> Here it was that one day an old countrywoman asked her to what manner of mankind she belonged and at Helga's replying: 'I'm a Negro,' had become indignant, retorting angrily that, just because she was old and a countrywoman she could not be so easily fooled, for she knew as well as everyone else that Negroes were black and had woolly hair. (76)

In this construction, Helga is *not* a Negro; she does not conform to stereotyped expectations and again, questions over who has the power to define become confused. Is Helga's self-definition sufficient, or does a stranger, an old Danish countrywoman, hold more power? Significantly, Larsen slides over this question, and the encounter is never remarked upon again, except in relation to the fact that Helga's Danish family find her wandering ways unsettling.

For some, this refusal to comment may appear to be politically naïve, but Wall argues that Larsen's task was always insurmountable, since 'examining the intersection of race, class, and gender was a perilous business. She could derive no safe or simple truths.'[20] Wall further suggests that though ambiguity is seen as a hallmark of modernist literature, for writers of the Harlem Renaissance, no such allowances were made; instead, such writers were supposed to be very clear on their allegiances. Yet Larsen, like many other African-American artists of the time, felt strongly that Europe offered opportunities to forge transnational identities. Paul Gilroy argues that experiences of transatlantic travel:

> raise in the sharpest possible form a question common to the lives of almost all of these figures who begin as African-Americans or Caribbean people and are then changed into something else which evades those specific labels and with them all fixed notions of nationality and national identity.[21]

Thus Helga, as a fictional construction of a woman who may or may not herself have travelled to Europe, is not alone in her 'desire to escape the restrictive bonds of ethnicity, national identification, and sometimes even "race" itself', a transcendent desire that Gilroy links specifically to the Black Atlantic.[22]

Yet such transcendence is more dream than reality, as the encounter above denotes, or an even earlier encounter shows. The first Dane whom Helga meets on disembarking from the ship is Fru Fisher, a woman whom Helga believes to be worldly since she had once lived in England; yet even this apparently cultured woman eventually betrays herself as racist, deriding the 'Bolsheviks and Japs and things' who populate a particular restaurant (80). Although she begs Helga's pardon for not liking American music, she does not think to try to excuse her racism. The griefs that Helga turns her back on in the US continue to confront her face to face in Denmark.

Clearly, however much Helga attempts to define herself with a stable identity, a host of perceptions combine to undermine that stability. Larsen's novel suggests that there is a particular difficulty in considering the 'foreign' or the 'exotic' in a diasporic context like that of the Black Atlantic, in which one's foreignness is as pervasive at 'home' as it is 'away', when it is mapped by friends, strangers and family alike. More than one critic has noted that Helga has no living black family; her only known family – including, of course, in Denmark – is white.[23]

What Larsen is able to do in this novel, as Chip Rhodes and other scholars note, is compress into a relatively short novel a number of encounters with ideological systems, with the opportunity to defamiliarise subject positions and reveal their contingent nature.[24] Such movement also suggests the particularly narrow definition of race in the US.[25] Yet to set up the US as corrupt and Europe as a new Eden is also shown to be a false comparison. Helga cannot escape the construction of race by traversing the Atlantic, or by becoming an immigrant. In fact, Gray argues that Helga, as a 'travelling mulatto figure' serves to 'heighten our awareness of that absence of determined essence, and of the reality that the construction of the Self goes on, home and abroad, subject to forces that crowd the body with contradictory representations – pleasant and disturbing, limiting and enabling'.[26]

Helga comes closest to this realisation herself when she admits that her life will be forever divided:

> [T]his certainty of the division of her life into two parts in two lands, into physical freedom in Europe and spiritual freedom in America, was unfortunate, inconvenient, expensive. It was, too, as she was uncomfortably aware, even a trifle ridiculous . . . (96)

A trifle ridiculous. Helga is indeed made ridiculous in this text, no more so than when she is painted as a lascivious African by a famous Danish artist, Axel Olsen. Olsen, described in the text as 'brilliant, bored, elegant, urbane, cynical, worldly' (77), is almost anything but; his worldliness is more aligned with worlding, or the construction of the world in colonialist and restrictive nationalist terms.[27] In fact, though he believes otherwise, he knows little of Helga or her society, yet when he paints her, he claims to know the truth of her:

> He had made, one morning, while holding his brush poised for a last, a very last stroke on the portrait, one admirably draped suggestion, speaking seemingly to the pictured face. Had he insinuated marriage, or something less – and easier? Or had he paid her only a rather florid compliment, in somewhat dubious taste? Helga, who had not at the time been quite sure, had remained silent, striving to appear unhearing. (84)

Despite her unwillingness to hear his comment (which mirrors her willed blindness elsewhere), she has to face it once he both proposes marriage to her and unveils the painting. His portrait is that of a prostitute. At this point, she can no longer be blind to the spectacle she has been made into, nor the reality of her transatlantic sojourn. She is no more able to leave race behind in Denmark than she is in the US.

The five middle chapters of *Quicksand* provide a central focal point for exploring the problematics of location within the Atlantic world. Helga, who first conceals her difference to her Harlem friends and then, on her return, accentuates it, and who is othered in Denmark in both admiring and sinister ways, eventually learns that she cannot control her own reception. In trying to leave race behind, she misreads the racial politics abroad and is herself, therefore, misread. Within Helga, Gray argues, 'the two questions of indeterminacy and of geographical "place" are not only equally paramount but finally become a single question'.[28]

Ultimately, of course, Helga abandons her dream of shuttling across the transatlantic space, in order to mire herself in that which she has always avoided, maternity and poverty. Always positioned as a consumer, she is now consumed by an identity that does not sit easily on her shoulders. Ironically, perhaps, Helga is as foreign in Alabama as she was in Denmark, and is, moreover, disregarded as an ' "uppity, meddlin' No'the'nah" ' (119). This is another space in which she does not belong, and another example of how her textual wandering equates with instability – at least in the eyes of others. As Karen Lawrence maintains, women's wandering is too often associated with promiscuity,[29] a link that Helga has never herself been able to break. Lawrence asks:

> Can women writers revise the various plots of wandering (in romance, adventure, exploration, and travel narratives) without succumbing to the traditional pitfalls of these plots for a female protagonist? Such a question intersects feminist concerns about whether women will 'get caught' in their own imitation of patriarchal discourse and myth, unable to repeat with a difference.[30]

If a kind of liberation politics is being asked for here, *Quicksand* does not provide it, as its very title seems to suggest. Yet if this is a disappointing end to the text, it remains somehow appropriate. As Hostetler argues, 'Structured as a journey, the novel appears to criticize the narrative closure of the journey motif as well as the path to

success mapped out by popular notions of racial uplift.'[31] Helga,
who has set herself apart and who thinks she controls her image, is
continually defined in opposition to herself. *Quicksand* reveals
that however optimistically the transatlantic embrace is forged, its
reshaping of identities is not always positive, long-term or beneficial.
There is no idealistic resolution to this text, nor any sense that Helga
can step outside of her complicated and complicating cultural
inheritance.

As with Helga, so it also was, to a certain extent, with Nella
Larsen. In 1930, Larsen became the first African-American woman to
receive a Guggenheim Fellowship for Creative Writing. The prize was
$2,000 to travel to Europe and to write a novel about '"the different
effects of Europe and the United States on the intellectual and physical freedom of the Negro" '.[32] It was a novel that Larsen never wrote.
Perhaps her flirtation with the transatlantic narrative had already
been played out, like Axel's clumsy wooing of Helga; perhaps there
are other reasons why her journeys did not result in further literature.
Clifford suggests that 'many people choose to limit their mobility, and
even more are kept "in their place" by repressive forces.'[33] For both
Larsen and her fictional counterpart, transatlantic travel is fraught
with such repressive forces, which bleed into the narrative of space
and agency, to show how both race and gender shape the journey. In
Quicksand, the significant image is one of the grey waters of the
Atlantic, which offer a fit and final metaphor for Helga's muddled,
seething journey.

NOTES

1. Nella Larsen, *Quicksand and Passing* (London: Serpent's Tail, 1995).
   Originally published in 1928. All references to this text will be cited parenthetically.
2. See, for example, Pamela E. Barnett, Linda Dittmar and Cheryl Wall on
   colour and artistry, Claudia Tate on biography, and Deborah E.
   McDowell on the conclusion of *Quicksand*.
3. Toni Morrison, *Beloved* (London: Picador, 1988), p. 190. Originally
   published in 1987.
4. Charles R. Larson, *Invisible Darkness: Jean Toomer and Nella Larsen*
   (Iowa City, IA: University of Iowa, 1993), p. 189.
5. See, amongst other sources, *The United States Passport: Past, Present,
   and Future* (Washington, DC: US Government Printing Office, 1976)
   and http://www.archives.gov/genealogy/passport/, accessed 23 March
   2008.

6. George Hutchinson, 'Nella Larsen and the Veil of Race', *American Literary History* 9 (2) (1997): 329–49.
7. Langston Hughes, *I Wonder as I Wander*, in Alasdair Pettinger (ed.), *Always Elsewhere: Travels of the Black Atlantic* (London: Cassell, 1998), p. 252.
8. Judith Butler, *Gender Trouble: Feminism and the Subversion of Identity* (New York: Routledge, 1999), pp. 173–4. Originally published in 1990.
9. Linda Dittmar, 'When Privilege is No Protection: The Woman Artist in *Quicksand* and *The House of Mirth*', in Suzanne W. Jones (ed.), *Writing the Woman Artist: Essays on Poetics, Politics and Portraiture* (Philadelphia, PA: University of Pennsylvania Press, 1991), p. 147.
10. Cheryl A. Wall, *Women of the Harlem Renaissance* (Bloomington, IN: Indiana University Press, 1995), p. 87.
11. Ann E. Hostetler, 'The Aesthetics of Race and Gender in Nella Larsen's *Quicksand*', *PMLA* 105 (1) (1990): 41.
12. Kimberley Roberts, 'The Clothes Make the Woman: The Symbolics of Prostitution in Nella Larsen's *Quicksand* and Claude McKay's *Home to Harlem*', *Tulsa Studies in Women's Literature* 16 (1) (1997): 108.
13. Wall, *Women*, p. 96.
14. Kimberly Monda, 'Self-Delusion and Self-Sacrifice in Nella Larsen's *Quicksand*', *African American Review* 31 (1) (1997): 32.
15. Jeffrey Gray, 'Essence and the Mulatto Traveler: Europe as Embodiment in Nella Larsen's "Quicksand"', *Novel: A Forum on Fiction* 27 (3) (1994): 260.
16. Wall, *Women*, p. 109.
17. Gray, 'Essence', p. 258.
18. Debra B. Silverman, 'Nella Larsen's *Quicksand*: Untangling the Webs of Exoticism', *African American Review* 27 (4) (1993): 599.
19. Yves W. A. Clemmen, 'Nella Larsen's *Quicksand*: A Narrative of Difference', *CLA Journal* 40 (4) (1997): 465.
20. Wall, *Women*, p. 138.
21. Paul Gilroy, *The Black Atlantic: Modernity and Double Consciousness* (London: Verso, 1993), p. 19.
22. Ibid.
23. See Gray, 'Essence', p. 258, and Hostetler, 'Aesthetics', p. 35, for example.
24. Chip Rhodes, 'Writing of the New Negro: The Construction of Consumer Desire in the Twenties', *Journal of American Studies* 28 (2) (1994): 201.
25. Hosetler, 'Aesthetics', p. 38.
26. Gary, 'Essence', p 268.
27. See the Introduction for a discussion of the problematics of worlding.
28. Gray, 'Essence', p. 259.

29. Karen Lawrence, *Penelope Voyages: Women and Travel in the British Literary Tradition* (Ithaca, NY: Cornell University Press, 1994), p. 16 n. 18.
30. Ibid. p. 17.
31. Hostetler, 'Aesthetics', p. 37.
32. Wall, *Women*, p. 135.
33. James Clifford, *Routes: Travel and Translation in the Late Twentieth Century* (Cambridge, MA: Harvard University Press, 1999), p. 28. Originally published in 1997.

CHAPTER 2

ASSIMILATION IN THE (FICTIONAL) HEARTLAND: BHARATI MUKHERJEE'S *JASMINE*

> There are no harmless, compassionate ways to remake oneself. We murder who we were so we can rebirth ourselves in the images of dreams.
> Bharati Mukherjee, *Jasmine* (1989)[1]

The above quotation from Bharati Mukherjee's *Jasmine* (1989) in many ways encapsulates the novel, especially in the way that it highlights both the violence of identity shifts and the mythical embrace of the American Dream, an embrace that Mukherjee deconstructs in the narrative of her peripatetic and eponymous heroine. *Jasmine* is the story of a young woman named, variously, Jyoti, Jasmine, Jazzy, Jase and Jane, who travels from India to the US on an ever-westward trek that finally sees her lighting out for the territory into an unknown future. In the novel, Mukherjee relies on familiar American myths and images, altering them strategically to acknowledge the impact of gender and ethnicity on transatlantic travel. As a result, Jasmine's encounters with 'America' – both mythic and real – affect her negotiations of her transatlantic, gendered identity.

In its archetypal configuration, the American Dream sites the solitary white male as the hero of the tale. Mukherjee's novel records the necessary alteration of the dream when its principal figure is an illegal female immigrant who both seeks and resists assimilation. Unlike Huck Finn, for example, Jasmine cannot fully abandon culture, home and other people on her journey; she is, after all, a pregnant woman by the end of the text, and in the process of recreating a hybrid family made up of her lover, his adopted daughter and her unborn child (by her common-in-law husband); she is also hoping to reunite with her own adopted Vietnamese son (who, uncomfortably, has also been constructed as a brother figure, given their age gap of only seven years).[2] Hers is thus a multiple migration, one filled with encumbrances, so even as this multiply-defined woman leaves, she does so with the weight of culture attached to her. Yet as Mukherjee makes clear, Jasmine is implicated in the myths promulgated by the US. When living in Iowa, Jasmine notes, 'Every night the frontier creeps a little closer' (20), and this is just one example of how American myths creep into her narrative, a fact that critics find some fault with, as they seek a different kind of immigrant narrative from the one that Mukherjee presents.

Inderpal Grewal argues that

> The consumption of narratives of distance and alterity has a long history in the West in relation to knowledges produced by European colonization, but American race and gender politics produced a specific version. The immigrant novel written by and about the 'Asian' and 'Asian-American' woman constituted a particular genre whose production, marketing, and regulation revealed a great deal about the transnational circulation of knowledges of nation, race, and gender.[3]

This transnational circulation of knowledges, Grewal suggests, promotes the idea of freedom from patriarchy (signified by the original home) and movement into a liberal America that embraces the woman traveller. It is not accidental that Grewal traces this narrative in a chapter entitled 'Becoming American', nor that she, like many other critics, finds fault with this rather too easy assumption of American promise, an assumption that feeds into, rather than critiques, myths of the welcoming shores.[4]

I have elsewhere argued that female escape rarely conforms to the models set out by male adventure stories or the critical texts that accompany (and recapitulate) them.[5] Never is this clearer than in this novel, in which women's movement is critiqued as negative and selfish; both by characters with whom Jasmine comes into contact, who almost never want her to leave (even when her presence is disruptive), and also by critics who dislike the narrative's apparently problematic trajectory.[6] Whether based in India or Iowa, Jasmine is expected to stay put, defined by her familial roles; in neither place does she live by society's precepts, but instead, she moves beyond the reach of a single narrative into a mythical encounter with 'America'. That this encounter is a love story troubles critics who want the novel – and the author – to provide a more realistic account of an illegal immigrant's experience. This chapter will explore how Jasmine's status – as a woman, and an illegal immigrant – impacts upon her transatlantic exploration of space and identity, creating conflict as well as apparent resolution in her journey. Gender and ethnicity are thus central to the novel, and the ways in which each intersects with travel is at the heart of my reading of Mukherjee's text. Also central to my reading is the encounter with critics who resist Jasmine's immigrant tale because its location is, at some level, too familiar: residence in the America of dreams.

The Transatlantic Body

Early in the novel, Jasmine proclaims, 'I couldn't marry a man who didn't speak English, or at least who didn't want to speak English. To want English was to want more than you had been given at birth, it was to want the world' (68). As this quotation demonstrates, travel, desire and gender interact in important ways in the novel. For Jasmine, such desire is never easy, and travel implies movement which is dangerous both culturally and individually. Roger Bromley goes so far as to suggest Mukherjee's texts represent, at some level, the space accorded the illegal immigrant:

> The gaps in documentation, the 'illegal' status of women, have been extended beyond the literal sense to produce a work of breaks, passages, and bridges at a metaphorical level. Written against homogeneity, each text in its irregular and interstitial form is an irruption, a threshold crossing, a renewal of valorization.[7]

The very body of the illegal immigrant is thus reformed in the narrative, and it is certainly the case that Jasmine's body is invaded, abused and remade by her encounters and cultural clashes before and after she reaches the US. As a child, she is marked by her encounter with an astrologer who foretells her fate of widowhood and exile, a fate she denies; as a result, she is scarred on the forehead after the man pushes her away, a scar that she renames her third eye (5). As an adolescent bride, she is covered in the blood of her husband when Sikh terrorists plant a bomb that is meant to kill her, rather than him. As a young woman in the US, Jasmine is 'raped and raped and raped in boats and cars and motel rooms' (127). The narrative jumps between times and places as Jasmine is remade – and renamed – by these encounters.

At first, transatlantic travel is a goal her husband Prakash has, and Jyoti, a teenager at the time and newly named by him as Jasmine, assumes the role of supportive Indian wife. Asked what she thinks, she muses, 'I didn't know what to think of America. I'd read only *Shane*, and seen only one movie. It was too big a country, too complicated a question. I said, "If you're there, I'll manage. When you're at work in America, I'll stay inside"' (81). Despite her intention to remain domesticated and indoors (and it is unclear at this point whether Jasmine actually sees herself waiting in the US or waiting back in India), Jasmine eventually allows his goal to become hers: ' "If you want me to have a real life, I want it, too" ' (81). While she characterises the US as a site of the 'real', the fact that she knows it only through the media and through carefully constructed propaganda is readily apparent. Indeed, her experience of America initially comes through others' depictions and others' desires, and always at one remove. For example, Prakash offers her a US aerogramme written by his former tutor to help persuade her, and instead of reading the contents, she focuses on the package. The aerogram is 'velvety', not 'rough and fibrous' like her more familiar Indian ones, and she is quickly seduced by its appearance and its message: 'CELEBRATE AMERICA, the American postal service commanded. TRAVEL . . . THE PERFECT FREEDOM' (83, ellipses in original). What Jasmine cannot recognise is that these aerogrammes promote the myth of welcoming shores precisely because they erase ethnicity; after all, the aerogrammes can be sent by anyone (in America) to anyone (outside of America). Thus, 'America' as a construct can be consumed by anyone, regardless of national or ethnic background, and travel is seen as an openly liberating gesture, not the frightening, coerced or dangerous venture that it becomes for Jasmine, as for others.

However, if *this* America is unethnicised, other versions are explicit in inscribing ethnicity. Perusing an American university brochure for 'international students', Jasmine notes, 'For the first time in my life I was looking at familiar Indian faces and seeing them as strange, a kind of tribe of intense men with oily hair, heavy-rimmed glasses, and mustaches' (92). Here, even the *thought* of transatlantic travel changes her perceptions. What Jasmine has yet to realise is that this tribe is also manufactured, designed to appeal to those who wish to join these 'international' students, and is just the first of many different kinds of 'Indians' constructed by, through and in the US that Jasmine will encounter. She later meets the less financially and educationally successful Indians who cling to their outsidership and whom she rejects in her desire to become Americanised, as well as professional medical personnel, whom she embraces: 'I trust only Asian doctors, Asian professionals. What we've gone through must count for something' (32). Yet even here, Jasmine's recreation of a bond is suspect: it depends on ignoring differences (of both class and nationality) in her desire to embrace an America of hope and good fortune.

When her husband is murdered before they can depart, Jasmine decides to fulfil his dream anyway, and travels – illegally – to the United States, commenting derisively on tourists who seek migration as 'adventure' (102). Revealing that for transients like her, 'the zigzag route is straightest' (101), Jasmine records the *necessity* rather than the luxury of travel. Her many reinventions also foreground the way that gender constructs her journey; as a woman (much less as a widow), she is identified frequently as at risk. Unlike the tourists, Jasmine is part of a different kind of tribe, a word that recurs with various meanings throughout the novel:

> We are the outcasts and deportees, strange pilgrims visiting outlandish shrines, landing at the end of tarmacs, ferried in old army trucks where we are roughly handled and taken to roped-off corners of waiting rooms where surly, barely wakened customs guards await their bribe. We are dressed in shreds of national costumes, out of season, the wilted plumage of intercontinental vagabondage. We ask only one thing: to be allowed to land; to pass through; to continue. We sneak a look at the big departure board, the one the tourists use. Our cities are there, too, our destinations are so close! But not yet, not so directly. We must sneak in, land by night in little-used strips. (101)

Jasmine's only aim in reaching the US is to commit *sati*, thereby fulfilling her cultural role as a Hindu widow, even while disrupting it by travelling alone and against her family's wishes. To do so, however, would be to slip back into the role of Jyoti, her first incarnation as a rural, under-educated Indian girl, and Jasmine instead begins a series of reinventions in the US, with each place she travels to producing a new identity – and a new relationship with a man. Through this process of relocation, Jasmine comes to represent postmodern fluid identity, though she is never able to rid herself of the label of exoticism that her visible ethnic heritage engenders in the minds of her American companions (nor, to be fair, does she always want to).

The novel itself takes on her highlighted zigzag construction, moving back and forth between the India of Jasmine's past and the

Iowa of her present in the first few chapters of the book, before adopting a more chronological structure for the middle chapters (6–17), which are devoted almost exclusively to the narrative of her childhood and adolescence, and subsequent trip to the US, at the age of 17, by which time she is already a widow. The final sections of the text zigzag across the United States: from Florida, her point of entry, where she recovers from a violent rape; to New York where she lives two distinctly different kinds of lives, first with an Indian family who maintain their Indianness against a perceived slide into US mores, and then with an American family where she takes on the role of caregiver; to Iowa, where she starts a complicated family of her own.

In the US sections of the novel, Jasmine both embraces and rejects the construction of herself as foreign, as from a generic 'over there'. Once settled – albeit temporarily – in Iowa, America's heartland, she takes *gobi aloo* to a Lutheran Relief Fund craft fair, serves *matar panir* with pork, and feeds neighbouring farmers on 'oriental' spices and herbs bought, mail order, from California (thereby complicating her Eastern associations). She is bemused when Midwestern Americans link 'away' with a variety of unconnected European spaces: Ireland, France, Italy. Her rural neighbours have no purchase on where India is, or that she is Indian at all. Such ignorance recalls an earlier observation by Lillian Gordon, a Quaker woman who originally offered Jasmine shelter, and rescued her from appearing like an illegal alien. Lillian argued that if Jasmine could ' "walk and talk American, they'll think you were born here. Most Americans can't imagine anything else" ' (134–5). Although this is a clear swipe at US citizens who focus only on America and remain blind to the nations and cultures outside it, this sentiment equally exposes the artifice of Jasmine's performance: it is built from the outside, though she also later internalises the message that Lillian imparts. In this way, Jasmine learns to construct herself as American, even though she herself first equates Americanness with being white. Returning again to the postgraduate student brochure mentioned above, Jasmine commented, when seeing the faces of the students there, 'Everyone on the cover and in the pictures inside was Indian or Chinese, with a couple of Africans. It didn't look anything like the America I'd read about' (90). She is, however, reassured by her husband's pronunciation of Tampa as 'Tam-pah': 'It sounded like a Punjabi village name, the way he pronounced it' (90). Here as elsewhere, Jasmine's America is overlaid with images of India, and her eventual embracing of it is not, as some critics suggest, a rejection of home, but a melding of images that sometimes sit comfortably together and at other times do not.

For example, Jasmine recognises that how she herself is constructed depends upon who does the assessing. Educated people from New York to Iowa assign exotic knowledge to her, despite the fact that she is, in her own translated terms, a 'sixth grade drop out' (180). Her Eastern origins speak to them of mystery and depth, wisdom and peace, ideas that are far removed from her actual beginnings. How she is constructed is also dependent on where she is located. For example, in India, her complexion is considered ' "wheatish" ' (33), whereas in Iowa, as she muses, 'they'll admit that I might look a little different, that I'm a "dark-haired girl" in a naturally blond county. I have a "darkish complexion" . . . as though I might be Greek from one grandparent' (33).

Thus, her transatlantic body is malleable not only because of violent encounters (terrorism, rape), but because of encounters with people who categorise her in ways that fit their own world view (or lack thereof). Jasmine further muses, 'Educated people are interested in differences; they assume that I'm different from them but exempted from being one of "them," the knife-wielding undocumenteds hiding in basements' (33). Yet she is not as different as these people think: she was indeed a knife-wielding undocumented alien, who, on her first day in the US, killed the man who raped her. This is a secret she shares with her adopted Vietnamese son Du in an attempt to build cultural bridges with him. Significantly, she hides this fact from the rest of her family, who cannot imagine any of her previous identities, so fixated are they on the construction of her as Jane.

Critics are uncomfortable with Jasmine's recourse to silence, or her apparent denial of the past. Debjani Bannerjee, for example, claims that 'Jasmine's complete erasure of her Indian past once she is embroiled in the melting-pot dynamic of North America is interesting. As she assimilates into the dominant culture, she casts aside her identity as an Indian.'[8] Even if one accepted that this were true, Jasmine shows how, in fact, many of those around her (if not her closest family) refuse to allow this identity erasure. They want her to connect with them on the basis of her Indian past, by teaching them how to cook spicy food, or even, more problematically, how to connect with their Americanised versions of Eastern philosophy and reincarnation. Moreover, with her subversive food and her ironic comments that her neighbours do not understand where she is from, Jasmine mocks the idea that she has left behind her

Indianness; it is simply that it is misrecognised by those around her. Yet because this critical discomfort recurs so regularly, it needs to be explored further. This is especially true given the claims that Mukherjee writes an assimilationist text that erases the transatlantic space that I argue creates her heroine's most important identity markers.

Critical Conflict

Mukherjee's novel has most frequently been read – and fiercely critiqued – as an assimilationist text that depends upon (false) constructions of romance, love and the powerful presence of a saving hero. For example, Grewal's view of the novel is easily established in this acerbic summary: 'Miraculously all white men fall in love with her, and she possesses an ability to obliterate racism with the taste of the curry she makes for them.'[9] In other words, according to this view, *Jasmine* falls into the category of feel-good multiculturalism-lite, a culture-clash novel with a happy ending. Anu Aneja similarly critiques the novel for fostering a stereotypical version of Indian femininity, just the sort, Aneja suggests, that makes Western feminists want to 'rescue' Indian women from oppression.[10] Aneja also suggests that Western readers are therefore 'relieved at the freedom achieved at the end by Jasmine',[11] yet I would argue that this stance offers up an implied reader who may not exist. After all, Jasmine's final lighting out for the territory is actually a fraught one. She rather blithely abandons her disabled husband despite carrying his genetic child, thereby forcing readers to encounter the destructive elements of her narrative, and few readers, I would suggest, find comfort in her ability to discard the past (and present) with such selfish abandon.[12] Indeed, Samir Dayal goes as far as to suggest that Jasmine's actions reveal 'a desperately selfish nomadism, a continual urge to "homelessness" and exile' and despite postmodern embracing of such terms, it is clear that they are considered negative when applied to this female character.[13]

Like Aneja, Anindyo Roy similarly suggests that Mukherjee caters to Western readers, for her own gain:

> The reading public in the West and the literary press are quick to seize the opportunity of promoting a Third World artist who is a believer in the American Dream. Moreover, an immigrant writer's work like Mukherjee's narrative contains enough exotic elements to preserve the

curious differences posited by an Orientalist discourse, which can be easily appreciated by the Western reading public.[14]

Read simplistically, the novel does seem to suggest that Jasmine is an oppressed Indian woman who finds liberation when she reaches the shores of America, and it is possible that some readers do connect with the text on this level alone. Read with a more critical eye, however, it is clear that this is a text of uncomfortable negotiation, where desire for connection is met with resistance and misinterpretation (including exoticism), and where liberation is partial and easily lost.

Unlike the critics above, Rosanne Kanhai offers a rather idealistic look at *Jasmine*, suggesting that it is a novel particularly suited to a postcolonial female reader; it therefore becomes a novel 'through which [such a reader] evaluates her own place in the U.S. environment and the trajectory of her own quest'.[15] This, if nothing else, suggests that different (critically) imagined readers encounter different texts.

Susan Koshy finds another reason to critique Mukherjee's work, arguing that her texts 'are assimilationist because they reconstruct their emancipation within hegemonic feminist narratives'.[16] Although this is allied with the arguments above, it is also subtly different: Koshy suggests that Mukherjee pays scant attention to race and ethnicity, preferring instead to write a text with gender as its primary concern. This way, Koshy suggests, Mukherjee falls into the critical trap of a feminist narrative which must seek success and resolution at the end. I would argue that such a critique misrepresents feminism, since even early second-wave feminist texts are rarely as wholeheartedly optimistic and full of 'positive role models' as later critics sometimes would have us believe. Moreover, it seems to me that rather than ignore race and ethnicity, Mukherjee frequently acknowledges Jasmine's 'difference' from white America and how it is perceived, not to promote an Orientalist discourse, but to explore how one might try to adapt to and overcome (and sometimes strategically exploit) such views. Jasmine is not held up as a perfect feminist (if such a creature exists), but is rather a character who, in her own unplanned and haphazard way, seeks pleasure and release even whilst being aware of responsibilities and conventional expectations. In addition, the way that Koshy allies feminism with assimilation is problematic in itself, given that most versions of feminism promote counter politics and seek to undermine easy inculcations of the status quo. In fact, it is Jasmine's very breaking out of expected patterns that both challenges and rewards the feminist reader.

Kristin Carter-Sanborn, who like Grewal, Roy and Aneja, dislikes Mukherjee's politics, argues that *Jasmine* is nothing more than a 'sort of pop multiculturalist prop' that focuses on exoticism.[17] Certainly there are passages that make such a reading tenable, as when Jasmine admits that her American common-law husband Bud 'courts me because I am alien. I am darkness, mystery, inscrutability. The East plugs me into instant vitality and wisdom. I rejuvenate him simply by being who I am' (200). Rather than read this as unthinking Orientalism, I would argue that Mukherjee's stance here is a knowing one that takes a familiar narrative and infuses it with contingent and uncomfortable crosscurrents. Bud *may* be influenced by Orientalism and therefore invoking its presence in their relationship; Jasmine is not (or at least, not consistently). Mukherjee plays with Orientalism in the same way that she plays with familiar American myths such as lighting out for the territory, the American Dream and the metaphor of the wretched refuse welcomed to the shores of America. She does this in order to defamiliarise the issues so that the reader is invited to consider them afresh.

It is certainly the case that Jasmine obviously performs her transat-lantic exoticism at times, as when she unsettles Iowan taste buds; she knows the reactions she will get when she does so, as her neighbours fan their mouths and find her food too spicy for their Midwestern palates. She purposely becomes foreign in these instances (even if they misread that foreignness as something else). At other times, however, Jasmine longs for an invisible assimilation that does not mark her as other: 'Plain Jane is all I want to be. Plain Jane is a role, like any other. My *genuine* foreignness frightens [Bud]. I don't hold that against him. It frightens me, too' (26, my italics). Such a desire for the erasure of difference, of 'foreignness' in this example, is naïve, perhaps, but nev-ertheless a recurring image in many women's texts of transatlantic immigration, including those which do not feature heroines whose 'difference' is ethnically visible.[18] Moreover, while it is not hard to read Mukherjee's heroine as naïve, it is problematic to read the author in the same light. To berate Mukherjee for her delineation of Jasmine's passing desire seems to suggest that only 'approved' feelings are acceptable in postcolonial fiction, a critical stance that is retrogressive at best. A more useful stance would be to reflect on performance theory and apply it to the performance of transatlantic identity, espe-cially since Jasmine's body is and remains gendered.

Judith Butler's complicated exploration of performativity ack-nowledges the pull of fantasy:

According to the understanding of identification as an enacted fantasy or incorporation, however, it is clear that coherence is desired, wished for, idealized, and that this idealization is an effect of a corporeal significa-tion. In other words, acts, gestures and desire produce the effect of an internal core or substance, but produce this *on the surface* of the body, through the play of signifying absences that suggest, but never reveal, the organizing principle of identity as a cause. Such acts, gestures, enact-ments, generally construed, are *performative* in the sense that the essence or identity that they otherwise purport to express are *fabrications* man-ufactured and sustained through corporeal signs and other discursive means.[19]

Butler's work is focused on the performance and performativity of gender rather than ethnic difference, yet it is clear that Jasmine fits within this framework because she enacts both performance (a knowing display) and performativity (less consciously chosen behav-iour that is publicly regulated), and that both of these are regulated by her gender, too. (Du, her adopted Vietnamese son, is not expected to enact his foreignness in the same way as Jasmine does, for example, and his sexuality is never made an issue in the text, whereas Jasmine's is.)

Throughout the book, Jasmine is caught up in performing her (many, varied) roles, ranging from faithful Hindu wife to abandoning American wife; and hers is a performance that she only partially con-trols. Helena Grice argues that Mukherjee, in both her fictional and her polemical writing, enacts a ' "performative patriotism" ',[20] and this may be closely linked to questions of assimilation and the poli-tics behind it. Indeed, Roger Bromley suggests that critics who take issue with *Jasmine* misread the protagonist's desires for the US. He suggests that what appears to be assimilation is really 'a refusal of nostalgia and exoticism'.[21] For example, Jasmine's first home in New York is with her husband Prakash's former teacher, Devinder Vadhera, whose family welcomes her into their lives as an unpaid servant as befits her position as a widow. They live in 'an apartment of artificially maintained Indianness' (145) and keep 'a certain kind of Punjab alive, even if that Punjab no longer existed' (162). Jasmine begins to realise that the man she calls Professorji feels that 'his real life was in an unlivable land across oceans' (153). This contrasts sharply with Jasmine, who sees the US as the site of the 'real', yet both are caught up in performances of their roles that they find hard to break. (Devinder renames himself Dave, pronounces his surname as if it is Americanised, and lies to his extended family about his job; he is a sorter of human hair, not the academic they think he is, and that he was back in India.)

Such intense attachment to the past reminds Jasmine only too well of her own family, who endlessly replayed their lost life in Lahore, before partition: 'the loss survives in the instant replay of family story: forever Lahore smokes, forever my parents flee' (41). In living with the Vadheras, Jasmine discovers that they are only able to teach her 'about surviving as an *Indian* in New York' (162, my italics). In fact, 'they let nothing go, lest everything be lost' (162). This assertion of culture as a dam against American influence is not a possible narrative for Jasmine, as it does not allow for movement, travel or (in her eyes) growth. It is not accidental that it is only once she moves in with an American family, Wylie and Taylor Hayes – again, as a quasi-servant, though Wylie calls her a 'caregiver' and Jasmine's own name for her role, 'day mummy', evokes family attachments – that Jasmine considers herself as having fully arrived in the US. This is where she claims to have become American herself (165), a process that is not subject to official sanction, but instead is one that she alone recognises. This process begins early in her sojourn in America, but is not complete until she can 'pass' as American.

In order to pass, Jasmine and other female immigrants are initially helped by Lillian Gordon, who 'made possible the lives of absolute *ordinariness* that we ached for' (131, italics in original). This tension between ordinariness and foreignness is not easily accommodated,[22] and Jasmine's desire to blend in leads her to manufacture and reconfigure aspects of her life. Lillian teaches Jasmine to walk, talk and act American in order to avoid detection from Immigration and Nationalization Service (INS) agents. Whilst 'naturalisation' has a specific political meaning (and the service has now been swallowed up by the Department for Homeland Security, a title which puts an altogether different spin on its remit), it is fitting that it is from such agents that Jasmine attempts to shield herself, by acting as *naturally* as possible in an alien environment. That 'ordinariness' equates with acting American speaks volumes and is not lost on critics who take issue with the text. Roy, for example, argues that this passing is unavailable to real women like Jasmine, women without education or funds, and that Mukherjee 'not only suppresses the complex realities of economic, political, and historical exigencies of immigration, but also "forgets" the implications of the post-colonial subject's authorising of such aesthetics'.[23] It is certainly true that Jasmine embraces America wholeheartedly, yet Mukherjee also shows the negative

effects of such devotion. In one passage, after Jasmine has transformed herself into a nanny, she becomes temporarily addicted to a
home shopping network, so much so that she begins to dread the
mail, which brings her evidence of her addiction. Here, her benefac-
tor (and eventual lover) Taylor manages to extricate her from excess
by returning the unwanted items and ensuring that Jasmine knows
her rights. Crying, 'America! America!' (186), Taylor recognises the
obsession for what it is: an obsession with a country (or a dream of a
country), not its reality. Jasmine's devotion is destructive when it
becomes all consuming.

Lillian even teaches Jasmine how to use an escalator with ease, and
this series of lessons does seem to set up America as a site of technology as opposed to India; yet throughout, Jasmine records Indian interactions with advanced technology (her husband and brothers repair
electronic goods), and indeed it is her claim that she is familiar with
American technology that partly inflames her violent rapist 'Half-
face' when she first enters the US: 'He dragged me to the television
and pressed my forehead against the screen. Then he brought my head
back and slammed it against the set, again and again. "Don't tell me
you ever *seen* a television . . ."' (112). Jasmine is thus read as tech-
nologically inactive or backward, and even the otherwise progressive
Wylie assumes that she is not entirely au fait with the latest gadgets.
What is key, however, is that Mukherjee allows these gaps and mis-
representations to be situated in the text, and to stand alongside more
accurate representations of Jasmine's past. Thus Mukherjee is not, as
some critics have suggested, setting up a clear demarcation between
the progressiveness of America and the backwardness of India, but
she is exploring how *perceptions* of this binary opposition are an
underlying factor of Jasmine's US life.

Although as earlier noted, Jasmine's fate seems wrapped up with
the men with whom she forms intimate relationships, it is also clear
that her fate is transformed by American women who, from her perspective, offer positive interventions. Lillian Gordon is one such
woman, and again, the fact that she is a white woman seems to reinforce the hierarchical positioning of the races that Mukherjee's critics
dislike. However, Jasmine's perspective and the reader's own may be
different. After all, Mukherjee cleverly inserts a later acknowledgement that at least some people feel that Lillian may have had
less savoury motives than pure altruism in assisting Jasmine; she
is eventually arrested for exploiting illegal immigrants for free work
and sent to jail. Whilst there is a later attempt to recuperate her (a

made-for-tv movie about her, entitled *An American Kind of Saint* is planned, but eventually dropped), and while Jasmine clings to the belief in her essential goodness, Lillian, like the concept of 'America', is subject to at least two opposing readings.

Another older woman, Mother Ripplemeyer, offers Jasmine a new start in Iowa by presenting Jasmine to her son as a potential bank teller; eventually Mother Ripplemeyer becomes her mother-in-law. Neither woman wants Jasmine to focus on her time before. Jasmine cautiously notes, 'I have to be careful about these stories. I have to be careful about nearly everything I say' (16). This is because Mother Ripplemeyer 'can't begin to picture a village in Punjab. She doesn't mind my stories about New York and Florida because she's been to Florida many times and seen enough pictures of New York' (16). The implicit injunction against speech indicates anew the ways in which Jasmine's carefully constructed American identity is just that: constructed, and that living in America requires that she does violence to her memories. It is worth repeating the passage that introduced this chapter: 'There are no harmless, compassionate ways to remake oneself. We murder who we were so we can rebirth ourselves in the images of dreams' (29). Mukherjee's choice of words here indicates that this is a painful process, and any attempt at assimilation is fraught with difficulties.

Yet Jasmine acknowledges ties beyond ethnicity when she states, 'Lillian Gordon, Mother Ripplemeyer: one day I want to belong to that tribe' (197). She seeks to see herself as an enabler, not a destroyer (and she seeks to see these older familiars only in this positive light as well). However, it is clear that despite the positive spin Jasmine insists upon, there are darker readings available in relation to these women's motives, and for America as a whole.

Encountering America

John K. Hoppe argues that Mukherjee 'separates "America" – as an ideal space/temporality of continuous self-invention – from America's dominant citizens'.[24] He further argues that 'Mukherjee's concept of violent personal, trans-cultural transformation is different from the attempts at total erasure practiced by the colonising powers on their conquests.'[25] Thus, unlike the critics above, Hoppe sees Mukherjee's aim as one that recognises the disjuncture between myth and reality. Indeed, Mukherjee seems to focus upon the discovery of America as a process that is neither wholly positive nor wholly negative. For example, Jasmine notes, '[W]hen I listed my discoveries [about New York] to Taylor he listened carefully, as though I were describing an unmapped, exotic metropolis' (184). In many respects, she is: her New York consists of nannies from outside the US who make the country their own, and is different from the New York of the Vadheras and of Wylie and Taylor Hayes, too.

Jasmine's transnational desire for America doesn't negate the harsh realities of the country. After all, it is always clear that the shores of America are themselves under scrutiny. Consider the description of Jasmine's entry into the US aboard a shrimper named *The Gulf Shuttle*. Jasmine smells 'unrinsed waters of a distant shore' and her first sight is of the pollution from nuclear power plants. She does not ride the shrimper onto shore, but disembarks early to avoid detection: 'I waded through Eden's waste: plastic bottles, floating oranges, boards, sodden boxes, white and green plastic sacks tied shut but picked open by birds and pulled apart by crabs' (107). This is no paradise, no grateful entry into the promised land. The 'wretched refuse of your teeming shore'[26] takes on an entirely different meaning here, and it is important to recognise Mukherjee's deliberate invocation and disruption of familiar and nostalgic American iconography. Later, this 'scummy, collared cove' is repackaged as a 'private marina' by a developer who buys not only the run-down hotel where Jasmine was first raped, but also Lillian Gordon's 'safe house'. As Jasmine muses, 'A sanctuary transformed into a hotel; hell turned into paradise – to me this seems very American' (138).

Everywhere, then, the America of dreams is set alongside the America of nightmares, and it is this palimpsestic vision that becomes the true America to Jasmine. In another example, driving in her adopted county in Iowa, Jasmine asks, 'I wonder if Bud even sees the America I do' (109). In looking at half-built houses, Jasmine imagines undocumented runaways ensconced inside, whereas Bud, a banker, wonders how the buildings are financed and does not think to enquire who might be hiding within. In another passage, talking to a high school history teacher who 'tried a little Vietnamese' on her adopted son and is surprised that he 'just froze up', Jasmine seethes, 'This country has so many ways of humiliating, of disappointing' (29). She recognises, if the teacher does not, that Du can never hear his native tongue spoken by a white American man without wondering how the speaker came to know his language, or snippets of it. That the man is a history teacher reinforces the error that he makes and does not recognise.

Never is Jasmine's America the same America as it is for others. In her own life writing Mukherjee suggests that the issue lies partly in the difference between 'America' and the US. In an article in *Mother Jones* aptly entitled 'American Dreamer', Mukherjee confesses an overwhelming desire for ' "America" ' or what she calls 'the stage for the drama of self-transformation'. She also notes, 'The United States exists as a sovereign nation. "America," in contrast, exists as a myth of democracy and equal opportunity to live by, or as an ideal goal to reach.'[27] As I have demonstrated, the division between myth and reality – and between different views of America – is reiterated compulsively in *Jasmine*, a factor that not all critics have fully recognised.

What is also key to the novel is that, despite its quasi-realism, it is a transatlantic fantasy, combining narratives of fate, reincarnation and, specifically, gods and goddesses. Jennifer Drake perceptively argues that Mukherjee 'fabulizes America, Hinduizes assimilation, and represents the real pleasures and violences of cultural exchange'.[28] Moreover, '[T]o read *Jasmine* only through the lens of assimilation ignores that when a goddess transforms, she doesn't lose herself: she is no singular self; she contains the cosmos.'[29] No fewer than five times, Jasmine refers explicitly to Bud and herself as gods and goddesses (and at one point, even assigns the role of a god to a pet iguana), thereby reinforcing this layered unreality. Carmen Wickramagamage links the provisionality of Jasmine's identity to the tenets of Hinduism and sees Mukherjee's aim as a positive integration of Eastern religion with Western postmodern cultural critique.[30] It is thus in line with Homi Bhabha's concept of hybridity. Bhabha suggests that 'the borderline engagements of cultural difference may as often be consensual as conflictual; they may confound our definitions of tradition and modernity; realign the customary boundaries between the private and the public, high and low; and challenge normative expectations of development and progress.'[31] Mukherjee's narrative, despite claims to the contrary, engages with just this sort of hybridity in delineating the love story of an illegal immigrant and her quest for America.[32]

If, as Baudrillard suggests, 'What you have to do is enter the fiction of America, enter America as fiction,'[33] then this is precisely what Mukherjee attempts in her delineation of the protean Jasmine. Such a character, who refuses fixity whilst paradoxically longing for ordinariness, becomes the ultimate traveller. Jasmine argues, 'The world is divided between those who stay and those who leave' (228). Jane Ripplemeyer, the significantly non-Eastern name Jasmine adopts in the

Midwest, may be someone who stays; after all, she usurps the position and the name of the first Mrs Ripplemeyer, Karin, a woman who 'never got to travel' (204). But Jasmine is only Jane temporarily, and 'adventure, risk, transformation' – not to mention 'the frontier' – call to her, 'pushing indoors through uncaulked windows' (240). The final lines of the novel see the traveller Jasmine taking flight again: 'I am out the door and in the potholed and rutted driveway, scrambling ahead . . . greedy with wants and reckless from hope' (241).

The last vision of Jasmine, then, is one of flight, as she and her lover head West; the frontier is invoked and challenged, as this Eastern immigrant retraces the steps of former migrants. If the traveller is, in Michael Kowalewski's words, 'the reader's surrogate, a cultural outsider who moves into, through and finally beyond the places and events encountered',[34] then it is ironically appropriate that it is an Americanised non-American – an illegal female immigrant – who takes centre stage in this narrative of travel across the United States. By offering up not the expected hero of an archetypal journey of escape, but a complicated, encumbered woman whose flight is couched in negative terms as well as positive ones, Mukherjee negotiates the myths of America and the ways in which transatlantic identity is negotiated, understood and, in some cases, endlessly deferred.

NOTES

1. Bharati Mukherjee, *Jasmine* (London: Virago, 1990), p. 29. Originally published in 1989. Subsequent page references to this text will be cited parenthetically.
2. Du, significantly, has a transpacific rather than transatlantic crossing. He is a Vietnamese refugee, 'rescued' from a refugee camp where some of his family members died. He arrives in Iowa by way of Honolulu. Bud's adoption of him is motivated by a desire to embrace Asia, a desire that might be rendered suspect, and fits in with Aneja's claim about Westerners seeking to save individuals from third world countries without recognising their own complicity within a narrative of Western heroism. Victoria Carchidi takes another viewpoint when she suggests that 'the motley recipients of [Jasmine's] love have remade themselves into an atypical – and therefore more truly American – family unit.' Victoria Carchidi, ' "Orbiting": Bharati Mukherjee's Kaleidoscope Vision', *MELUS* 20 (4) (1995): 93.
3. Inderpal Grewal, *Transnational America: Feminisms, Disaporas, Neoliberalisms* (Durham, NC: Duke University Press, 2005), p. 62.
4. Ibid. p. 63.

5. See Heidi Slettedahl Macpherson, *Women's Movement: Escape as Transgression in North American Feminist Fiction* (Amsterdam: Rodopi, 2000).

6. It is not an accidental that Wylie is also critiqued for leaving home, particularly as she leaves behind Taylor, the man of Jasmine's dreams. Although this is of course convenient for Jasmine, it is nevertheless harshly viewed.

7. Roger Bromley, 'A Concluding Essay: Narratives for a New Belonging-Writing in the Borderlands', in John C. Hawley (ed.), *Cross-Addressing: Resistance Literature and Cultural Borders* (Albany, NY: State University of New York Press, 1996), p. 296.

8. Debjani Bannerjee, ' "In the Presence of History": The Representation of Past and Present Indias in Bharati Mukherjee's Fiction', in Emmanuel S. Nelson (ed.), *Bharati Mukherjee: Critical Perspectives* (New York: Garland, 1993), p. 170.

9. Grewal, *Transnational*, p. 68.

10. Anu Aneja, ' "Jasmine", the Sweet Scent of Exile', *Pacific Coast Philology* 28 (1) (1993): 75.

11. Ibid. p. 77.

12. Indeed, any text in which a woman leaves home to pursue 'selfish' goals tends to be critiqued quite heavily. To explore this issue in more depth, see Chapter 4 of Macpherson, *Women's Movement*.

13. Samir Dayal, 'Creating, Preserving, Destroying: Violence in Bharati Mukherjee's *Jasmine*', in Emmanuel S. Nelson (ed.), *Bharati Mukherjee: Critical Perspectives* (New York: Garland, 1993), p. 75. For a discussion of nomadism and exile, see, amongst others, Edward Said, *Reflections on Exile and Other Literary and Cultural Essays* (London: Granta, 2000) and Caren Kaplan, *Questions of Travel: Postmodern Discourses of Displacement* (Durham, NC: Duke University Press, 1996).

14. Anindyo Roy, 'The Aesthetics of an (Un)willing Immigrant: Bharati Mukherjee's *Days and Nights in Calcutta* and *Jasmine*', in Emmanuel S. Nelson (ed.), *Bharati Mukherjee: Critical Perspectives* (New York: Garland, 1993), p. 133.

15. Rosanne Kanhai, ' "Sensing Designs in History's Muddles": Global Feminism and the Postcolonial Novel', *Modern Language Studies* 26 (4) (1996): 121.

16. Susan Koshy, 'The Geography of Female Subjectivity: Ethnicity, Gender, and Diaspora', *Diaspora* 3 (1) (1994): 71.

17. Kristin Carter-Sanborn, ' "We Murder Who We Were": *Jasmine* and the Violence of Identity', *American Literature* 66 (3) (1994): 575.

18. See, for example, Eva Hoffman's desire to 'give up the condition of being a foreigner' in her memoir *Lost in Translation*, p. 202.

19. Judith Butler, *Gender Trouble: Feminism and the Subversion of Identity* (New York: Routledge, 1999), p. 173, italics in original. Originally published in 1990.

20. Helena Grice, 'Who Speaks for US? Bharati Mukherjee's Fictions and the Politics of Immigration', *Comparative American Studies* 1 (1) (2003): 87.

21. Bromley, 'Concluding Essay', p. 282.

22. See also Eva Hoffman's *Lost in Translation*, where the narrator aches for a sense of the ordinary:

> I want to figure out, more urgently than before, where I belong in this America that's made up of so many sub-Americas. I want, somehow, to give up the condition of being a foreigner . . . *I no longer want to have the prickly, unrelenting consciousness that I'm living in the medium of a specific culture. It's time to roll down the scrim and see the world directly, as the world.* I want to reenter, through whatever Looking Glass will take me there, a state of ordinary reality. (202, italics mine)

23. Roy, 'Aesthetics', p. 130.

24. John K. Hoppe, 'The Technological Hybrid as Post-American: Cross-Cultural Genetics in *Jasmine*', *MELUS* 24 (4) (1999): 138.

25. Ibid.

26. See Emma Lazarus's famous poem 'The New Colossus' (1903), which commemorates the Statue of Liberty, http://www.legallanguage.com/poems/statuelibertypoem.html, accessed 29 January 2007.

27. Bharati Mukherjee, 'American Dreamer', *Mother Jones* (January/February 1997), www.motherjones.com/commentary/columns/1992/01/mukherjee.html, accessed 16 October 2006.

28. Jennifer Drake, 'Looting American Culture: Bharati Mukherjee's Immigrant Narratives', *Contemporary Literature* 40 (1) (1999): 61.

29. Ibid. pp. 63–4.

30. Carmen Wickramagamage, 'Relocation as Positive Act: The Immigrant Experience in Bharati Mukherjee's Novels', *Diaspora: A Journal of Transnational Studies* 2 (2) (1992): 174.

31. Homi K. Bhabha, *The Location of Culture* (London: Routledge, 2006), p. 3. Originally published in 1994.

32. In contrast, Kristin Carter-Sanborn claims that 'fluidity in *Jasmine* is theorized not as hybridity but as a perpetual gesture toward absolute otherness' (' "We Murder" ', p. 582).

33. Jean Baudrillard, *America*, trans. Chris Turner (London: Verso, 1998), p. 29.

34. Michael Kowalewski, 'Introduction', in Michael Kowalewski (ed.), *Temperamental Journeys: Essays on the Modern Literature of Travel* (Athens, GA: University of Georgia Press, 1992b), p. 9.

PART 2
MEMOIRS AND TRANSATLANTIC TRAVEL

INTRODUCTION

Trinh T. Minh-ha argues that 'travelling perpetuates a discontinuous state of being, [but] it also satisfies, despite the existential difficulties it entails, one's insatiable need for detours and displacements in postmodern culture.'[1] To travel is to invent not only the destination, but also the traveller, as identity becomes a performance which tailors itself to whatever audience it encounters. The performance of travelling gender has already been introduced, but in the two chapters that follow, this performance moves into other arenas, and specifically into memoir. If late twentieth- and early twenty-first-century women travellers are (on the whole) less concerned with their appearance as manifested through dress and clothing, they are nevertheless still cognisant of their roles as travelling women, and of how gender as well as other social markers influence the way they are received. In what follows, I will explore two very different memoirs of travel: one focused on a reluctant and resistant immigrant, and one on a resistant tourist, who denies her position as tourist even as she inhabits it.

Although there may not, at first, seem to be a lot of connection between the exile's nostalgia for the past and the tourist's present tense focus on elsewhere, in fact, there does seem to be a connection worth probing further. As Dean MacCannell argues, despite the tourist's desire for non-routine activities on holiday, the fact is that they 'often *do* see routine aspects of life as it is really lived in the places they visit, although few tourists express much interest in this'.[2] Diski is the obvious exception, particularly in her overt performance of the anti-tourist, the individual who refuses to conform to the label she knows is placed upon her (she is similarly resistant to the label travel writer, despite the fact that she is writing about her travel).

Eva Hoffman 'performs' her complicated national allegiances in her move from Poland to North America in her first memoir, learning as well how to be a girl and then a woman in North America, whereas Jenny Diski 'performs' the role of the anti-tourist in her travel books and resists her role as healing rescuer of fellow travellers, as seductive as she occasionally finds that (gendered) task. Hoffman is a reluctant inhabitant of new nations, first Canada and then the US, and holds onto an evocative remembrance of her original country of Poland; Diski, in contrast, gives herself over to almost continuous motion and residing in the present, noting in her second travel book that 'to be a train passenger in America is to be in an altered state, the fifty-first and the only mobile state in the Union.'[3] Although Diski also traces her own history in the first travel book, alternating her physical travels with mental travels into her past, by the second she has considerably reduced the amount of space she offers over to her own lived life. Hoffman seeks roots nostalgically, defining herself as exilic; Diski plans routes, and tries not to deviate from them even as, at some level, she resists their template of travel. Both, however, are defined by their travel, and their gender as travellers.

What is clear for both texts, as well as other travel memoirs, is that within them, 'shifts of identity are highly complex, sometimes unstable, and often have reversible elements built into them.'[4] Transatlantic memoirs of (chosen or forced) dislocation within the twentieth century discuss this very instability, and Hoffman's memoirs and Diski's travel books offer the opportunity to explore a range of the spectrum from unwilling to deliberate traveller. Both writers are also self-consciously aware of themselves as narrators of their own journeys, as creators of a written version of themselves. Both explicitly engage with literary criticism in doing so, and are aware of antecedent texts that partially determine their own responses to travel.

Heather Henderson argues that the very genre of travel memoir constrains the author or ensures a replication of already encountered moments,[5] and this is something that Diski herself notes overtly in *Skating to Antarctica*, when, for example, she reads the sea through the lens of already-viewed films of the sea itself. Given this sense of the re-enactment, it is particularly important to focus on the role of identity selection and conscious performance in relation to memoirs of travel. As Sara Mills reminds us: '[I]t is not necessary to read travel writing as expressing the truth of the author's life, but rather, it is the result of a configuration of discursive structures with which the author negotiates.'[6] Moving away from the two texts of focus in the following chapters, an example of this discursive structure is readily apparent in Alain de Botton's *The Art of Travel*, which is a travel narrative with a difference. De Botton travels with the wonderfully undefined M, but more importantly, perhaps, with philosophers, painters and poets. M provides the curious reader with a glimpse of de Botton's (carefully constructed) personality – so even travel writers argue with their partners on holiday and feel the 'mutual terrors of incompatibility and infidelity'[7] – that is, potential abandonment and unexpected departure. Even more, reading outside the boundaries of the narrative, M is, presumably, the Michele Hutchison of the dedication, so the reader can be relieved to find she is not reading about the demise of a relationship, and that these mutual terrors are, after all, just figments of the author's imagination. The information around de Botton's text is, therefore, read as much as the interior text, and de Botton's gender, though not explicitly foregrounded, is nonetheless in evidence here.

Reading around Diski's second memoir, the reader is confronted with the image on the cover either of the profile of a woman smoking on the original hardback, or, perhaps more evocatively, the image of a travelling woman in an old-fashioned train compartment in the paperback version. This latter image focuses on the woman's legs, crossed neatly at the knee, in a sepia-coloured tint to indicate nostalgia or the past, and indeed, the reader is able to glimpse an old-fashioned hat on the woman, thus confirming the image's focus on an earlier era (or a replication of this era). Though the image bears no resemblance to any image one manufactures of Diski herself through reading the memoir, its use signals the ongoing concern with gender in travel. Similarly, the Minerva paperback edition of Hoffman's first memoir includes a (presumably real) photograph of the author and her sister, again in sepia tones, which is juxtaposed with images of skyscrapers in colour. Hoffman's imaged self is as a small and uncertain girl, rather than the successful woman writer she becomes through the experience of emigrating. The image is therefore a 'before' image, with the book itself indicating the 'after' side of the equation. Thus the choice to focus on gender in relating travel experiences is a crucial one, as it tells us something about how these women writers continue to focus on the politics of location.

Though Hoffman's text is one of exile, and Diski's one of chosen travel, both authors spend time articulating the sense of strangeness attached to being elsewhere. Iain Chambers argues that 'cut off from the homelands of tradition, experiencing a constantly challenged identity, the stranger is perpetually required to make herself at home in an interminable discussion between a scattered historical inheritance and a heterogeneous present.'[8] Although perhaps not intentional, Chambers's use of the generic 'she' here is instructive; the strange woman (as opposed to the strange man) has a different experience of travel and movement, and a different register on which to record these experiences.

Carla Freeman is particularly concerned with ensuring that women's stories are not simply an addition to discussions of globalisation, but are instead central to the understanding of globalisation's processes and effects: '[P]roducers, consumers, and bystanders of globalization are not generic bodies or invisible practitioners of labor and desire but are situated within social and economic processes and cultural meanings that are central to globalization itself.'[9] Both social travellers and migrants participate in the global economy, as Diski makes clear when she visits tourist sites which are predicated on the market, and as Hoffman makes explicit when she discusses how her family and its Polish community support themselves both prior to and just after emigration. Similarly, travellers themselves are gendered, racialised and classed, and it is precisely for this reason that James Clifford suggests that the term travel – with all its 'historical taintedness' – is a better word to use than the 'more apparently neutral, and "theoretical" terms, such as "displacement," which can make the drawing of equivalences across different historical experiences too easy'.[10] Debates over terminology (as seen from the Introduction) are perhaps inevitable, but what is key here is that the authors of these memoirs acknowledge and play with language to guide understanding about their own positions as travellers and, for Hoffman, as an exile.

Almost inevitably, then, what comes into play for Hoffman is a focus on nostalgia for places that are lost or transformed. Roberta Rubenstein, in her book *Home Matters*, suggests that 'while homesickness refers to a spatial/geographical separation, nostalgia more accurately refers to a temporal one.'[11] *Lost in Translation* offers both, as Hoffman first poses as her younger self mourning her lost homeland, and then moves forward through to adulthood, where she mourns the kind of child she might have been, had she stayed in Poland. Chelva Kanaganayakam argues that literature of exile has as one of its 'thematic preoccupations' a 'propensity to place remembered realities above immediate, referential ones', whereas Edward Said suggests that the 'exile's new world, logically enough, is unnatural and its unreality resembles fiction'.[12] Taken together, these arguments offer a compelling reading against which we can place Hoffman's narrative, as the child Eva learns a new language, consciously determines a writing self in English, and then eventually applies New Critical Theory to her understanding not just of literature, but of life as well. Although Caren Kaplan for one is suspicious of nostalgia, linking it to a kind of modernist validation of detachment, for Hoffman, this detachment is both a result of dislocation and a condition of continuing to reside in a transnational space, where Canada, Poland and the US all rub up against each other in her lived life and where she is forced to confront their very different presence for her as opposed to others.

Kaplan queries the notion that there should be longing for the 'mother tongue' or 'it is "natural" to be at "home" and that separation from that location can never be assuaged by anything but return.'[13] In contrast, Rubenstein would argue that failure to attend to issues of home is a consequence of second-wave feminism's rejection of the home, or the refiguring of it as a site of imprisonment. She argues further that:

> longing for home may be understood as a yearning for recovery or return to the idea of a nurturing, unconditionally accepting place/space that has been repressed in contemporary feminism. Narratives that excavate and recover the positive meanings of home and nostalgia represent 'the return of the repressed' in that they foreground, confront, and attempt to resolve that subversive longing.[14]

Given feminism's counter-cultural stance, it is perhaps ironic that a feminist critic such as Rubenstein would see a claim to domesticity and a reclamation of home as an area for subversive twenty-first century feminist intervention. Though perhaps not: one of feminism's strengths is its ability to read anew spaces and places that have been denied sufficient critical attention. Questions of home are also of importance in Part 3, in the move back to fictional representations of movement and change which are traced over generations rather than focused solely on individual travellers. This movement towards and away from home in diverse texts suggest its ongoing importance not just for transatlantic fiction, but for women's fiction as a whole. For this next section, however, the emphasis is firmly on the factual, as

Hoffman and Diski offer up their written selves for transatlantic reflection.

NOTES

1. Trinh T. Minh-ha, 'Other Than Myself/ My Other Self', in George Robertson et al. (eds), *Travellers' Tales: Narratives of Home and Displacement* (London: Routledge, 1994), p. 21.
2. Dean MacCannell, *The Tourist: A New Theory of the Leisure Class* (Berkeley, CA: University of California Press, 1999), p. 106, italics in original. Originally published in 1976.
3. Jenny Diski, *Stranger on a Train: Daydreaming and Smoking around America with Interruptions* (London: Virago, 2004), p. 73. Originally published in 2002.
4. Paul White, 'Geography, Literature and Migration', in Russell King et al. (eds), *Writing across Worlds: Literature and Migration* (London: Routledge, 1995), p. 3.
5. Heather Henderson, 'The Travel Writer and the Text: "My Giant Goes with Me Wherever I Go"', in Michael Kowalewski (ed.), *Temperamental Journeys: Essays on the Modern Literature of Travel* (Athens, GA: University of Georgia Press, 1992), p. 239.
6. Sara Mills, *Discourses of Difference: An Analysis of Women's Travel Writing and Colonialism* (London: Routledge, 1993), p. 9. Originally published in 1991.
7. Alain de Botton, *The Art of Travel* (London: Hamish Hamilton, 2002), p. 24.
8. Iain Chambers, *Migrancy, Culture, Identity* (London: Routledge, 1994), p. 6.
9. Carla Freeman, 'Is Local: Global as Feminine: Masculine? Rethinking the Gender of Globalizations', *Signs* 26 (4) (2001): 1010.
10. James Clifford, *Routes: Travel and Translation in the Late Twentieth Century* (Cambridge, MA: Harvard University Press, 1999), p. 39. Originally published in 1997.
11. Roberta Rubenstein, *Home Matters: Longing and Belonging, Nostalgia and Mourning in Women's Fiction* (Houndmills: Palgrave, 2004), p. 4.
12. Chelva Kanaganayakam, 'Exiles and Expatriates', in Bruce King (ed.), *New National and Post-Colonial Literatures* (Oxford: Oxford University Press, 1996), p. 201; Edward Said, *Reflections on Exile and Other Literary and Cultural Essays* (London: Granta, 2000), p. 181.
13. Caren Kaplan, *Questions of Travel: Postmodern Discourses of Displacement* (Durham, NC: Duke University Press, 1996), p. 33.
14. Rubenstein, *Home*, p. 4.

CHAPTER 3

'THERE IS NO WORLD OUTSIDE THE TEXT':
TRANSATLANTIC SLIPPAGE IN EVA HOFFMAN'S
LOST IN TRANSLATION

Jennifer Browdy de Hernandez argues that, for postcolonial autobi-
ographers, home is a 'contested site on which the cultural conflicts of
the larger society are played out in microcosm'.[1] Such a recognition is
important for an exploration of Eva Hoffman's transatlantic memoir,
Lost in Translation. In this text, Hoffman's childhood home, Poland,
becomes a landscape of desire, a place she can neither return to nor
abandon. Indeed, part way through the memoir Hoffman expands at
length on her desire for Poland, and its continual pull on her:

> The country of my childhood lives within me with a primacy that is a
> form of love. It lives within me despite my knowledge of our marginal-
> ity, and its primitive, unpretty emotions. Is it blind and self-deceptive of
> me to hold on to its memory? I think it would be blind and self-deceptive
> not to. All it has given me is the world, but that is enough. It has fed me
> language, perceptions, sounds, the human kind . . . no geometry of land-
> scape, no haze in the air, will live in us as intensely as the landscapes that
> we saw as the first, and to which we gave ourselves wholly, without
> reservation.[2]

Indeed, the very blurring of locations within Hoffman's memoir, as
she moves from past to present almost seamlessly at times, indicates
the way in which spaces are influenced, if not infected, by other
spaces, and as home itself becomes a multiple site that resists final
definition. Hoffman follows in a long line of critics and writers who
see places as if on a continuum of being. Ernest Hemingway, in his
memoir of life in Paris, argued that 'Paris was never to be the same

again although it was always Paris and you changed as it changed.'[3] Hoffman, too, discovers this odd double image, as the Poland of her youth – Paradise – is reread by others and herself, in a continually evolving depiction of place.

In the acknowledgements page of his collected essays, *The Lovely Treachery of Words*, Canadian critic Robert Kroetsch argues that he 'wear[s] geography next to [his] skin' and that he 'speak[s] out of the play of surfaces against and with each other'.[4] These poetic phrases, buried in his list of thanks, could as easily be applied to Polish-Canadian/American writer Eva Hoffman. *Lost in Translation*, her first memoir,[5] examines the necessity of wearing geography next to one's skin; the way in which the surfaces and depths of her beloved lost country and her grudgingly gained new one(s) slip against each other to form a palimpsestic narrative where America as a concept obtrudes upon both Canada and Poland. Hoffman limns the landscapes of Poland, Canada and the United States in her Woolfian memoir that traces the space of childhood and young adulthood, alternating between a geographic and a linguistic structuring of her memories. This chapter explores the discourses of 'here' and 'there' invoked by her multilayered images, and maps the transatlantic, linguistic signs of Poland, Canada and 'America' – however this last term is defined. It also argues that Hoffman's text, positioned in one or other of the defining geographical spaces by critics who attempt to circumscribe the memoir and label it as an American, or Jewish, or immigrant narrative, actually offers a more nuanced, transnational reading of space.

Hoffman herself has defined transnational literature as one where 'multiple cultural references collide and collude',[6] and the reader encounters a variety of cultural collisions in negotiating the memoir's meaning. These collisions problematise Hoffman's other assertion, that 'there is no world outside the text' (182). This position, developed during her study of New Criticism, is ultimately undermined precisely through reading Hoffman's memoir, in which the multifaceted world outside the text is skilfully created and recreated in a series of competing discourses about how memory itself is constructed and place is negotiated. As Susan Fanetti argues: 'Only when she is adept at "reading" the culture in which she resides is she able to come to know and understand her place within that culture.'[7] The process of reading and misreading her transatlantic self – a process that is both internal and external – comes to structure the narrative as a whole.

In the very first paragraph of the book, posing as her 13-year-old self, Hoffman observes that leaving Poland 'is a notion of such crushing, definitive finality that to me it might as well mean the end of the world' (3). However, Hoffman's text reveals that the process of emigration – or, indeed, exile – can never be complete. It is always the subject of regrets, memories and transitions. Indeed, Hoffman's text is not a chronological account of coming to the 'New World', but a tapestry of ideas, flowing like a transatlantic stream of consciousness narrative back and forth between Poland and Canada or the US. As the ship taking her from Poland moves away, Hoffman notes that her 'being is engaged in a stubborn refusal to move' (4) – yet move she does; what the book celebrates and analyses is that very movement, even by way of its elliptical structure, which fluidly melds past and present. Such images reinforce the transatlantic tides which move in different directions, and which carry Hoffman both back and forth across this (imagined) oceanic space.

The book is, as the subtitle 'Life in a New Language' suggests, principally a memoir of dislocation. In it, Hoffman examines individual words and whole languages in a bid to understand her own sense of exile; she uses literary criticism and theory to structure her responses to the 'new' world, invoking structuralism, postmodernism and references to theatre. This 'New World' is an amalgam of Canada and the US; indeed, Canada is at first vaguely interpreted and mistakenly associated with an 'America' that erases its cultural specificity. Canada itself only invokes an undefined sense of a cultural desert: 'There are vague outlines of half a continent, a sense of vast spaces and little habitation' (4).

In contrast, Poland is writ large and lovely, though Hoffman problematises her 'paradise' construction through acknowledging that Poland itself is a shifting entity. Where Lvov was once Polish, it becomes Russian and necessitates a move for her parents who were 'trying as quickly as possible to cross the new borders so they could remain within their old nationality even at the cost of leaving home' (8). What is more, political change two years after the publication of Hoffman's text now situates Lvov in the independent Ukraine, indicating again the shifting nature of national boundaries, and the fact that one's lived experience may or may not equate with political positionings. Poland is a country revisited in the text, both sentimentalised and exposed as unforgiving. Its meaning is not singularly wrapped up in paradise, but constantly alters until it becomes such a diffuse image that Hoffman cannot contain it. Hoffman uses the term 'geography of emotions' to explain and explore her own feelings, acknowledging as she does so that for her Canadian contemporaries, Poland is a 'gray patch of land inhabited by ghosts' (132). She finds her own poltergeist in Mary Antin, author of an immigrant narrative that she feels maps onto her own, despite the fact that Antin's transatlantic tale is a Russian-US one; again, cultural and country borders are here problematised, and the metaphorical maps that Hoffman uses as guides do not necessarily relate to political geography.

It is formally appropriate that questions of 'here' dominate Hoffman's memoir, given that her first emigration is to Canada, a country that critics have argued is preoccupied with margins and dislocations, a place which, rather than loudly proclaiming a sense of place and space (as perhaps its southern neighbour does), expends its critical energies on the tensions between 'here' and 'there'. Indeed, it has long been a commonplace that Canada's primary question is 'Where is here?'[8] If contemporary critics unpack the assumptions behind Northrop Frye's momentous statement, they nevertheless acknowledge the potency of the image, whether it be mythic or more pragmatically 'real'.

Geography, again, becomes metaphorical, and Kroetsch's construction of it as skin links with Hoffman's construction of it as emotion. Geography here extends beyond definable, if changing borders, and is not necessarily linked to political nation-states; after all, Hoffman's text frequently conflates Canada with the US, and the short author biography in later texts suggests that Hoffman moved to 'America' at the age of 13, a shorthand assertion that offers no national differentiation, and indeed encourages a misrecognition of place.[9] From Hoffman's perspective, one of the difficulties of being an immigrant is dealing with 'the strangeness of glimpsing internal landscapes that are arranged in different formations as well' (265); thus it is unsurprising that external landscapes and divisions are not rigidly maintained. What further complicates Hoffman's half-wished-for, half-resisted assimilation into the 'New World' is her adolescence at the time of emigration. She is a child lost in the mores and attitudes of a new culture, where dating, make-up, and the ways to conduct oneself in public all require performing a role to which she is unaccustomed. Hoffman's own sense of national and personal identities become fragmented when she moves from being a Polish child, to a Canadian adolescent, to an American adult, and these various, indeed sometimes imaginary identities bleed into each other to form the tapestry of her memoir.

If not Where, then Who?

R. Barbara Gitenstein argues that 'critics who write of Hoffman try to confine or limit her identity,' yet it is significant that in Gitenstein's list of possible constructions of Hoffman ('Polish, Jewish, female and developing American'), the identity tag 'Canadian' is not even mentioned.[10] Indeed, Gitenstein refers to Canada only twice, in two short passages. In one, Gitenstein notes that 'after her teenage passage in Canada, where she begins to learn the niceties of being a female in the New World and a modern visionary with a memory and nostalgia for the Old World, Hoffman comes to see herself as a special interpreter of America to her friends, her family and herself.'[11] A second reference is even briefer, simply noting that it was in Canada that Hoffman 'begins to lose her sense of self – her ability to speak and be'.[12] For Gitenstein, then, the contrast is between the sharply divided Old and New Worlds, rather than between the nations that constitute this 'New World'; Canada is merely the transitional space that gets superseded by the US. Given that Gitenstein's article appears in a collection subtitled 'American Women Writers of Polish Descent', the elision of Canada is perhaps not surprising.

It is also the case, as Danuta Zadworna Fjellestad notes, that Hoffman herself is slippery in relation to the term 'America', which sometimes seems to encompass Canada and sometimes does not.[13] Hoffman acknowledges the slippage early on: 'America – Canada in our minds is automatically subsumed under that category – has for us the old fabulous associations: streets paved with gold, the goose that laid the golden egg' (84). Furthermore, as Jerzy Durczak points out, 'Though the reader has occasional glimpses of the Canadian school, the Canadian society or the autobiographer's family life, the bulk of the author's observations has to do with "living in a new language".'[14] Thus, it may be Hoffman's own construction of Canada as space of transit, or as part and parcel of 'America', that encourages critics to focus elsewhere.

Nevertheless, it is remains surprising how few writers even acknowledge Hoffman's transitional Canadianness. Several articles in *MELUS*, the journal attached to the *Society of Multiethnic Literature* (which therefore might be expected to engage with the multi-national nature of Hoffman's identity), do not focus on Hoffman's 'other' other nationality, Canadian, at all, while one article from the same journal makes only passing reference to Hoffman's Canadianness – and even this occurs in the footnotes. Other articles focus on

Hoffman's Jewish identity, on the genre of immigrant novels in general, or on the connections between Hoffman's narrative and Mary Antin's.[15] Mary Besemeres is thus unusual in explicitly isolating Hoffman's Polish-Canadian identity. Besemeres justifies her usage of the term 'Polish-Canadian' by noting that her article considers Hoffman Polish-Canadian 'because her original emigration from Poland was to Canada'.[16] Besemeres then notes that she will refer to Hoffman's ' "Polish" and "Anglo" senses of self', and that the latter term covers both the US and the Canadian portions of this identity, thus then conflating her Canadianness with her Americanness (and stirring up other critical debates about the contested term 'Anglo').[17] Furthermore, whilst Besemeres offers a comprehensive account of Hoffman's national identity, this discussion is confined to a footnote. Moreover, Besemeres is likely to need to justify such a claim, given that the article is published in *Canadian Slavonic Papers*.

Perhaps the most extensive treatment of Hoffman's Canadianness comes from *Canadian Ethnic Studies* – again, the site of publication perhaps ensures such discussion. Eva Karpinski's critically acute, if at times scathing analysis of Hoffman's memoir acknowledges Canada's 'transitional' space for Hoffman, and engages more extensively with the country and its meanings for Hoffman. Karpinski argues that 'Canada to her becomes a place of exile primarily because it is associated with linguistic uprooting.'[18] It is, moreover, 'a place inhabited by her *immigrant* self and her "ethnic" parents'.[19] Karpinski clearly sees a self that moves beyond an immigrant status, yet paradoxically, she lambasts Hoffman for not attending sufficiently to the importance of her outsider status. It is worth exploring Karpinski's objections in more detail. The passage that Karpinski focuses her critique upon runs thus:

> I want to figure out, more urgently than before, where I belong in this America that's made up of so many sub-Americas. I want, somehow, to give up the condition of being a foreigner . . . *I no longer want to have the prickly, unrelenting consciousness that I'm living in the medium of a specific culture. It's time to roll down the scrim and see the world directly, as the world.* I want to reenter, through whatever Looking Glass will take me there, a state of ordinary reality. (202, my italics)

Karpinski argues that, in this passage, Hoffman 'confuses "ordinary reality" with the ethnocentric "norms" of American culture, thus implying that the immigrant reality is peripheral and somehow less real'.[20] A different reading simply locates the desire to belong, the desire to exist not as a type, but as an individual – a desire endlessly deferred for a visible or aurally-identifiable immigrant. Hoffman here wishes to locate the unthinking sense of place that individuals who have not been uprooted seem to maintain as if without effort.

If such a place is more mythic than real, it is still a powerful symbol of one's ability (or inability) to fix location. It is perhaps significant that Karpinski cuts the section in italics here.[21] The tensions between 'here' and 'there' are, in this passage, between two states of being: an idealised, unaware sense of rootedness, and an overwhelming awareness of displacement. Such binaries structure much of Hoffman's memoir. Nowhere is this clearer than in her positioning of her Polish childhood as 'paradise' and her Canadian adolescence as 'exile'.

In his discussion of the difficulties of distinguishing between fact and fiction in autobiography, Ihab Hassan trenchantly asks: 'Isn't memory sister to imagination, kin to nostalgia, desire, and deceit? Isn't memory sometimes even an agent to mendacity, meant consciously to mislead or manipulate history?'[22] Thus Hoffman's memories of her homeland must always be seen through the screen of doubt, their constructed nature foregrounded. She herself admits that:

> to some extent, one has to rewrite the past in order to understand it. I have to see Cracow in the dimensions it has to my adult eye in order to perceive that my story has been only a story, that none of its events has been so big or so scary. It is the price of emigration, as of any radical discontinuity, that it makes such reviews and re-readings difficult; being cut off from one part of one's own story is apt to veil it in the haze of nostalgia, which is an ineffectual relationship to the past, and the haze of alienation, which is an ineffectual relationship to the present. (242)

It is to her credit that Hoffman acknowledges her own process of reinscription as both a willed and a wilful one. She is not, as some critics have mistakenly believed, unaware of her own critical and creative manipulations. Indeed, her careful linguistic and structural plotting of a sense of exile and emigration attests to the fact that, if anything, she is hyperaware of the creation and construction of her memories. Hassan notes that ' "paradise" is made in the mind, precisely to be lost and perpetually regained.'[23] Such awareness is crucial to Hoffman's own construction of her Edenic Poland, a Poland which is irrevocably lost to her, especially after a visit 'home' in which her childhood friend suggests that she is at least half-American now.

Hoffman's own gloss on her eventual 'Americanness' is telling: 'I've become a partial American, a sort of resident alien' (221). Lacking a sense of completeness, Hoffman concedes a partial representation of herself as allied with her new environment, but significantly sites herself outside any normative framework. She is, at best, an *alien* American, with all of the otherness that such a designation encodes.

The near 'double-consciousness' that Hoffman experiences as a returning stranger – that iconic position so closely allied with Canadian postcolonialism – is implicitly contrasted to her Poland of childhood, which appears (in places) as whole and unreflective. Marianne Hirsch, herself a multiply-displaced immigrant, criticises Hoffman's stance in this respect, arguing that she wants Hoffman to acknowledge that 'in Poland, as a child, she was already divided.'[24] Hirsch's difficulty comes with her mistaken assumption that Poland is 'unequivocally' located as paradise in Hoffman's text. Indeed, Hirsch asks a series of piercing questions:

> What does it take for Hoffman to consider this place paradise? Why would she want to recapture a childhood that rests on such [an anti-Semitic] legacy? Hoffman's denial is painful to read, yet it is basic to her construction of her narrative and her world, of her self . . . With her evocation of childhood plenitude, Hoffman has displaced the reality of the war, of the anti-Semitism she admittedly still experiences, but which she simply dismisses by calling it *primitive*.[25]

Hirsch's passionate discomfiture with Hoffman's text is compelling, but, as Besemeres rightly notes, this criticism of Hoffman is flawed: 'Hoffman's declaration about childhood's non-dividedness should be read not as an absolute or descriptive statement but as an experiential one, relative to her own life "in" the Polish language.'[26] Moreover, Besemeres also notes Hirsch's own conflation of places within the Polish landscape, an elision that makes a powerful argument, but not an entirely accurate one. Yet perhaps Hirsch needs a more complete answer to her questions of how Cracow can be constructed as paradise. The text offers one: it is a paradise constructed of 'shimmering light and shadow, with the shadow only adding more brilliance to the patches of wind and sun' (38). Thus, despite superficial appearances, this is no Pollyanna-ish stance, but a carefully considered one, which evokes the play of light and dark in order to hollow out a more deeply felt understanding of a sense of homeland and place.

Karpinski offers another critique of Hoffman's 'personal mythology' as she calls it. She argues that, in the memoir, childhood is 'coded'
as 'the place of the familiar' whereas adulthood 'connotes fragmentation and divisiveness, splintering and insecurity'.[27] The most important words here, I believe, are 'mythology' and 'coded', in that they
specifically indicate the constructed nature of Hoffman's version of
her childhood. If Hirsch faults such binaries, Karpinski recognises
their self-conscious use. Furthermore, as Marianne Friedrich notes:
'[T]he paradise motif provides an ideal supportive structure due to its
inherent potential to *build oppositions*.'[28] This 'supportive structure'
is deliberately invoked, as Hoffman's text moves from a structuralist
position through many different levels of literary and cultural criticism to arrive at a post-structuralist, postmodern stance towards
identity. Fjellestad identifies the movement thus:

> The book speaks of the results of the loss of what poststructuralist
> wisdom would call a romantic illusion of unity and center and of the costs
> and rewards, the joys and terrors, of being thrown into the postmodern
> world of constantly shifting boundaries and borderless possibilities.[29]

Hoffman's text engages with the myth of wholeness in order, I
believe, to acknowledge that childhood is full of illusions; her text
allows them a space, even as or when there is another, ironic voice
behind such idyllic memories. A clear example of such dual-coding
occurs in her recollection of a summer holiday in Bialy Dunajec, a
small village near the Tatry Mountains. The village is considered
'primitive' by the city folk who elect to spend their leisure time there,
yet overlaying any sense of having to *put up* with 'roughing it' is the
'good, strong smell of raw wood and hay and clear mountain air'
(18); here we have a clear sense of the primitive as close to nature, and
therefore 'good'. The journey to Dunajec is expressed in similarly idealised terms. Hoffman is 'hypnotized' by the train and sees 'golden
haystacks baked by the sun, and the peasants unbending from their
work to wave at the passing-by train' (18). This Edenic version of the
Polish countryside is a highly stylised one, with peasants acting out
picturesque and friendly scenes, rather than toiling hard with little
reward. Indeed, even the work they perform seems a rich part of a
child's happy life. To consider this carefully-crafted idealism as less
than consciously constructed is to misread Hoffman's narrative. As
she bluntly acknowledges at the beginning of the book: '[T]he wonder
is what you can make a paradise out of' (5). Here then, as elsewhere,

Hoffman is overtly conscious of the *desire* for plenitude, as well as the myth behind such a wish for wholeness.

Hoffman's use of binaries – admittedly and perhaps strategically disrupted through her conflation of the US and Canada in places – follows not only from an immigrant-tale template in which Old and New Worlds are explicitly compared and contrasted, but from her own education in structuralist and then post-structuralist thought. Indeed, it is perhaps this overt awareness that prods Hoffman to undermine any sort of binary opposition here, even as she herself sets them up. If the immigrant template calls for a text which sees the Old World as 'bad' and the New World as 'good', she calls her Old World 'Paradise' and her New World 'Exile'. If the immigrant template of a resident of a former Communist country calls for a denunciation of the Old World political view, Hoffman 'complicates the popular picture by focusing on the charms and blessings of the System and the terrors and curses of the Promised Land',[30] going so far as to use the image of the smiling peasant – a Communist propaganda tool if there ever was one – for her own ends. Hoffman's memoir is thus more than a personal narrative; indeed, her inclusion of cultural and literary analysis makes it possible to isolate lines which come as if from literary criticism, rather than autobiography, and it is to her linguistic and theoretical structuring of 'exile' that I now turn.

Words and the World: The Literary Interpretation of Exile

As a child, Eva reads *Anne of Green Gables*, the archetypal story of the growing-up girl in Canada: 'As long as I am reading, I assume I am this girl growing up on Prince Edward Island; the novel's words enter my head as if they were emanating from it. Since I experience what they describe so vividly, they must be mine' (28). Hoffman here constructs the naïve reader who wishes to sink into a 'realist' text and be transported. Indeed, she notes that 'I love words insofar as they correspond to the world, insofar as they give it to me in a heightened form' (28). As yet unaware of the contingency of meaning, or of Saussure's linguistic signs, Hoffman allows words to stand in for real things. Indeed, she even goes so far as to evoke her own, nonsensical language in order to tell 'A Story, Every Story, everything all at once' (11).

Once she is in exile, however, she understands the inability to articulate everything, and her literary critical language takes over. She becomes a 'living avatar of structuralist wisdom' fully aware that 'words are just themselves' (107). Indeed, she sees as one of her biggest problems the fact that 'the signifier has become severed from the signified' (106). Moreover, she understands that immigrant stories are just that, stories, 'models for immigrant fates' which most likely feel unnatural to those that live them (95). Unsurprisingly, then, she actually incorporates an example of an immigrant story within her larger narrative of immigration – the story of Irena, a young woman who plays out her love on board the ship carrying them from Europe to North America, only to be 'sold' into marriage upon reaching the 'promised land'. Here, Hoffman again reveals how things only 'mean' contingently. After all, what is political freedom in such an environment? Moreover, the young Eva makes this 'story' into part of her own story; she notes that Irena 'completes the novel I'm temporarily living in perfectly' (89) and she later imagines contradictory fates for her heroine, who fittingly disappears into Canada without a backwards glance. Irena as fictional heroine is set alongside Eva as factual traveller who wishes her narrative to be less real herself. If she is able to read her life as a novel, she can step outside of it and return to her original space: Poland, home.

Hoffman suggests that life becomes a series of translations, not necessarily between two different languages, but 'from the word back to its source' (107). For the young woman who revels in language – her own, childhood language – there is the sudden disconnection that comes from experiencing words only in their 'literary value', words 'that exist only as signs on the page' (106). Indeed, in her exile from language, Hoffman learns through *text* rather than experience. Given a diary, she makes a conscious decision to write in English: 'I learn English through writing, and, in turn, writing gives me a written self. Refracted through the double distance of English and writing, this self – my English self – becomes oddly objective; more than anything, it perceives' (121). Petra Fachinger berates Hoffman for the choice to write autobiographically in a mode that suggests objectivity, and for taking Benjamin Franklin as a model: 'Hoffman fails to acknowledge the inadequacy of an eighteenth-century male vision which, among other things, assumes the absence of racial and sexual prejudice and discrimination in a classless society in the contemporary context.'[31] This objective, perceiving self is one that Fachinger perceives as primarily male, and she bemoans Hoffman's apparent 'privileging of the "public" over the "private", her refusal to reflect on the androcentric tradition of autobiography, her adoption of the male model of self-representation, and her endorsement of the American story of successful assimilation'.[32] Yet to read Hoffman's story as one that

promotes an easy assimilation is to misread it, and to suggest that it
denies the effects of gender is to ignore not only the story of Irena, but
also Hoffman's own unhappy forays into trying to be a 'normal'
Canadian adolescent, learning (if faultily) the performances required
to be considered date-worthy. In Canada, Eva takes on the 'manner-
isms of a marginal, off-centered person who wants both to be taken
in and to fend off the threatening others' (110). This is no easy assimilation; learning to be North American is a process that confuses and
dismays Eva, and one that she finds not a little unfaithful to her past.
In asking, 'Can I jump continents as if skipping rope?' (115),
Hoffman retains a sense of her female childhood, and, contrary to
Fachinger's suppositions, never lets go of the fact of being a classed
and gendered body.

As Hoffman moves from Canada, to Rice University in Texas, to
Harvard graduate school and on to New York, she retains her sense
of being an immigrant. Indeed, as she notes: '[B]eing "an immigrant,"
I begin to learn, is considered a sort of location in itself – and sometimes a highly advantageous one at that' (133). In this context,
though, Vancouver itself is never transformed into a homeland, a
place of comfortable return, because it was there that Hoffman 'fell
out of the net of meaning into the weightlessness of chaos' (151).

If in Poland, she read the narrative of a young girl's life in Canada
as realism, she cannot, in America, read an immigrant's tale with
such abandon. Mary Antin, her alter-ego, 'amusing poltergeist' and
'ancestress', is unpicked by her newly-aware structuralist and post-
structuralist objective, perceiving self. Taking the stance of a resisting reader, Hoffman unpicks the triumphalist tone of *The Promised
Land* in order to interrogate the 'trace of another story behind
the story' (162). With great irony, Hoffman notes the similarities
between their tales, yet Antin focuses on triumph and assimilation,
whereas Hoffman – a spectacularly successful woman by any definition – appears to revel in her own maladaptions, her own sense of
dislocation.

Perhaps appropriately, Hoffman uses the language of pop psy-
chology and contemporary theatrical performance to explore her
transatlantic dislocation. In inventing and reinventing herself, she
finds her own desires are as uncontrollable as 'an infant's id' (160).
Moreover, she invokes the idea of a 'Canadian superego' secretly
observing Polish immigrants that conform, or at least behave as
though they do (141). Her text is interrupted and infused with inter-
polated dialogues between the versions of herself, existential passages

that speak of fragmentation and loss. In one example, the young Eva imagines what she would have been like had she never left Poland, how she would have looked, how she would have acted.

> But you would have been different, very different.
>> No question.
>> And you prefer her, the Cracow Ewa.
>> Yes, I prefer her. But I can't be her. I'm losing track of her. In a few years, I'll have no idea what her hairdo would have been like.
>> But she's more real, anyway.
>> Yes, she's the real one. (120)

Yet even this 'real' Eva is constructed, as an adult version of Hoffman acknowledges over a 100 pages later. Judith Oster argues that Hoffman is thus 'combining a past *place* with her present *time* and thus constructing a "self" that cannot possibly exist'.[33] She is, rather, suspended transatlantically between these two constructions of self, and it is only later, as an adult, that Hoffman acknowledges that 'the space *between* cultures is the only viable space for actuality and identity.'[34] In Hoffman's internal struggle, various Evas co-exist, and neither is awarded an identifiable tag that suggests the Polish 'Ewa' versus the 'American' Eva, though the reader is able to disentangle who is who:

> Leave me alone. It's you who's playing the charade now. Your kind of knowledge doesn't apply to my condition.
>> I'll never leave you quite alone . . .
>> But I don't have to listen to you any longer. I'm as real as you are now. I'm the real one. (231, ellipses in original)

This linguistic and existential construction of the 'real' across the transatlantic space indicates slippage as well as demarcations of identity. In her travel book-cum-memoir *Exit into History*, Hoffman suggests that every immigrant has 'a second, spectral autobiography, and in my revision of my own history I would have stayed in Poland long enough to become involved in the oppositional politics of my generation'.[35] Instead, she revisits Poland – here as elsewhere – in an attempt to make sense not only of the country she has left behind, but the person that she might have become as well.

Hoffman also sets out as theatrical dialogue conversations between (one version of) herself and MAF, 'My American Friend', a nameless Everywoman; these dialogues point to a postmodern sense of identity as process, not product, and, perhaps more to the point, performance, not being. Hoffman's text moves between genres as quickly as she moves between continents, setting down only momentarily in one style before hurling herself in another direction.

At Rice University, she is taught New Criticism, a form of literary criticism that allows her to shine: 'Luckily for me, there is no world outside the text; luckily, for I know so little of the world to which the literature I read refers' (182). In exploring American literature, she prefers once again to focus on the word, the 'world' being too remote, too unknowable, to capture successfully. New Criticism, she argues, 'is an alienated way of reading meant for people who are aliens in the country of literature' (183): here, form and content, literature and life intermingle, offering mirror images that reinforce Hoffman's sense of exile. It is only when she becomes a teacher of literature herself that she jumps back into a space almost akin to her childhood where words become 'beautiful things – except this is better, because they're now crosshatched with a complexity of meaning, with the sonorities of felt, sensuous thought' (186). It is no coincidence that Hoffman experiences this moment of epiphany when she is reading and interpreting T. S. Eliot, himself a transplanted national.

New Criticism and the like are never enough, though, for a complete understanding of her own 'here' and 'there' tensions, and she plunders the discourses of Foucault, Bakhtin and others in her search for a literary description of exile. She refers to Adorno, Nabokov and Milan Kundera with ease, locating within their dislocations a sense of camaraderie. Clearly, as Fjellestad notes, Hoffman is 'conscious of her *experience* of a linguistic construction of her self'.[36] She is, moreover, conscious of others' constructions as well.

Karpinski maintains that Hoffman's narrative never gets beyond 'a nostalgia trip, a piece of cultural anthropology that flaunts cultural generalities'. Furthermore, she argues that 'despite her appropriation of poststructuralist rhetoric, she is still committed to the concept of essential selfhood whose experience can be of universal value.'[37] I would argue, however, that Hoffman rejects the universal time and time again, and this rejection is one of the key facets of her memoir. Nowhere is this more apparent than in her refusal to concede to her friends' decisions to draw universal connections from specific texts. While she and MAF both find a particular Hungarian movie powerful, MAF extrapolates its plot to encompass the notion of everyone's co-option in the system. Hoffman reacts angrily: 'But it wasn't about

all of us. It was about the Communist party in Hungary circa 1948.'
She fiercely notes: 'I'm loyal to some notion of accuracy, which is more
than I can say for you! The world isn't just a projection screen for your
ideas, highly correct though they may be' (205–6). If such language
bespeaks the righteous indignation of youth, it also sets up a running
argument that the specific is the specific; the myth of universality must
indeed be abandoned. Clearly, there *is* a world outside the text, despite earlier protestations otherwise, and clearly, Hoffman's literary
sensibilities reject a casual transference of meaning across space and
time.

At the same time, the fabulated nature of Hoffman's early construction of North America ('streets paved with gold') is revisited near
the end of the book, where Hoffman's Polish compatriots gather in
New York, and ironically reconstruct a Polish-inspired vision of the
US: ' "Someday you'll get there, and then you'll see what it's like. Tall
men in cowboy hats, producers throwing deals at your feet, a swim-
ming pool in every penthouse, and a TV with remote control in every
room . . . I tell you, it's quite a country, America" ' (259, ellipses in
original). This description is followed by the statement, ' "Oh well,
maybe I'll apply for a visa to go there, I hear they're easier to get these
days," Jurek says and raises his glass' (259). Already inhabiting *an*
America, Hoffman's Polish friends step back ironically to reinhabit
the fantasy version of it, to acknowledge the gap between the actual
country and their transatlantic versions of it. Hoffman even compares
and contrasts the differing interpretations of space that immigrants
from various countries hold.[38] She compares a Polish friend to her
cleaner, Maria; for her unnamed friend, '[T]he world is too small to
sustain the fabulous America of people's dreams; there is no America
any longer, no place the mind can turn to for fantastic hope. But for
Maria, who nurtures no fantastic hopes, it's still America you emi-
grate to – this all-too-real America' (261).

Lost in Translation is, as Karpinski rightly notes, composed of a
privileged narrative voice; its discourse *is* that of Western autobiography. What Hoffman does with the immigrant narrative, however, is
extend it beyond her own 'essential selfhood' through the very discourses of power and criticism that she invokes. Poland, Canada and
the US become both particularised places and metaphorical ones in
her capable hands. Paradise, Exile and the New World correspond to
these countries respectively, and yet even these designations slip and
tumble into each other. Poland is both the 'gray patch of land' imagined by her Vancouver classmates and the whole globe imagined by

her adolescent self. Hoffman is eventually, however, able to see it as her classmates do, as 'a distant spot, somewhere on the peripheries of the imagination, crowded together with countless other hard to remember places of equal insignificance' (132). This realisation, in turn, recalls her own first view of Canada as 'an enormous, cold blankness' (4).

These two views, similar in perspective yet diametrically opposed at the same time, mark her moment of realisation that reference points necessarily shift.[39] Indeed, as Hoffman notes: 'The reference points inside my head are beginning to do a flickering dance. I suppose this is the most palatable meaning of displacement. I have been dislocated from my own centre of the world, and that world has been shifted away from my center' (132). The world is larger than she is; its centre is not her and never will be. Indeed, 'there is no geographic center pulling the world together and glowing with the allure of the real thing; there are, instead, scattered nodules competing for our attention' (275).

Hoffman is searching, through words, for her 'blank white center' (275), yet paradoxically, it is only through black marks transgressing this white space that any story can be written at all. What Hoffman does in her memoir is inscribe Poland onto a transatlantically produced Canadian and American literary landscape (and vice versa). She asserts connections and disruptions between all three countries, relocating specific geography within a linguistic and emotional geography, juxtaposing, for instructive comparison, the worlds inside – and outside – the text.

NOTES

1. Jennifer Browdy de Hernandez, 'On Home Ground: Politics, Location, and the Construction of Identity in Four American Women's Autobiographies', *MELUS* 22 (4) (1997): 21.
2. Eva Hoffman, *Lost in Translation* (London: Minerva, 1991), p. 74. Originally published in 1989. All subsequent references to this text will be cited parenthetically.
3. Ernest Hemingway, *A Moveable Feast* (London: Vintage, 2000), p. 182. Originally published in 1960.
4. Robert Kroetsch, *The Lovely Treachery of Words: Essays Selected and New* (Toronto: Oxford University Press, 1989), p. ix.
5. Hoffman followed publication of *Lost in Translation* with her travel memoir *Exit into History: A Journey through New Eastern Europe* (1993), an account of her return to Poland after the fall of Communism.

The book begins by noting that 'Poland has taken a leap away from me, not in distance, but in time' (p. 1), indicating Hoffman's continuing engagement with emotional rather than literal geographies of place. She has also published *Shtetl: The History of a Small Town and an Extinguished World* (1998) and *After Such Knowledge: Where Memory of the Holocaust Ends and History Begins* (2004), as well as one novel, *The Secret* (2001), and various essays, including 'The New Nomads' in André Aciman's *Letters of Transit: Reflections on Exile, Identity, Language and Loss* (New York: The New Press, 1999).

6. Hoffman, 'New Nomads', p. 56.
7. Susan Fanetti, 'Translating Self into Liminal Space: Eva Hoffman's Acculturation in/to a Postmodern World', *Women's Studies* 34 (2005): 405.
8. The question comes originally from Northrop Frye:

   It seems to me that Canadian sensibility has been profoundly disturbed, not so much by our famous problem of identity, important as that is, as by a series of paradoxes in what confronts that identity. It is less perplexed by the question 'Who am I?' than by some riddle such as 'Where is here?' (Northrop Frye, *The Bush Garden: Essays on the Canadian Imagination* (Toronto: Anansi, 1971), p. 220)

9. See, for example, the Vintage editions of *After Such Knowledge*, *Shtetl* and *Exit into History*.
10. R. Barbara Gitenstein, 'Eva Hoffman: Conflicts and Continuities of Self', in Thomas S. Gladsky and Rita Holmes Gladsky (eds), *Something of My Very Own to Say: American Women Writers of Polish Descent* (New York: Eastern European Monographs/Columbia University Press, 1997), p. 261.
11. Ibid. p. 266.
12. Ibid. p. 271.
13. Danuta Zadworna Fjellestad, ' "The Insertion of the Self into the Space of Borderless Possibility": Eva Hoffman's Exiled Body', *MELUS* 20 (2) (1995): 146 n. 12.
14. Jerzy Durczak, 'Multicultural Autobiography and Language: Richard Rodriguez and Eva Hoffman', in Jadwiga Maszewska (ed.), *Crossing Borders: American Literature and Other Artistic Media* (Lodz: Wydawnictwo Naukowe PWN, 1992), p. 27.
15. See, amongst others, William A. Proefriedt, 'The Immigrant or "Outsider" Experience as Metaphor for becoming an Educated Person in the Modern World: Mary Antin, Richard Wright and Eva Hoffman', *MELUS* 16 (2) (1989–90): 77–89; Fjellestad, 'Insertion'; Mark Krupnick, 'Assimilation in Recent American Jewish Autobiographies', *Contemporary Literature* 34 (3) (1993): 451–74; Eva C. Karpinski,

'Negotiating the Self: Eva Hoffman's *Lost in Translation* and the Question of Immigrant Autobiography', *Canadian Ethnic Studies* 28 (1) (1996): 127–35; Steven G. Kellman, 'Lost in the Promised Land: Eva Hoffman Revises Mary Antin', *Proof Texts: A Journal of Jewish Literary History* 18 (2) (1998): 149–59.

16. Mary Besemeres, 'Language and Self in Cross-Cultural Autobiography: Eva Hoffman's *Lost in Translation*', *Canadian Slavonic Papers* 40 (3–4) (1998): 327.

17. Ibid.

18. Karpinski, 'Negotiating', p. 128.

19. Ibid. p. 132, italics mine.

20. Ibid.

21. I have similarly cut some of the words Karpinski quotes. The missing words are as follows:

> I no longer want to tell people quaint stories from the Old Country, I don't want to be told that 'exotic is erotic,' or that I have Eastern European intensity, or brooding Galician eyes. I no longer want to be propelled by immigrant chutzpah or desperado energy or usurper's ambition. (202)

22. Ihab Hassan, *Selves at Risk: Patterns of Quest in Contemporary American Letters* (Madison, WI: University of Wisconsin Press, 1990), p. 30.

23. Hassan, *Selves*, p. 68.

24. Marianne Hirsch, 'Pictures of a Displaced Girlhood', in Angelika Bammer (ed.), *Displacements: Cultural Identities in Question* (Bloomington, IN: Indiana University Press, 1994), pp. 76–7.

25. Hirsch, 'Pictures', p. 77, italics in original.

26. Besemeres, 'Language', p. 330 n. 8

27. Karpinski, 'Negotiating', p. 128.

28. Marianne M. Friedrich, 'Reconstructing Paradise: Eva Hoffman's *Lost in Translation*', *Yiddish* 11 (3–4) (1999): 164, italics in original.

29. Fjellestad, 'Insertion', p. 136.

30. Ibid.

31. Petra Fachinger, 'Lost in Nostalgia: The Autobiographies of Eva Hoffman and Richard Rodriguez', *MELUS* 265 (2) (2001): 118.

32. Ibid. p. 119.

33. Judith Oster, 'See(k)ing the Self: Mirrors and Mirroring in Bicultural Texts', *MELUS* 23 (4) (1998): 64, italics in original.

34. Fanetti, 'Translating', p. 406, italics in original.

35. Eva Hoffman, *Exit Into History: A Journey through the New Eastern Europe* (London: Vintage, 1999), p. 36. Originally published in 1993.

36. Fjellestad, 'Insertion', p. 139, italics in original.

37. Karpinski, 'Negotiating', p. 133.

38. This discussion can be compared with Josef Skvorecky's exploration of nations, in his novel *The Engineer of Human Souls* (1977), where he writes: 'I also know about their real country, the one they carry in their hearts' (p. 299), referring to immigrants' views of their native Czechoslovakia, or to Hoffman's own *Exit into History*, in which she is told that she is visiting Poland's Harlem while visiting an impoverished part of Warsaw.

39. Hoffman notes in *Exit into History* that for the 'new' Eastern Europe, engagement with the 'West', for example, includes both Japan and Hong Kong (25), revealing again the contingency of meaning that isn't necessarily connected to geographical 'reality'.

CHAPTER 4

THE ANTI-TOURIST: JENNY DISKI'S *SKATING TO ANTARCTICA* AND *STRANGER ON A TRAIN: DAYDREAMING AND SMOKING AROUND AMERICA WITH INTERRUPTIONS*

If Eva Hoffman's memoir about dislocation in language and space is one that rails against such disjunctures (if unevenly, and with the knowledge that dislocation can also be beneficial), Jenny Diski's travel memoirs go so far as to *celebrate* the dislocating nature of travel, as well as the urge to position oneself as an outsider, peering in (or, turning away). Diski's travels to Antarctica and America, her encounters with strangers, and her determined proposition to remain a stranger herself, combine to offer up a narrator no less self-aware than Hoffman, and *Skating to Antarctica* and *Stranger on a Train* are texts that both engage in and resist their truth-telling tag.[1] Indeed, though she offers up a portrait of herself as knowing, Diski is also a withholding author, who plays with the idea of discovery and revelation only to deny the ultimate effectiveness of both.

Like Hoffman, Diski is engaged with questions of mediated reality, and indeed at times in both travel memoirs, she offers up a Baudrillardian reading of her experience. In his travelogue *America*, Baudrillard suggests that:

> It may be that the truth of America can only be seen by a European, since he [*sic*] alone will discover here the perfect simulacrum – that of the immanence and material transcription of all values. The Americans, for their part, have no sense of simulation. They are themselves simulation in its most developed state, but they have no language in which to describe it, since they themselves are the model.[2]

Baudrillard's overstated 'observations' about the nature of Americans have been seen as the hyperbole that they are, particularly given his decision to focus on 'astral' America or the America of surfaces (and empty spaces); but it is clear that there is an affinity between Diski's observations and Baudrillard's own. It is not accidental that Diski recounts, in her second memoir, the experience of visiting Savannah, Georgia to sit on a bench that *replaces* the bench that Tom Hanks sat on in *Forrest Gump*: 'The actual bench has been taken away back to Hollywood by the studio. Still tourists come to stare and click their cameras at the substitute. It's a fake bench, but it's a fake bench in the right place' (53). If she doesn't precisely name Baudrillard, it is clear that she is familiar with his principles of hyperreality and simulacra, indeed so much so that when, on her travels around the US, she discovers that Las Vegas is indeed a 'home town' for some, she is disappointed; she would much rather it remain in her mind as a 'theme park of American toomuchness' (160).

Similarly, Baudrillard's conception of his American journey is one of visiting an (un)culture, a desert, and his trip is one without a plan, much as Diski's US trips are without a final destination in mind (apart from an acknowledgement that she will fly home on a particular day, and that her destination, therefore, is return). Threaded throughout both texts is an awareness of the nature of travel as somehow less real than travellers desire it to be, less authentic than (pre)supposed. Given that a long-running tourist campaign in the US has the tag line, 'You've seen the films. Now visit the set', it is perhaps not surprising that there is a conflation of reality and unreality in criticisms of the US, though the advertisement puts paid to the notion that Americans have no sense of humour.[3]

The transatlantic nature of Diski's work is apparent in both of her travel memoirs, though only in the second does she actually spend any amount of time in the Americas. The transatlanticity of *Skating to Antarctica* mainly resides in encounters with Americans on board the vessel taking her to Antarctica, and their preconceptions of what England and the English are like; indeed, though the majority of the text takes place in the Southern Oceanic space, it is the Atlantic encounters that determine the trajectory of the text.

In *Stranger on a Train*, Diski goes even further in tracking the habits of US travellers, concentrating almost exclusively on those who share her penchant for smoking, a defiant pleasure that is engaged in, denied, delayed and celebrated. It is the smoking carriage that gets the most space, as indeed Diski almost lovingly limns the interiors of the carriages as a way of identifying the varied reactions to smoking offered by smokers and non-smoking travellers alike. Diski's motives for travelling are much like Baudrillard's – to see, but also not to see, and to refuse at some level to see what is meant to capture the tourist/traveller's imagination.

'Like the Best of Times Being at Home, Only with an Upgraded View'

In her 1997 memoir *Skating to Antarctica*, Jenny Diski unsettles a number of assumptions about the motives for long-distance travel, as she explores her desire to head to the bottom of the world. Noting, for example, that travel can be associated with a search for roots or an investigation of alternative lifestyles – potentially if unrealistically noble pursuits – Diski admits that neither of these reasons could be attached to a visit to the Antarctic, an ex-centric place to desire to see. Moreover, as Margaret Atwood has her protagonist Rennie say in *Bodily Harm*, 'Those who'd lately been clamouring for roots had never seen a root up close . . . She had, and she'd rather be some other part of the plant.'[4] Diski's roots lie elsewhere, and though they are also the subject of the memoir, she spends at least as much time ruminating on the nature of travel itself, and engineering a complete avoidance of roots.

Diski's desire for the Antarctic is at some level undefinable. As she explains:

> I didn't plan this journey as a pilgrimage of any kind, just a hopeful journey into whiteness. My motives were as indistinct as the landscape I was wishing to travel to. There was simply an irrational desire to be at the bottom of the world in a land of ice and snow. I wanted to write *white* and shades of white, though even this did not necessarily require me to go to such lengths. (126–7, italics in original)

The final line notes that even this motive is suspect; her desire for whiteness is not absolutely connected to a desire for the Antarctic, which is merely a convenient destination to attach to this desire for blankness – or, as it turns out, an inconvenient one. The Antarctic is a series of places, not a specific destination; it is best defined as 'a position on a navigation chart' (232) and travelling to it is problematic: 'It turned out not to be so easy to go to Antarctica. There isn't anywhere exactly to go' (5). Moreover, the continent is reserved for scientists, people who are seen to have a legitimate reason to go; when Diski half-jokingly asks the British Antarctic Survey if there is a writer-in-residence programme available,[5] she is plainly told that her presence would not be allowed:

> The scientists, it seemed, had wrapped up the entire continent for their own purposes. No one could go without their say-so, because their objectives were pure, and being pure they were entrusted with the last pure place on earth. The rest of us are frivolous despoilers who need to be controlled. (6–7)

Nevertheless (or potentially as a result of this refusal), she resolves to go there, and *Skating to Antarctica* becomes the record of her trip. However, as Diski discovers, any destination is the fantasy of its creator. Throughout her journey, Diski finds the dream of her perfect white world disturbed by grey skies, blue icebergs and insufficiently satisfactory implements. Of the ship, for example, Diski notes that the wheel of the craft 'was actually a small semicircle, not the satisfactory great wagon wheel of my imagination' (142). Moreover, her travelling companions disturb her desired contemplation, not only with their own neuroses, but with their colonising gazes and tourist desires. Diski's fantasy of the Antarctic is of an *uninhabited* space, 'never mind the penguins, seals and base camp personnel for the time being' (5), but in contrast to her fantasy, her Antarctic adventure is a corralled and crowded experience in which transatlantic encounters cannot be avoided.

Diski divides her narrative equally between a search for her mother (undertaken by her daughter, and with no overt approval offered) which entails the remembrance of her past as an unhappy child of unhappy parents, and this journey into whiteness, oblivion and release: the physical journey to Antarctica. Despite the assumed differences in these foci, the sense of journey is apparent in both, and the very separate elements bleed into each other: in her remembrance of things past, she navigates around London, explores past car journeys with her father in travelling terms, and considers the implications of travel; in her journey to Antarctica, she almost unwillingly considers her mother and her mother's influence on her. At this vantage point of adulthood and distance, however, she recognises her position as the child of immigrants, and that this is a particular location in itself (105).

If a memoir is a search for the truth about a remembered past (however debated the term 'truth' has become in the postmodern world) and a travel book is an exploration of place, Diski manipulates both designatory titles as she withholds and defers the reader's knowledge of each aspect of the text. Becoming anti-truthseeker and an anti-tourist, Diski confounds the reader's expectations of each genre and as a result produces a text which navigates a postmodern route to both kinds of journeying.

A central question of the text is whether Diski's long-abandoned and abandoning mother is alive or dead; this question is eventually answered (though by Diski's daughter Chloe, rather than herself). The central *assumption* of the text, however – that a trip to the Antarctic is executed – remains unresolved. On reaching her destination, Diski plays with the idea of turning away, and she never finally records the truth or otherwise of her final disembarking.

The memoir is divided into alternate sections, juxtaposing the 'fixed landscape of [her] early childhood' (10) with sections entitled 'At Sea'. Both literally and metaphorically, this repeated chapter title works, especially given the fact that the central traveller dislikes travel and hates to be disturbed from her preferred indolence and stasis. Flux is not a state she enjoys, which makes her decision to travel to a position on a navigation chart all the more remarkable. Comparing her desire to a 'sexual compulsion' (5), Diski finds it hard to identify the reasons for her journey. George Robertson argues that:

> The imperative to travel signifies the quest for the acquisition of knowledge and a desire to return to a utopian space of freedom, abundance and transparency. Psychic desires are displaced in partial and vicarious participation in another set of relations (another place and time), and the self becomes realized as the hero of its own narrative of departure and return.[6]

Such a reading is perhaps appropriate, given Diski's unarticulated, perhaps subconscious desires, as well as her frequent denial of psychoanalytic 'truth'. For example, if, on board ship, Diski compares the swaying of the boat to the space of her mother's womb, she is also quick to deny any real connections.

Diski's journey to Antarctica is a long one, with spaces in between of absolute waiting or lull. 'I have it in my head,' she says, 'that I like being suspended in travel from one place to another, but it doesn't seem to be the case. The urge to get somewhere, even if it's only the next stage on the journey is quite strong' (40). Particularly on her transatlantic flight, she finds the signs of her travelling somewhat difficult to decipher. Knowing from the display monitor that she is travelling at over 500 miles an hour, she cannot reconcile this fact with the concomitant fact that the icon of the plane appears not to move between her glances at it, despite her determination 'not to look for a decent length of time' (39). Indeed, her entire concept of place and the idea of travel become somehow unreadable: 'I idled the time away, up in the air between there and there; here but nowhere, not even a border check to give me the feeling that I was passing through several heres on the way to there' (40). The border checks of her child-hood, and the recognition that living on an island meant that 'it was the sea that said a country was a country' (9), have not prepared her for the (apparently) endless suspension of destination that transatlantic flight entails.

Her first real 'here' is Ushuaia, the capital of Tierra del Fuego. Ushuaia, the city at the end of the world, becomes, ironically for our literate and discerning traveller, a tourist spot. Diski notes that the city built a golf course, despite the fact that local residents do not play, simply to ensure that it had the southernmost golf course in the world. In 2003, the official online tourist site for Ushuaia had a section enti-tled 'History', but the legend under it read, 'Under construction'.[7] Jamaica Kincaid, the anti-tourism essayist, might appreciate the irony here; she would certainly recognise the position of the golf course, along with the fact that the main street is lined with duty-free elec-tronic outlets and tourist shops, though only intermittent pavement. It is a place, ultimately, for tourists, not natives. Diski's tour guide through the city notes, ' "People think you have to be rugged to live here . . . But it's easy living here these days. We lose water and elec-tricity sometimes, but that happens everywhere. Well, everywhere in Argentina. We get HBO, MTV and CNN. Just like anywhere else" ' (53). That the place is defined by its resident as 'anywhere else' pre-cisely through its reception of American entertainment packages speaks volumes, as does its occasional lack of basic amenities.

Ushuaia is a waystation on the way to somewhere else, the land of glaciers, penguins and seals. On this trip, Diski hones her identity an anti-tourist, though this is not an entirely new stance. (Having several times been to Paris, she has always made sure that she has avoided seeing the Eiffel Tower.) Diski carries no camera, and manages to avoid seeing the sights she is supposed to, including glaciers and whales, simply because she gets waylaid, or she finds that she cannot be bothered to move to the side of the ship that proffers the best view. Paul Fussell argues that the anti-tourist's determination to define him- or herself in opposition to a tourist (aligning themselves more with the elevated traveller) is a 'symptom and cause' of *'tourist angst,* defined as "a gnawing suspicion that after all . . . you are still a tourist like every other tourist" '.[8] Diski's project to be an anti-tourist is perhaps heightened by the fact that she is writing about her journey, thus making what is a tourist journey into an element of her work and therefore conflating two apparently unrelated activities. John Urry maintains that tourism 'is one manifestation of how work and leisure are organised as separate and regulated spheres of social practice in "modern" society',[9] and this is very much the case with most tourism, which is seen as a break from routine and daily life. However, for Diski, the conflation of work and tourism has its benefits. By using the tour through the Antarctic as the basis of her book – her *work* – Diski protects her status as not one of *them*, her touristy companions.

Diski's companions are birders, or history buffs who want to know about Shackleton or disapprove of whale hunting. One is a Canadian postgraduate who travels south because ' "being Canadian, [she] felt it was important to go to the Arctic, as a matter of national solidarity" ' (183). One is an elderly Scot who refuses to offer her age to those who question her; but most are Americans. They are less people than types, and indeed Diski assigns them imaginary names, such as Butch for the American leader, or Big Jim and Less Big Jim for two of the overweight men on the trip. These elements of unreality and potential fabrication remind the reader of Diski's manipulation of fact in her supposedly true memoir, her first non-fiction book. She is also, however, clear about the way in which all of her fellow travellers imagine and misread their companions. She notes, for example, an encounter between two sets of people:

> the Ur-American John and James were delighted by Ur-British Margaret and Peter; they were like characters from their English novel-reading come to life. Both of them were very partial to some imaginary England where decency, they believed, was born and still lives. (135)

Thus, it is not just the Antarctic that is being imagined into existence, but other places as well, in particular England and the US – hence the designation of this text as a transatlantic one despite the primacy of the Antarctic space.

Although the original transatlantic flight is from England to South America, the primary transatlanticism is the one that flows between the passengers themselves. As Diski ruefully notes, after suggesting that travelling with so many Americans was beginning to be a nuisance, 'People kept informing me of these facts [about Britain], as if they were true and, if they were true, as if I wouldn't know them' (136). Thus, fittingly, the contested nature of truth is as much under observation as anything else in this memoir.

It is Diski's examination of the process of looking that gets the most attention in her text, and whilst this is to be expected in a travel book, her exploration is more along the lines of Roland Barthes's explication of *The Blue Guide* than *The Blue Guide* itself. Barthes sets out to reveal how travel guides, by suggesting that readers explore particular sights and sites, therefore downgrade or deny other, equally important ones.[10] Indeed, Antarctica fascinates Diski precisely because of its position as the 'unseen' (169).

Her focus on looking means that she carefully identifies the way that specific viewpoints determine and change the picture. For example, she records that 'the abandoned whaling station at Grytviken is either lovingly preserved in its natural state or derelict, depending on how you choose to look at it' (146). Diski therefore reminds us of the choice attached to what we see; being a tourist is not simply a passive experience, but one informed by guidebooks, routes taken, and the searching out of objects. As Urry contends: 'The viewing of . . . tourist sights often involves different forms of social patterning, with a much greater sensitivity to visual elements of landscape or townscape than normally found in everyday life.'[11] Diski's description of this process is somewhat different, however, and again recalls Barthes's own work to some extent. She argues: 'You have to stop looking in order to point a camera at something. And why peer through a lens which limits your vision? You can't see if you're always composing what's in front of you into a fancy shot' (151–2).

Moreover, on one of their landings, though only seventy or so people climb onto the desolate, virtually uninhabited section of land, they find themselves in each other's frames, either wandering accidentally into photographs as they are being taken, or having to be frozen in place, with a fixed smile, for future recollections. In their use of cameras and camcorders, Diski's companions translate the present into the past, adding a commentary or a frame to an experience before they have an opportunity to evaluate its significance:

> The present experience was already in the past to them, they had skipped over time, and were seeing the world through their video lenses, as it would look when the current moment was dead and gone. Things were named and described, sentences formed, a final draft written, without

that first-draft struggle to transform wordless impressions into language. There was no translation of world into words, just the direct commentary, cutting out all the processes that might have added up to the reflection. The memories being created now would exist, frozen in the future as lens-framed news reports. (153–4)

Given Diski's profession, it is not surprising that she prioritises the script over view, words over images, or that she mourns the loss of editing as a necessary art. But photographic evidence is not required for Diski. Moreover, even when such photographic evidence is offered, the way in which it is offered remains somehow suspect. Midway through the book, Diski suggests that she has but one photograph of her mother, and proceeds (almost lovingly, despite the apparent hostility she maintains towards her absent mother) to relate its details. The description – of Diski and her mother together, in London, wearing respectable gloves and dresses – mirrors the image on the cover of the 1998 Granta paperback, which again leads the reader to ponder the truth (or simulacrum) of the image. Just as the reader can never be sure that this is a real photograph (or, a real photograph of Diski, at any rate), so too does the reader question the narrative itself, which aims to depict a journey to Antarctica but at the same time refuses to do so. After all, even when the images of it are not frozen onto film, the experiences of the Antarctic, for Diski, merely resemble the Antarctic in a clear example of Baudrillard's simulacra.

> Sometimes, looking out to sea, I had to shake away the films I had seen, the sense of remembering without having ever actually experienced the event. I had seen such a sea many times on television, film and in photographs. The sea outside my cabin looked remarkably like those pictures. It was, well, a copy. And here we all were, taking films of what we had already seen on film so that our children and grandchildren and our friends would once again not see it all afresh for themselves. And if they do go off to strange places, it will be, like us, to confirm what is already known. (157–8)

It is perhaps for this reason that Diski plays with the notion of going to the Antarctic and not finally seeing it:

> I located a subterranean knot of unwillingness to set foot on the last continent just because I happened to be there. Though of course I didn't just

happen to be there. This was a place where no one just happens to be. Which made it all the more pleasing and/or distressing (the two emotions were inextricable) to consider the possibility of not stepping on to the land. There was considerable satisfaction at the thought that I might not set foot on the continent that I had taken a good deal of trouble to get to. (227)

Perhaps it is not entirely surprising, then, that Diski contemplates both outcomes, and chooses not to tell the truth. Indeed, she plays with saying one thing and doing another: saying she has landed, when she has not, or claiming that she hasn't, when she has. It is, finally, she argues, a private matter whether or not she disembarks on the last continent, despite the fact that she is writing a travel memoir about it. Her truth, she says, 'depends not on arriving at a destination. Nor in failing to arrive' (230).

Somehow, it seems that Diski is right – the book retains its power even though one does not know the truth of the final disembarking or staying put; or perhaps precisely because one does not know. Indeed, this is an important metaphor for what travelling means to Diski, who terms herself a 'resistant traveller' (227). In her construction, the tourist knows what there is to see, and sees it, frames it and turns away; the traveller may also know what there is to see, but may understand there is no direct translation of it, no final framing possible. The tourist is self-enclosed, perhaps destructive. Of course, the traveller (or anti-tourist, or expeditioner) may also be destructive – after all, even Diski and her environmentalist companions had to be reminded not to touch the wildlife or to leave litter, which would suggest that, at some level, the British Antarctic Survey was right; they were 'frivolous despoilers who need to be controlled' (7).

The paradigmatic moments of *being* elsewhere – the consuming, both as a body and as an economic participant, and the looking, if not always well – define the *activities* of elsewhere when you are there. They do not, however, define elsewhere, or firmly position who you are when you are there. This is the point on a navigation chart, but such positions mean something only contingently, and the positions of traveller and tourist are contingently defined as well. If readers do not need quite such ex-centric spaces to understand this, nevertheless Diski is able to explore issues of travel, looking and power more overtly because of the eccentric position she takes: someone who saw, and turned away – or who at least pretended to.

'A Magical Combination of Ease and Discomfort. That, Actually, Was How I Found Americans'

In *Skating to Antarctica*, Diski notes the way in which the cabin on the ship signifies something different to her than it does to her companions. For them, she assumes, 'entering their cabins signified departure, but for me it was the moment of arrival, the very definition of the distinction between being not in the right place and arriving' (59). This somewhat perverse way of looking at her interior space, the thing that encloses her from the experience she has paid to have, is perhaps the same thing that drives her, a few years later, to entertain the notion of travelling through and around the US on a train, not looking for or locating destinations, but merely investing in travel itself, and in writing a book about ' "nothing happening" ' (7). Although there are obvious stops along the way, the point of the journey is the journey itself: to pass through. Yet this plan, like the earlier plan to inhabit whiteness, is ultimately flawed: despite treasuring her strangerhood, or her outsidership, Diski ends up sharing her journey with many other similar strangers, and inevitably offers up snippets of their own stories, told through and beside hers.

Despite her annoyance with the overbearing nature of Americans, articulated throughout *Skating to Antarctica*, she chooses to spend a considerable amount of time in their company (even breaking her train journeys occasionally, to spend time with Phoenix John from the first travel memoir, and, latterly and less successfully, with a fellow traveller, Bet). In *Stranger on a Train*, Diski explores the mythic landscape of America, and the sense that train travel is the great adventure of the twenty-first century even as her journey, in a sense, signifies the end of the dream of rail travel, retrospectively seen as a nineteenth-century folly. She mourns the way in which 'the passion and drama that had gone into creating a comprehensive rail network in a country so large that you had to be slightly crazy to dream of it in the first place, had just died away' (163). Her dreams of travel are set alongside reality with jarring regularity, just as her desire for outsidership is set alongside a multitude of strangers conversing in the smoking carriages and drawing her reluctantly into their stories.

If Americans irk her, America itself does not. Just as Hoffman records an ironic and continuing desire for 'America' by settled immigrants in *Lost in Translation*, so, too, does Diski suggest that there is something magical about the US, its temptations rich and varied, and its pull a historic one:

As a child in fifties London, America was as distant a reality to me as ancient Egypt, yet present in my life in a way that those who had carved the remnants of mighty statuary I knew from my visits to the British Museum could never be. Distant was not quite the word. America was like the moon: its remoteness was irrelevant, what mattered was the light it bathed me in, its universal but private reach. The moon was the moon, and mine; familiar and personal, shining over me wherever I was, whenever I looked at it. America, too, was light. It beamed above my head from the cinema projection booth, particles dancing in its rays, ungraspable as a ghost, but resolving finally on the screen into gigantic images of a world I longed for, yet only half believed in. If I walked directly in front of the screen and got caught in its light, my very own shadow was projected up there . . . People in the audience shouted at me to duck down and get out of the way as if I hadn't realized what had happened, but I knew exactly what I was doing. I wanted to be in the way of all that. (8–9)

Paul Giles's theoretical interpretation of transatlanticism can be applied to passages like these. Giles argues: 'To reconsider American . . . culture in a transnational context, then, is not to abandon the idea of nationalism, but to reimagine it as a virtual construction, a residual narrative rather than a unifying social power.'[12] Diski's incorporation of a (virtual) US culture, her willingness and indeed overpowering desire to be included in it, shows how this culture expands beyond its borders to bump into and jar against the expectations of those outside the US. Diski's childhood desire to be 'in the way of all that' and her concurrent belief and disbelief in this other place, so clearly made 'other' and yet also made familiar, also displays the image of misreading, or, perhaps, misviewing that is central to my argument.

Throughout her trip, Diski certainly does misread her companions, from Bet, who first appears to be a frightened woman who has no cause for fear, and who is later revealed to be the sister of a recently murdered man, to various others, people whom Diski cannot quite work out; indeed, she is sometimes not even sure if they harbour good or ill will towards her (including, in the end, Bet again). Diski cyclically returns to images and ideas along her route(s), refashioning some of the material she first explored in *Skating to Antarctica*, but applying it now to the US rather than just its inhabitants, and reiterating images of movies and film clips, Americans as actors and the entire journey as a Baudrillardian construction of a pseudo-experience.

The first of her two US journeys begins at sea. Eschewing another transatlantic flight, she prefers a transatlantic crossing, and on this unconventional mode of transport, again wishes for stillness and aloneness and is denied both. Two of her companions end up being 'insular Americans [who] had taken a peek at Europe, but were uneasy at finding themselves in a strange world, in strange company' (27), thereby confirming Diski's suspicions of the US, whereas the other couple are almost stereotypically rude Germans who fail to leave her alone. When she does find space simply to view the seascape, it becomes impossible for her not to read the journey in metaphorical terms: '[A]ll I really wanted was for the sea simply to be the sea. I found myself constantly thinking of it in terms of something else, as if I were reading it for meaning, which was not what I thought I wanted to do at all' (14).

In reading the ocean, she cannot help but notice that the vessel makes little impact on its surroundings, besides a temporary displacement of water: 'The frothy turbulence of the wake proved our movement, but the record of it was continually lost, rubbed out by the vast body of water that healed all the scars scored by whatever made its way through it' (15). That she begins her narrative in this way is significant, for this metaphor of movement that is erased essentially comes to bear on all that follows. As Diski passes through areas, they remain virtually untouched by her presence, and if in environmental terms this is inaccurate, in cultural terms it remains the case, particularly when, at various points, she pointedly refuses to take up the tourist mantle and make compulsory purchases of useless tourist junk. She makes one one lone exception, where, in Old Sacramento, she makes a connection between tourist purchases and what Americans have done to their culture and their history:

> I slouched around, killing time before I could return to the interior of a train that was in every way more of a destination than any of this, staring at stuff made of plastic that lit up, or made a sound, or turned out to be something it didn't look like, and came away, eventually, with a small rubber replica of a brain, the size of a walnut, which was guaranteed to swell to twenty times its size when placed in water. (231)

This is the only purchase Diski identifies at length, and the line break at the end of this passage suggests that she has said all she can about the power of consumerism and the inauthenticity of much of what passes for the real. In a reworking of the famous and fatuous statement that travel broadens one's horizons, Diski clearly suggests that only when one moves away from the tourist trap can one expand one's mind. Yet travel remains her focal point, much more than in the first travel memoir. Here there is much less moving back and forth between the past and the present – her focus is on the here-and-now (or, the here-and-gone). The three focal points of her narrative become landscape, people and story, and the ways in which they intertwine. If, as Said argues, what most identifies the traveller is not power but motion,[13] then Diski becomes a traveller par excellence here, almost constantly in motion.

Ulrike Stamm criticises Isabella Bird and other nineteenth-century travel writers for focusing more on landscape than people in their narratives,[14] but Diski has the opposite problem. Upon returning to the UK at the end of her first US train journey, she emails her travelogue to the US fashion magazine which had commissioned an article about her trip, only to be told to cut details of the people and the actual train and focus more on the scenery itself (97). That fashion focuses on surfaces is not in doubt, but the command to reduce the space offered to Diski's companions appears to suggest that Americans themselves get in the way of viewing America. Yet the land from Diski's carriage becomes a blur, with several states passing by over two days, the image of unrelenting land becoming a partner to the unrelenting water of her sea voyage. Here, too, though, Diski is unable to view it without reading it into some context she has already prepared for. Comparing the US landscape to Shakespeare's plays or well-known biblical phrases, she argues that 'they are already read, so that when you come across them in their proper context, they jar and falsify the moment' (99).

What is also jarring for Diski is to discover that although many outside of the US feel they know the country's landscape, having seen it on celluloid ad infinitum, many within its borders do not:

> It is astonishing how many Americans tell you of longing for American landscapes but fail to get to them decade after decade. The remarkably untravelled lives of many of the people I met on the train quite pulled against the notion of a continent in flux, all its people on the move. (203)

Diski's outsider perspective fails to see the cultural conditions that militate against the US being this nation of travellers. Not only do the open spaces and vast distances make travel difficult, but the lack of statutory vacation time for those in work puts up additional barriers, and the historical hobo seems to have no real current counterpart.[15] Though America looks large on a map, Diski discovers that 'for many people it's as small as their local town, beyond which is an uncharted wilderness inhabited by monsters' (57). Furthermore, anyone who travels by train in the US is unlikely to be a standard traveller in any case. Since many Americans do not travel extensively, it is not surprising that most Americans do not travel by methods that are long and unreliable (more than once Diski feels like she's trapped in a '51st state' on the train, which leaches time during the entire journey). Ironically, perhaps, given Stamm's quotation above, Diski's friend John, whom she visits in Phoenix, likens her travelling by train to an epic adventure of a nineteenth-century English lady traveller; here again Diski is re-imagined in other terms, and indeed, much like Bird before her, her reputation precedes her, so much so that, once her random travelling companions know that she is a writer, people offer her their stories for posterity. She sometimes obliges, with an odd nod to a fellow traveller.

In *Skating to Antarctica*, Diski found herself in photographs and reciprocated by inserting her fellow travellers into her narrative, suggesting that this was her way of colonising the world. She finished one section of *Skating to Antarctica* with the innocuous phrase, 'Hi Jim' (160). In *Stranger on a Train*, instead of waving to her fellow companions in print, she maintains her strangerhood by sometimes refusing to comment on the stories she hears, though she repeats them nonetheless. At one point, Diski is confronted by an 'ordinary-looking' man who forces his story upon her: ' "People should hear about what happened to me. About the Prozac and depression. You're a writer. So you can write my story" ' (209). Write it she does, apparently verbatim, but it is significant that she makes no comment on it at all. After a short space break, the narrative returns to landscape.

If Diski is an anti-tourist in *Skating to Antarctica*, she is an anti-travel writer in *Stranger on a Train*. She professes not to know what a travel writer does, and speaks of them as somehow different from herself. She suggests that travel writers 'must put their faith in the inevitability of incident' (7), but of course she attempts to define stasis within travel, and at times avoids incident by remaining in her own carriage, venturing out solely for food and cigarettes. Indeed, she denies that her book contract (awarded for the second journey) is the reason for her circumnavigation of the US by train; it is, at best 'a useful cover' that allows her to get on with doing what she wants (153). Moreover, she confesses to a certain amount of fraudulence;

assuming that a *real* travel writer would undertake detours along the way, she carefully plots her journey in advance, in order to avoid disruption and, most importantly, to ensure a sleeping carriage. Just as she discovered the made up element to her Antarctic adventure, so she understands that her initial view of the train as a space of unscheduled freedom is itself flawed.

Throughout her journey through what she considers 'mythic places' (45), she comes across people who both reinforce and undermine her stereotypes. The young American man who books her train journey becomes as excited to hear her British accent as did the Ur-Americans of the Antarctic trip, and she is counselled to ' "imagine you're de Tocqueville. What do you think of us Americans?" ' (44). Yet for every (would-be) traveller interested in the outside world and its view of the US, she encounters people for whom travel is an unwanted gift, people for whom the smallness of the world makes it safe and homely, and Diski almost unaccountably considers this 'quite exotic' (169). Travelling for a time on a bus, with companions Bet and Troy, she recognises that not only do Americans not travel by train, but many who have a choice do not travel by bus, either. Thus she finds herself in the ethnic minority amongst African Americans, a fact that her white travelling companions obviously find frightening: 'In their America a bus full of black people was a rumour, a story they'd heard about an America in which they did not, and were pleased not to, live' (57).

The idea of many Americas alongside each other becomes more real the more she travels, never more apparent than when she sits in the smoking carriages (when they have one) or jumps off the train for a quick cigarette when the whole train is smoke free. She details encounters (or, rather, non-encounters) with Amish people, whose dress provokes interest but feigned indifference, recording that all the other travellers 'made a point of ignoring them, as if their quaint clothes and manners were a form of disability that was not to be remarked upon or stared at' (164–5). She also encounters a range of passengers whose real disabilities provoke alarm in others, whether they are physically or mentally affected.

Not all of her companions are Americans, of course. In one memorable encounter, Diski records a conversation between a black chef of uncertain ethnic origin (he claims he has 'ethnic' hands and knows many languages) and a Chinese boy. During this conversation (which is really more of a monologue), the linguist chef tells the boy, ' "She's from England. Where we all once came from. Well, not

you, or me, but America. She comes from the source of language" '
(167). The Chinese boy cannot speak English, with the result that
this rather odd embracing of the 'special relationship' remains
incomprehensible to him. This elision of all cultures into one
because of a common language misreads the US and its multiple her-
itages; yet Diski comments only that the chef appeared to be either
high or manic, and the narrative moves on, with no further unpack-
ing of the assertions made.

The most serious misreading of the journey occurs during a break
from train travel. Although what Diski most desires is the 'condition
of being always in transit, of never arriving, of being a travelling
stranger for as long as possible' (155), she inadvertently strikes up an
early relationship with Bet, whom she then visits on her second
journey. Bet becomes, in Diski's reading, a character from Stephen
King's *Misery*, a woman who, enjoying Diski's company so entirely,
never wishes her to leave. Although Diski is granted her own space in
a stationary trailer on Bet's driveway, a place to which she retreats
with regularity, this distance is never enough for her. Diski finds
herself at first irked by Bet's ability to talk continuously, and later concerned that Bet's joking references to keeping Diski are real. In this
space, Diski moves from 'America-in-the-movies to movie-America'
(255), and it is significant that it is the filmed version of *Misery*, not
the original novel, that is played out here. Diski descends into para-
noid gothic mode, at one level recognising her mania for what it is,
but at another level remaining deeply convinced that she is part of a
larger plot in which she never gets away: the horror of remaining in
this America is far too real for Diski, fed as it is from celluloid
nightmares.

Diski's decision to include this element in her travel narrative
is intriguing. If the recurring figures of Bet and her family are not
real but manufactured elements, no one is hurt by this fantasy of
American horror, but if they are indeed people whose hospitality she
endured for five days, her decision to recount this experience here suggests a payback beyond the apparent joke of their liking and wanting
to keep her. At the end of this section, Diski reveals she is leaving the
US early, and no longer wishes to spend time with Americans, even
with friends whom she knows well. Instead, she decides she has had
enough stories of America and seeks only to fast-forward through the
remaining days of her journey.

If the geography of America is, as she suggests, 'freed from
individual stories and script' (202), the book as a whole is full of

such scripts, laced together through references to smoking and the potential – never to be realised – to change lives and positions. She assigns various roles to individuals and even contemplates making one man, Chuck, the 'authorial voice of our journey' (126). Chuck is a man who, for reasons no one can fathom, helps to rescue two boys and a drunk man named Raymond. Diski recounts a fleeting rescue fantasy when she meets up with Raymond, who wants her to come home with him, and toys with the notion: 'What's to stop this story from being the one where she gets on a train, takes an unnecessary journey, meets a drunk and turns it deliberately into happily-ever-after?' (122). The happily-ever-after fantasy narrative is one she associates with the US and not with the UK:

> In America every story has happily-ever-after either as an ending or a howling opposition. The template story is known, how it should be, and all the stories told on the journey are exemplars of closeness or distance from the true tale. Is that solely American? Probably not, but the dream of meeting the stranger who is the completing half, the compensating force, takes a decidedly dystopian, misanthropic turn in the hands of the Englishman who made *Strangers on a Train*. (125)

And of course, Diski's last story is just such a compensating story, one where a woman married for almost two decades finds – she hopes, she thinks, she fears – her compensating force in a younger man, whom she leaves to return home to her husband – so we also get the train story of *An Affair to Remember* thrown in for good measure, alongside rather trashy Country and Western songs that talk of love and loss in 'two-minute stories of heartbreak' (278).

Diski's travel memoirs offer opportunities to explore the construction of national narratives, through film, song, story and imagination. First in *Skating to Antarctica* and later in *Stranger on a Train*, Diski maintains her own reticence about story, but engages with it nonetheless. If Hoffman's memoir is more explicitly literary and theoretical, Diski's travelling tales still engage with theoretical suppositions about travel, either fairly explicitly, in the passages that resemble Baudrillard's, or in the ways that she engages with the implications of gender and travel. Offering herself both as a wandering woman without a fixed agenda, and then revealing later how circumscribed her travel choices are, Diski explores potential narratives of harm and love, rescue and release. Karen Lawrence asks:

Can women writers revise the various plots of wandering (in romance, adventure, exploration, and travel narratives) without succumbing to the traditional pitfalls of these plots for a female protagonist? Such a question intersects feminist concerns about whether women will 'get caught' in their own imitation of patriarchal discourse and myth, unable to repeat with a difference.[16]

It seems to me that Diski is able to resist getting caught. Her desire for travel is not one of mastery, but stasis, not one of discovering what is out there, but what is inside: in small spaces, in carriages and corridors that are too frequently overlooked and unobserved. In some ways, she recapitulates the travels of Xavier de Maistre, who, some 200 years before Diski, published a book entitled *Journey around my Bedroom* (1790), in which he detailed the pleasures of staying in.[17] Diski explores the misdirected desires of the transatlantic gaze, seeing not only 'America as a text in circulation',[18] but also the circulation of other texts which are similarly misread. In doing so, she understands the value of travel, and of the frothy wake no longer being scarred.

NOTES

1. Jenny Diski, *Skating to Antarctica* (London: Granta, 1998). Originally published in 1997. Jenny Diski, *Stranger on a Train: Daydreaming and Smoking around America with Interruptions* (London: Virago, 2004). Originally published in 2002. Both texts will be cited parenthetically.
2. Jean Baudrillard, *America,* trans. Chris Turner (London: Verso, 1998), pp. 28–9.
3. The advertisement runs on UK television, directing viewers to www.discoveramerica.com, accessed 29 February 2008.
4. Margaret Atwood, *Bodily Harm* (London: Virago, 1991), p. 18. Originally published in 1981.
5. Diski's frivolous suggestion of a writer-in-residence position was oddly prescient. In November 2003, the Arts Council offered its first fellowship for artists to spend two months in Antarctica. The composer Craig Vear was the first recipient of the award.
6. George Robertson, 'As the World Turns', in George Robertson et al. (eds), *Travellers' Tales: Narratives of Home and Displacement* (London: Routledge, 1994), p. 5.
7. See www.tierradelfuego.org.ar, originally accessed 1 August 2003. The site has now been updated.
8. Paul Fussell, *Abroad* (Oxford: Oxford University Press, 1982), p. 49. Originally published in 1980.

9. John Urry, *The Tourist Gaze* (London: Sage, 2002), p. 2. Originally published in 1990.
10. Roland Barthes, 'The Blue Guide', *Mythologies*, trans. Annette Lavers (London: Cape, 1972), pp. 74–7.
11. Urry, *Tourist*, p. 3.
12. Paul Giles, *Virtual Americas: Transnational Fictions and the Transatlantic Imaginary* (Durham, NC: Duke University Press, 2002), p. 20.
13. Edward Said, *Reflections on Exile and Other Literary and Cultural Essays* (London: Granta, 2000), p. 404.
14. Ulrike Stamm, 'The Role of Nature in Two Women's Travel Accounts: Appropriate and Escape', in Liselotte Glage (ed.), *Being/s in Transit: Travelling, Migration, Dislocation* (Amsterdam: Rodopi, 2000), p. 158.
15. The National Hobo Convention is still held in August of every year in Britt, Iowa, and there are ongoing societies and websites dedicated to hobo life, but the population of people identifying themselves as hoboes is now very small.
16. Karen R. Lawrence, *Penelope Voyages: Women and Travel in the British Literary Tradition* (Ithaca, NY: Cornell University Press, 1994), p. 17.
17. Alain de Botton, *The Art of Travel* (London: Hamish Hamilton, 2002), pp. 243–4.
18. John Muthyala, ' "America" in Transit', *Comparative American Studies* 1 (4) (2003): 396.

NEGOTIATING THE FOREIGN/ RE-INVENTING HOME

INTRODUCTION

Kathleen Kirby suggests that space

> seems to offer a medium for articulating – speaking and intertwining –
> the many facets, or phases, of subjectivity that have interested different
> kinds of theory: national origin, geographic and territorial mobility
> (determined by class, gender, and race), bodily presence and limits, struc-
> tures of consciousness, and ideological formations of belonging and
> exclusion.[1]

As we have seen, space is central to the feminist construction of the
transatlantic, no more so than in relation to images of home and the
family, which are the focus of Part 3. As has been clear throughout,
individuals and characters in transatlantic narratives reconstruct the
transatlantic encounter as a rejection or continuation of 'home' and
engage with the concepts of movement and stasis in deceptively
simply or overtly complex ways. Moreover, the attempt to establish
'home' and 'not home' – especially through writing – inevitably
entails the mythological re-creation of both through some conception
of 'the foreign', whether that foreignness is one that is projected onto
new arrivals by those already in situ (even if they, themselves, once
occupied the role of new arrival or are children of such individuals),
or whether the arrivals themselves see their new surroundings as
foreign.

From Isabella Bird, who allowed others to think her Danish in
order to hear more revealing comments about the English, but who
also resisted making her temporary accommodations any more

homely in order to avoid being domesticated, to Nella Larsen's Helga, who resists learning Danish well in order to remain foreign, women writers offer complex and varied responses to questions of foreignness and home. Indeed, questions of home and away are central to all of these texts, not just the two novels that follow, but it is in relation to the work of Anne Tyler, an author who has been pejoratively considered a domestic realist writer who is uninterested in the wider world, and in relation to Isabel Allende's epic novel *Daughter of Fortune*, that questions of home and away become even more crystallised. Contrasting the work of a writer best known for rarely leaving home with the work of a writer who considers herself in exile offers up opportunities to explore *how* home means, as well as what it means. Neither Tyler nor Allende has yet received the sustained critical analysis that they deserve, and my exploration here seeks in part to remedy this critical neglect and to offer evidence that a variety of women writers, from best-selling authors to more critically acclaimed writers, engage with and identify issues to do with fluid spaces and identities.

In the two chapters that follow, I will explore how travellers seek or resist identification with the new cultures that they encounter and explore how this phenomenon is more complex than just a simple mapping of masculinity and femininity, ethnicity or nationality onto the transatlantic space. Indeed, in this final section, there is a more literal incorporation of the 'foreign' into the family, as adopted children are embraced, their foreignness either emphasised or explicitly denied. 'The foreigner is the other of the family,' claims Kristeva,[2] yet in the novels that follow, this is explicitly contested, as the foreigner *is* family, and joins the family at various points: at birth (or shortly thereafter), at adulthood, and indeed even late in the family's life cycle, following retirement.

Madan Sarup's musings on the nature of 'home' in his essay 'Home and Identity' are particularly relevant here, as is his exploration of foreignness as a condition that inculcates both welcome and resentment. Sarup argues that 'the foreigner is a "symptom": psychologically, s/he signifies the difficulty we have of living as an other and with others.'[3] Nowhere is this more apparent than within the family, which is always made up of those with blood ties and those with whom legal relationships imitate (and sometimes supersede) those blood ties. The idea of dwelling in families, and of travelling away and with them, complicates any notion of the lone traveller, who seeks enlightenment and peace. Although 'lone' travellers such as Bird and Diski do figure in my overall argument, more often the traveller is seen in connection, and indeed, even Bird and Diski travel with others (if not always well).

Exploring foreignness and home in the novels that follow also means exploring what it means to pass as 'other', to adopt a new costume, either to avoid detection or simply to blend in, to assimilate. At the same time, characters refuse to pass and resolutely assert their national identity: Maryam in Anne Tyler's *Digging to America* is a case in point, as are Rose and Jeremy Sommers in Isabel Allende's *Daughter of Fortune*. They are contrasted with Maryam's cousin, her son and her son's wife; and Eliza Sommers, and Tao Chi'en respectively, whose responses to their altered conditions include grappling with questions over assimilation (which we have already seen in Bharati Mukherjee's work). Sophia Lehmann argues that passing entails a deliberate forgetting, but also 'being cut off from one's community, the group with which one feels cultural and linguistics affinities'.[4] Certainly language itself becomes a fundamental issue for the texts that follow (and, again, showing how interlinked these issues are, the question of language has already been addressed in both Parts 1 and 2). Lehmann further argues that assimilation 'tends to exacerbate rather than alleviate the sense of marginality for which it was supposed to be the cure',[5] and the various responses to how to live as an other, in an other land, will be explored in what follows.

A variety of critics have explored how travel disrupts certain assumed stabilities, and one of the questions that therefore arises is precisely the question of who or what is 'other'. Trinh T. Minh-ha argues that identity is actually predicated on this unsettling, or 'inversion of one's identity', as she puts it: 'I become me via an other. Depending on who is looking, the exotic is the other, or it is me.'[6] For adopted children, particularly those adopted across ethnic and national boundaries, the exotic is always already located within, and how the family deals with such exoticism – by ignoring it, augmenting it or alternating between these reactions – is central to identity issues.

At the same time, Minh-ha provocatively argues that home is 'a place where one is compelled to find stability and happiness'.[7] Home, therefore, does not only include those happy resonances signified by homilies such as 'home is where the heart is', but also signifies a space in which identity issues are problematised and rearranged. That Minh-ha uses the word 'compelled' is not accidental; the family forms and reforms an individual's allegiance according to a variety of societal pressures; thus the psychic hold upon the individual in relation to questions of home, which are experienced variously. Rubenstein suggests, simply, that *home matters*:

> Home matters not simply as a place but as the imagination's *place marker* for a vision of personal (and cultural) re/union, encompassing both that which actually may have been experienced in the vanished past and that which never could have been. Even as the remembered/imagined vision of home is a construction, it also constructs – and stokes, and sometimes even heals – the longing for belonging. Home functions in the (literary) imagination not as a tangible place but as a liminal site . . .[8]

In what follows the various reactions to home, and various attempts at home-making and homecoming, will be explored in relation to the ever-present questions of foreignness and away. Lehmann suggests that 'the spaces *between* languages and countries become sites of new creation rather than marginality',[9] and indeed this insight is explored in relation to Tyler's characters' deliberately hesitant forays away, as well as Allende's more deliberate ones.

These final novels also explore transpacific as well as transatlantic encounters, opening out questions of identity and travel across other oceanic spaces. This movement to consider other cross-cultural moves offers an opportunity to compare and contrast the narratives attached to different oceanic spaces. The transatlantic has perhaps more immediate resonance than the transpacific for American histories and literatures (and by this I mean both North and South America): the Black Atlantic slavery route, the discovery of the 'New World' (acknowledging all of the attendant difficulties with that false designation), and the 'special relationship' asserted between the US and the UK conspire to suggest the primacy of this space. Indeed, it is significant that Duke University's 'Oceans Connect' project, funded by the Ford Foundation in the late 1990s, did not initially even consider the Pacific Ocean, focusing instead on the Indian Ocean, the Eurasian Seas, the Mediterranean and of course the Atlantic, though it later added a group entitled 'Pacific Visions' and changed the other groupings listed above.[10] The groups' aims, according to Ian Baucom, were 'not simply to trouble or reorganize but to multiply our maps of the "real," to render visible some additional fraction of all those worlds virtually present within the world'.[11] Likewise, my movement away from a sole focus on the Atlantic encounters in this final section suggests ways of rendering visible other, perhaps contestable meanings, and illuminating narratives of otherness that engage explicitly with what was once unproblematically considered the 'Orient'.

NOTES

1. Kathleen M. Kirby, 'Thinking through the Boundary: The Politics of Location, Subjects, and Space', *Boundary II* 20 (2) (1993): 174.
2. Julia Kristeva, *Strangers to Ourselves* (London: Harvester Wheatsheaf, 1991), p. 95.
3. Madan Sarup, 'Home and Identity', in George Robertson et al. (eds), *Travellers' Tales: Narratives of Home and Displacement* (London: Routledge, 1994), p. 100.
4. Sophia Lehmann, 'In Search of a Mother Tongue: Locating Home in Diaspora', *MELUS* 23 (4) (1998): 102–3.
5. Ibid. p. 103.
6. Trinh T. Minh-ha, 'Other Than Myself/ My Other Self' in George Robertson et al. (eds), *Travellers' Tales: Narratives of Home and Displacement* (London: Routledge, 1994), p. 23.
7. Ibid. p. 13.
8. Roberta Rubenstein, *Home Matters: Longing and Belonging, Nostalgia and Mourning in Women's Fiction* (Houndmills: Palgrave, 2004), pp. 164–5, italics in original.
9. Lehmann, 'In Search', p. 104, italics in original.
10. See Martin W. Lewis and Karen Wigen, 'A Maritime Response to the Crisis in Area Studies', *The Geographical Review* 89 (2) (1999): 161–8, for the claim that the Pacific was not an initial part of the plan, and see also the Duke University website dedicated to the project, which indicates the importance of the Pacific: http://www.duke.edu/web/oceans/project.html, accessed 10 March 2008.
11. Ian Baucom, 'Hydrographies', *The Geographical Review* 89 (2) (1999): 308.

CHAPTER 5

'AN INVENTION OF THE AMERICANS': NEGOTIATING THE FOREIGN IN ANNE TYLER'S NOVELS

According to Charles Vandersee, 'America is a site where people appear by accident and meet by accident rather than by ancestry and assignment.'[1] As if to prove this contention, Anne Tyler has developed a canon of accidental encounters, where individuals meet, form new, loose families with permeable boundaries, and, often, depart again. In doing so, they touch on the foreignness of others, outsiders who do not belong to genetic families but whose presence alters such families in dynamic and unstable ways. This chapter explores the construction of 'foreignness' in Anne Tyler's *The Accidental Tourist* (1985) and *Digging to America* (2006) in order to relate concepts of 'the foreign' to those of the 'familiar' in its literal sense: that is, relating to the family.[2] It will also assess the ways in which Tyler's conception of each has altered over the last twenty years, especially given her focus on a contested 'domestic realism', a critical framework that seems, by its very title, to focus on home rather than away. I argue that this 'convenient' critical framework is problematised throughout Tyler's oeuvre.

In *The Accidental Tourist*, home is shown to be a refuge that hinders growth: the central character, Macon Leary, returns to his original family home after the disintegration of his marriage, and on each of his travels, he is constructed as an archetypal (if exaggerated) American traveller who seeks the familiar and the 'American' as opposed to the 'foreign'; through him, I argue, Tyler offers a critique of Americanisation itself. Macon's refusal to encounter the foreign is not only a comment on American tourism, or on the 'safety' of modern travel that cocoons the tourist from the 'foreign' as much as possible, but also a comment on the nature of 'foreignness' itself.

Homesickness becomes an excuse to avoid seeking out the 'other'. When Macon does so, in the form of Muriel, an odd, working-class companion, he discovers that the 'foreign' can be found just as easily on Baltimore streets as in Paris or London. The text therefore grapples with the issues of how 'home' and 'away' can peacefully – even productively – co-exist.

In *Digging to America*, Tyler's famously narrow vision has widened to include political upheavals (first recorded overtly in her novel *The Amateur Marriage* which was published in 2004); here, the foreign is embraced in different ways by two US-based families who simultaneously adopt Korean baby girls. The 'American' couple attempt to inculcate otherness in their daughter, retaining her birth name Jin-ho to emphasise her cultural heritage, whereas the Iranian family seek an absorptive assimilation, naming their daughter Susan in an attempt at ordinary Americanness. Such differing approaches lead to inevitable conflict, particularly as the families come together to celebrate 'Arrival Day'. At this celebration, which replaces the traditional focus on birthday parties (which is an interesting exploration of 'origins' in itself), the families judge each other's relationship to Americanness and Americanisation.

Tyler's exploration of foreignness is a recurring concern, though it is not always addressed overtly. Similarly, her engagement with world politics is mostly under the radar. According to Charlotte Templin, Anne Tyler is not an apolitical writer; rather, 'she shares the politics of the American majority.'[3] C. Wright Mills argued in 1951 that the US middle class was politically 'inactionary',[4] a term that does seem to fit with Tyler's focus on a version of domestic realism.

Tyler herself has another view, suggesting in an interview with Paul Bail in 1997 that ' "much as I would love to think that a novel could make a positive political change, I've never seen it done, and I believe it is always a mistake to aim for anything more than pure storytelling when writing fiction." '[5] Templin argues that one's own ideology is invisible to one's self and this fact could be structuring Tyler's responses. Certainly Tyler's conservative, middle-of-the-road approach does not endear her to critics. Quite a few of the critical articles on Tyler are decidedly critical, particularly in relation to the fact that she apparently retells the same story in her novels – the story of departure and return – with seemingly little overt reference to political world events.

Yet Tyler's prose, which Donna Gerstenberger suggests 'often beguiles the unwary reader',[6] nevertheless negotiates a number of

politically charged situations, including the construction and mainte-
nance of the 'foreign', a trope that recurs throughout the canon of
her comic, quirky novels and has increasing significance from *The
Amateur Marriage* onwards. In her latest novel, *Digging to America*,
Tyler actually makes a non-American family central characters for the
first time, and even incorporates the explicitly 'foreign' into the
family, with the adoption of two Korean baby girls as well as, for one
family, a subsequent Chinese daughter. In relation to Tyler's earlier
novel, *Saint Maybe* (1991), the inclusion of foreign character is,
Judith Caesar argues, an 'integral part of the novel's exploration of
differentness and responsibility'[7] and these are certainly characteris-
tically Tylerian concerns. Whilst *Saint Maybe* is an important novel
that deals in a peripheral way with issues of foreigners and foreignness, it is in relation to Tyler's more explicitly transatlantic novels that
I want to address Tyler's recurring use of metaphors of foreignness,
particularly in what is perhaps her most famous novel to date, *The
Accidental Tourist* (1985) and her latest novel, *Digging to America*.
This first of these was made into an award-winning film starting
William Hurt, Geena Davis and Kathleen Turner. *The Accidental
Tourist* covers a year in the life of Macon Leary, a reluctant travel
writer who hates to travel yet finds himself constantly on the move,
whereas *Digging to America* explores what foreignness might mean
more at home, than abroad. If Tyler has a 9/11 novel, this is it.

Templin suggests that Tyler's critical reputation is higher in the UK
than in the US, and it is certainly the case that her reputation rose after
Nick Hornby and Roddy Doyle claimed that she was one of the best
living authors in a *Sunday Times* survey in 1994, a quotation which
is not only frequently repeated, but also used on the covers of her UK
published books. The reason for the disparity between US and UK
views of Tyler, Templin argues, has to do with national allegiance:
'Somehow ranking the artistic productions of one's own countrymen
and -women and evaluating their visions of one's own culture is
fraught with more emotion than making evaluations of writers that
represent another national literary tradition.'[8] Templin's rather
sweeping statement about the purpose or outcome of critical debates
could, itself, be debated. Indeed, there is an argument that distance
and outsidership offer an important vantage point for viewing literature, as recent debates about transnationalism in relation to American
Studies suggest. Paul Giles argues in *Virtual Americas*, that 'national
histories, of whatever kind, cannot be written simply from the
inside.'[9] Priscilla Wald, viewing the issue from another side, argues

that 'the impact of deterritorialization and transnational analyses on the field of American studies is that we are not yet – and no longer – sure where we are.'[10] This sense of critical displacement is neatly paralleled in *The Accidental Tourist*.

Exaggerated Americanness in The Accidental Tourist

At the beginning of the novel, Macon and his wife Sarah are returning from their summer holiday, though 'holiday' is the wrong word for what they have endured, principally because they are mourning the loss of their 12-year-old son Ethan, who was shot and killed the year before in a senseless, random act of violence. As Macon acknowledges, looking at their very different travelling outfits, 'They might have been returning from two entirely different trips' (1). Such an observation is more telling than even he realises, and sets up the remainder of the novel, not only because Sarah takes that moment to announce that she wishes to divorce Macon after twenty years, but because the novel as a whole is concerned with arrivals, departures and travel. What individual characters wear on their travels is a recurring concern, as well as what they eat, how they shop, and what they see – or refuse to see. Indeed, what Barry Curtis and Claire Pajaczkowska call the 'three paradigmatic moments of tourism: eating, shopping and sightseeing',[11] structure *The Accidental Tourist*.

Although relatively little time is spent on actual travel in the novel (Macon takes trips to England, Canada, France and various US cities, some named, such as New York, San Francisco and Philadelphia, others packaged into amorphous masses like 'the south'), the impact of displacement and movement is strongly felt throughout. Macon continually negotiates the foreign in his daily life, even on smaller journeys into unknown parts of Baltimore, resisting change and contamination from the outside as much as possible, yet inevitably becoming embroiled in the very things he tries to avoid. Emphasising food, money and language, *The Accidental Tourist* explores how Macon navigates around the unexpected results of travel, particularly after he breaks his leg and is forced to travel at a different pace.

The book is named for Macon Leary's travel series, guidebooks for businessmen who, on their travels, want to pretend that they have never actually left home. As Macon's publisher Julian Edge puts it, ' "While armchair travelers dream of going places . . . traveling armchairs dream of staying put." ' Then, pointing to a logo of a winged armchair, he says, ' "I thought we'd use this on the cover" ' (86) – and indeed, the cover of Tyler's novel itself features just such a chair. Originally the title of his series was 'The Reluctant Tourist', but the eventual title offers a closer parallel to what actually occurs, as Macon moves between places without a clear plan despite his almost obsessive desire for order. The series is anything but comprehensive, and his commissioning editor actually says, ' "I'm looking for the opposite of encyclopedic" ' (86). In perhaps one of the most telling comments in the book, the narrator notes, 'Other travelers hoped to discover distinctive local wines; Macon's readers searched for pasteurized and homogenized milk' (11). This image of safe, homely, familiar food is not accidental; the desire for sameness and safety runs as a constant thread in the series and the book, though next to it, danger and difference make their presence felt.

Although he is not credited as the author – there's only the logo on the front cover – Macon takes his writing job seriously, and finds it almost makes up for the fact that he is forced to travel to do so: 'As much as he hated travel, he loved the writing – the virtuous delights of organizing a disorganized country, stripping away the inessential and the second-rate, classifying all that remained in neat, terse paragraphs' (11). His desire for order and neatness cocoons him from experience. Macon is the archetypal American traveller, who puzzles over the question of why everywhere else is different from the US. His hatred of travel propels him anxiously through various European cities, only comfortable (and then, never quite) when he is eating in restaurants named Yankee Delight, US Open, or New America. His guidebook rates restaurants not by traditional stars, but by whether 'genuine' American food can be found there: 'Did Amsterdam have a McDonald's? Did Mexico have a Taco Bell? Did any place in Rome serve Chef Boyardee ravioli?' (11). That Macon's readers search for inauthentic replications of home across the Atlantic or below the US/Mexican border, in places which are thought by other travellers to contain the authentic or original version of such food, is telling. With no political concern over the creeping and overt Americanisation of these questions – indeed, if anything, attempting to celebrate it – Macon's series caters to the businessman who ask questions like, 'What hotels in Madrid boasted king-sized Beautyrest mattresses? What restaurants in Tokyo offered Sweet'n'Low?' (11).

Macon's written advice is repeated back to the reader, italicised, and focuses on minimising the disruption of travel. Macon's advice on what to wear while travelling is a grey suit, which he believes is *handy for sudden funerals and other formal events* (24, italics in original). In the filmed version, Macon's guidebook extracts are offered in voiceovers with images of Macon packing.

If Disney could create Europe, it would be so much tidier, so much less authentic, and therefore so much more comfortable for Macon. He would be the ultimate consumer of Baudrillard's hyperreality – if only he attempted to engage with any sort of 'real' at all. It is no coincidence that the Leary family's favourite game is a home-made card game they call Vaccination, a game that no one outside the family can master; or that, despite his extensive travelling, Macon's only foreign language is Latin, a language that cannot help him navigate around the world outside Baltimore. Macon desires most to be untouched, and his tourism is stereotypically, if exaggeratedly, American:

> *I am happy to say that it's now possible to buy Kentucky Fried Chicken in Stockholm. Pita bread, too, he added as an afterthought.* He wasn't sure how it had happened, but lately pita had grown to seem as American as hot dogs. (11, italics in original)

Macon's guidebooks cover only cities, since the businessmen for whom he writes never visit the countryside and mostly wish they had not left home at all. *The Accidental Tourist* is the logical extension of Roland Barthes's analysis of *The Blue Guide*, a travel guide that, by picking out only what there is to 'see', conveniently manages to become 'through an operation common to all mystifications, the very opposite of what it advertises, an agent of blindness'.[12] Similarly, Curtis and Pajaczkowska note that 'all guidebooks and tourist literature offer advice on what to "look out for", which implies the more interesting question of "what is to be overlooked."'[13] In Macon's case, this amounts to: just about everything.

That Macon's guide 'sees' something different from the traditional tourist guide – reminders of home rather than spectacular (foreign) beauty – is a comment on the nature of the stereotypical American tourist: selective, unbending, less willing to encounter a myriad of sites or experiences than anyone might admit (though Dean MacCannell's recuperation of the tourist figure in his seminal text *The Tourist* goes some way to dispelling the myths behind tourist desires).

As Heather Henderson writes of travel literature, '[T]he genre that by rights seems most likely to take both writer and reader out of their usual surroundings, is actually most at home with itself when it reveals how neither has ever really left the armchair.'[14] Macon, in looking for home, only ever encounters pale imitations, which leads to inevitable homesickness. Indeed, the article that brought him to the notice of his editor was a short piece in his weekly neighbourhood newspaper on a craft fair in Washington, subtitled, to Macon's chagrin, 'I Feel So Broke-up, I Want to Go Home': '*Getting there is difficult*, he wrote, *because the freeway is so blank you start feeling all lost and sad. And once you've arrived, it's worse. The streets are not like ours and don't even run at right angles*' (84, italics in original).

It is significant, though, that despite the 'geographic dyslexia' he claims to share with his siblings, which means that none of them can find their way around, he comes from a family that, at some level, desires to travel. His grandfather owned a well-thumbed book, *Tips for the Continent* (87), though Macon's reading of it is typically perverse:

> Travelers were advised to invert a wineglass on their hotel beds, testing the sheets for damp. Ladies should seal the corks of their perfume bottles with melted candlewax before packing. Something about that book implied that tourists were all in it together, equally anxious and defence-less. Macon might almost have enjoyed a trip in those days. (87)

In the filmed version, Macon's family house – which is much like a museum and treated as such by outsiders as well as by the inhabitants who religiously alphabetise and chronicle their belongings – includes several remnants of various foreign travels, though significantly, the placement of these objects is not overtly discussed. Instead, an interloper, Muriel, views and plays with these items, which the family itself seemingly ignore. In the novel itself, when Macon's grandfather begins to descend into senility, he plans a trip to Lassaque, an island that he believes is located off the coast of Bolivia, and he remains convinced of its presence even after Macon reminds him that Bolivia does not even have a coast, and after he is unable to find it in the encyclopaedia. His imagined country is telling for what it contains – and doesn't contain: ' "[T]he Lassaquans have no written language. In fact if you bring any reading matter they confiscate it. They say it's black magic" ' (139), Macon's grandfather pronounces. ' "They don't even allow, say, a checkbook with your name on it. Before you go ashore you have to soak the label off your deodorant. You have to get your money changed into little colored wafers" ' (139–40). Grandfather's confused image of this imaginary country, complete with an assumed native innocence that is reminiscent of many a colonial narrative – ' "I still intend to see Lassaque before it's corrupted" ' (140), the Leary grandfather claims – offers echoes of a kind of negative of his own life. In losing language himself, he seeks to strip it from others: ' "An intriguing effect of their illiteracy," he said, "is their reverence for the elderly. This is because Lassaquans' knowledge doesn't come from books but from living; so they hang on every word from those who have lived the longest" ' (140). He wishes to travel back to an imagined place (and a time) where his own knowledge was respected and listened to, where he was considered important, and none of Macon's reassurances offer him the succour he desires.

Whilst Macon was raised by Grandfather Leary, and in many respects becomes the exaggerated inheritor of his views, it is significant that Macon's mother (who is seen as flighty by her children) could never stay put, and Macon and his siblings credit their inability to find their way around to her constant movement. In order to avoid getting lost, 'None of them ever stepped outside without obsessively noting all available landmarks, clinging to a fixed and desperate mental map of the neighborhood' (111). Yet as Macon lets go of this mental image of himself, he also learns to navigate through unfamiliar emotional landscapes. To explore this further, it is necessary to offer a comparison between Macon's trips to Europe and his unexpectedly more compelling trips around Baltimore.

The Construction and Maintenance of the 'Foreign'

When travelling, Macon offers tips on how to avoid contamination from others: *'Always bring a book as protection against strangers. Magazines don't last. Newspapers from home will make you homesick, and newspapers from elsewhere will remind you you don't belong. You know how alien another paper's typeface seems'* (28, italics in original). In this as in all communication, Macon's word choice is precise: that which is alien is rejected. His guidebook has chapters entitled 'Trying to Sleep in England' and 'Trying to Eat in England'; his travels are, indeed, trying. The only part he really approves of is the plane itself:

> When the weather was calm, you couldn't even tell you were moving. You could pretend you were sitting safe at home. The view from the window was always the same – air and more air – and the interior of the plane was practically interchangeable with the interior of any other. (28)

What he dislikes is how people on the other side of the Atlantic assume that their time and their lives are equally authentic to his. 'In Macon's opinion, morning in other time zones was like something staged – a curtain painted with a rising sun, superimposed upon the real dark' (31). It is not so much that Macon sees himself as the centre of the universe as that Baltimore is, and the further away from it he gets, the less secure he feels. His response to time changes is remarked upon at several points, but the most significant passage on it comes as the plane prepares to land after the first transatlantic flight in the novel:

> The stewardess announced what time it was in London, and there was a stir as people reset their watches. Macon adjusted the digital alarm clock in his shaving kit. The watch on his wrist – which was not digital but real time, circular – he left as it was. (33)

Tyler's use of the circular motif offers a telling metaphor about Macon's contained life; his guidebooks force him to keep to the same schedule, revisiting the same locations on the same itinerary.

Yet none of it is real to him: when he visits hotels that afternoon, a parenthetical reference intrudes; it is afternoon 'so to speak' (35). By 8 p.m., he tells us, he is ready for bed, but then recalls that 'the English thought it was midnight' (36). Macon knows better. Macon's refusal to bend on the issue of time means that when he crosses the Atlantic, he is never able to be 'in the moment'; he is always elsewhere, or hoping to be, and in fact, he spends much of his journey attempting to get home, and failing, checking in and out of hotel rooms before resigning himself to his original schedule. To console himself (and to do research) he consumes American food, though he does acknowledge that English food, universally derided, is '*not as jarring as in other foreign countries. Nice cooked vegetables, things in white sauce, pudding for dessert . . . I don't know why some travelers complain about English food*' (52, italics and ellipsis in original). Later, visiting Paris, he warns his estranged lover Muriel not to expect her Burger King Woppaire to be the same as a Whopper at home (323). Unlike Macon, Muriel consumes foreignness (indeed, she becomes an obsessive consumer, visiting markets, bartering for goods and, because unlike the meticulous Macon, she does not really understand the exchange rate, she ends up with massive bargains as a result).

Indeed, before they travel there (and they are decidedly *not* travelling together as this point), Muriel urges Macon to take her with him on his Paris trip. When he says he hates Paris, she says, ' "I could show you the good parts" ' (100), and there is a sense that despite her lack of any travel experience at all, she could well be right: open to new experience, Muriel is offered as a clear counterpoint to Macon. Later, when she surprises him on the airplane, she claims to want to walk along the Seine, and significantly, despite the fact that he has been there many times, Macon pauses: 'Macon wasn't even sure it was possible to walk along the Seine' (315). Neither accidentally nor reluctantly a tourist, Muriel loves to travel, despite never really being anywhere else before. Caesar argues that characters like Muriel, whom she calls 'intrusive others', 'imply that otherness itself is normal and that acceptance of this otherness, whether with love or simply with an acknowledgement of the differentness, frees ones from the prison of the self'.[15] Thus Muriel is set up as a freeing figure, one who, despite not knowing the basics of foreign travel, embraces rather than endures the experience. Tyler herself claims that Muriel was 'very foreign to me at first' but the author 'did grow fond of her as I came to know her and I wanted people to see her in the best light'.[16]

What is intriguing in *The Accidental Tourist* is that Macon is a tourist in his own city, Baltimore, as well as elsewhere, as he navigates his way through Singleton Street, the aptly-named street on which Muriel lives with her 7-year-old son Alexander. Muriel, a dog trainer and odd jobs woman, is an unlikely match for Macon, but as Mary F. Robertson perceptively notes, 'Tyler does not seem to allow relationships between like and like to flourish.'[17] Rather, Tyler explores the negotiations that occur when outsiders transgress the boundaries of the family, with the result, Robertson argues, that 'the progress of Tyler's novels is felt more as an expansion of narrative disorder than as a movement toward resolution and clarification'.[18]

Certainly it is the case that Macon moves from an orderly universe to a disordered one, but along the way, he takes his travel experience and applies it to the working-class neighbourhood in which Muriel lives. Indeed, once he moves in with Muriel, and is visited by his brother Charles, Macon admits, 'He felt like someone demonstrating how well he got on with the natives' (233). In Singleton Street, Macon is required to deal with unfamiliar transport arrangements: for example, Muriel shares a car with a local boy who fixes its many and constant problems. Macon follows Muriel into thrift shops, negotiating for goods in ways that he is unaccustomed to, and in doing so, he recognises Muriel's very different strengths: 'He thought of the way she navigated a row of thrift shops – the way she cruised a street, deft and purposeful, greeting passersby by name . . . The places Muriel knew!' (319–20).

He tries to interest Muriel's son in new activities, including handy household repairs, and there's something not unlike the *Tips for the Continent* in how he approaches this role; certainly there is an element of inculcating a sense of stereotypical gendered behaviour in the boy, suggesting that he will one day be able to fix things for his own wife. He teaches Alexander about money; in the filmed version, this is done by trying to get him to see a maths transaction as somehow real by explaining how to figure out change from buying milk, thus combining two of the essential elements of dealing with foreignness: negotiating food and negotiating money. Indeed, Macon, in a change to his character, actually introduces food to Alexander; whilst this is the familiar American pizza (to which Alexander believes he is allergic), it nevertheless offers an opportunity for Macon to change the set patterns of his own life. As he acknowledges, 'In the foreign country that was Singleton Street he was an entirely different person' (202).

Finally, it is only when travelling with Muriel that Macon acknowledges that the real is located outside of him, and outside of his hometown: flying low over the American landscape, Macon has an epiphany: 'He saw then how real those lives were to the people who lived them – how intense and private and absorbing' (199). Macon, formerly an agent of blindness, has become instead, willing to engage with that which has always been foreign to him. Though at one point in the novel he accidentally returns to his wife (and indeed in Tyler's original conclusion, he ends up there permanently), in the published version Macon takes a chance on a new way of being, incorporating the foreign into his family – not only Muriel and her small son, but all of the inhabitants of Singleton Street, including Mrs. Patel, who signifies most explicitly the idea of foreignness at home.

The paradigmatic moments of being elsewhere – the consuming, both as a body and as an economic participant, and the looking, if not always well – define the activities of elsewhere when one is there. They do not, however, define elsewhere, or who you are when you are there. As Macon acknowledges, '[W]ho you are when you're with somebody may matter more than whether you love her' (307). Or, as Stout puts it, 'It is one of Tyler's central and governing principles that lives get intertwined and relationships are . . . more important than any relocations people may make.'[19]

' *"It's a lot of work, being foreign"* ': Digging to America

The Accidental Tourist begins with a return and ends with a departure – and throughout, explores how to negotiate the foreign, wherever it is encountered. *Digging to America*, on the other hand, begins at an airport arrivals hall, as two families wait to claim their adopted Korean baby girls, to incorporate the foreign, quite literally, into their families. Bitsy and Brad Donaldson, who are loud and brash and stereotypically American, identify themselves as part of a family, with 'laminated buttons such as you might see in an election year' proclaiming their relationships: 'MOM', 'DAD' and 'COUSIN' (4). They are contrasted with Sami and Ziba Yazdan, whose surname is repeatedly mispronounced in the text (as indeed, is Ziba's first name, which is accented on the second syllable, whereas mostly the Donaldsons accent the first).

When the Euro-American Donaldsons – who are filming the encounter – recognise that the Iranian-American Yazdans are also welcoming a baby into their family, they insist on maintaining contact, even though the families differ in religion, nationality, ethnicity and values. Their simultaneous adoption of baby daughters locks them into a relationship that extends years, with the Donaldsons enforcing a shared history and a need to create 'traditions', including the tradition of Arrival Day, ' "a ceremony, of sorts" ' (53) that Bitsy plans down to the last detail.

This joint Arrivals Party celebrates the girls' entry into the US (and becomes a competitive display of ethnicity and identity). For the first party, Bitsy envisions the girls coming in together, with a song playing in the background to announce their arrival; she also plans to replay the arrival video, but none of the parties goes to plan in this way, and she ends up stuck with the inappropriate but eventually raucous song, 'She'll be Coming Round the Mountain'.[20]

For all her focus on maintaining Jin-Ho's ethnic heritage and dedication to all things Korean, Bitsy baulks at including Korean desserts at her party, instead planning ' "a sheet cake frosted like an American flag" ' (53). It is perhaps this touch that allows Sami to voice his ambivalence towards the celebration, which becomes more important than the girls' birthdays, which differ by several months: ' "Behold! You've reached the Promised Land! The pinnacle of all glories!" ' (88). Later, when Ziba hosts the Arrivals Party, she serves a baklava 'spiked . . . all over with tiny American flags' (201) and this image is one that suggests an interesting alliance between cultures, even as it, like Bitsy's sheet cake, seems to ignore the girls' original nationality.

Despite Bitsy's concern that the Yazdans are Americanising Susan – she disapproves tremendously of their decision to rename the child and she also disapproves of the hairstyle they adopt for her – it is clear that the Yazdans are offering a hybrid space where Americanness (which has been, to a certain extent, adopted by all of them) works in concert with their ethnic heritage. Ziba is offended by Bitsy's suggestion that they are Americanising Susan, when in fact, the reality is that 'they chose a name that resembled the name she had come with, Sooki, and also it was a comfortable sound for Iranians to pronounce' (10). The name is thus one that suggests continuity between her Korean heritage and American nationality, whilst recognising her adoptive parents' ethnic heritage as well. Bitsy's assumed Americanisation is actually something else entirely.

Maryam, Sami's mother, who is by far the most interesting character in the novel, given her struggle with and against Americanness, is offered the most interesting gloss on Americanisation: '(As if anything could really Americanize a person, Maryam thought, having watched too many foreigners try to look natural in blue jeans)' (46). It is not accidental that her thoughts are placed in parenthesis. They remain unsaid, as does much in this novel where cultural misunderstandings occur.

The video of the girls' arrival clearly shows how sidelined the Yazdans initially are in this exchange. The Donaldsons take centre stage, literally marginalising the Yazdans, and it is no coincidence that Jin-Ho Donaldson grows up to be the larger of the two children; she metaphorically takes on the position of the attention-seeking Donaldsons. Susan Yazdan is alternately considered petite or just plain small, depending on who is doing the viewing, and each family prefers the look of their adopted daughter, imagining that the other family is jealous that they got the better deal.

This comparison is, however, largely unacknowledged, and acts as a metaphor for other unsaid or censored thoughts. For example, when Ziba suggests that she and Sami think that Susan's biological father might have been white, given her pale complexion, Bitsy reacts strongly: ' "Oh! Well! But actually that's not something we would *notice*, really!" ' (25, italics in original). This suggests, inaccurately, that choice is involved in what to notice about appearance, rather than that individuals are subconsciously prompted and programmed by culture to notice gender, size, age and ethnicity, amongst other things. Bitsy's overt political correctness is contrasted both with the Yazdans, who are frequently bemused by her posturing, as well as with her own father, Dave, who says things that could be construed as ignorant but who, ironically, becomes the vehicle for real incorporation of foreignness, when he falls in love with Maryam after the death of his wife. It is also the case that Sami and Ziba negotiate the line between being American and Iranian in their own marriage: when they meet at college, they feel that 'a cloak of shared background surrounded them invisibly' (84), and this is attractive for Sami despite the fact that 'in his heart he too had always thought his wife would be American' and he compulsively dated blondes before meeting Ziba. His desire for a blonde American wife is a desire for a manufactured view of family inculcated by television sitcoms: 'He assumed that his schoolmates enjoyed an endless round of weenie roasts and backyard football games and apple-bobbing parties, and his fantasy was that his wife would draw him into the same kind of life' (83). At each generational level, then, there is a struggle to acknowledge and negotiate aspects of foreignness and to contend with the manufactured image of a stable Americana as well.[21]

Bitsy's facile proclamation suggests that a refusal to notice is a guarantee of anti-racism. Yet Bitsy's reaction to Ziba and Maryam suggests that she *does* notice difference, and even accentuates it: '[S]he fell all over herself apologizing for her Americanness and her First Worldness and her "white-breadness," as she called it. She was forever complimenting Ziba's exotic appearance and asking for her viewpoint on various international issues' (189). The text counteracts this assumed exoticism and special knowledge in a typically understated way: 'Not that Ziba *had* much of a viewpoint, or any that was different from what she read in the *Baltimore Sun* if she could find the time. But somehow she was granted a kind of authority, even so' (189, italics in original). Bitsy is clearly as infected and affected by recognition of otherness as anyone else, though she prefers only to see the positive sides of this worldview.

For all her desire to incorporate the foreign into her family, and with the knowledge that such incorporation is not easy (especially after the adoption of a second child, Xiu-Mei, from China, which is far from smooth), Bitsy nonetheless displays her own ignorance at several strategic points in the text, particularly by insisting on Sami's foreignness, despite the fact that he is US-born and raised and has never even been to Iran. According to Bitsy:

> Sami had that very young habit of taking himself too seriously, although that could have been just his foreignness showing. (Even though his accent was dyed-in-the-wool Baltimore, something studiously, effortfully casual in his manner marked him as non-American.) (62)

Thus, although she does not – apparently – notice Susan's pale complexion, she clearly notices Sami's darker one. By virtue of his parentage, then, Sami is refused the comfortable belonging that Bitsy takes for granted. Yet even when Bitsy experiences this displacement for herself, she fails to understand the significance of it. Listening to Ziba's parents talking in Farsi, she notes, 'She had to guess at his meaning just from his tone, as if she were a foreigner in an unfamiliar country' (79). This is such an unusual occurrence for her that it merits mention, though clearly it does not merit any further exploration; like Macon to some extent, Bitsy does not easily step outside of her own cultural milieu.

What is striking about *Digging to America* is how unstable the terms 'foreign' and 'foreigner' are in the novel. Tyler carefully explores how it feels to be foreign, but also how those who are ethnically and nationally foreign in the US also use the term reciprocally in relation to the American majority. Sometimes 'foreign' is a designation accepted by an individual character about him- or herself, whereas at other times, it is assigned to the 'other', whether that other is Iranian or American.

This shifting reality is best explored through Maryam, Sami's mother, who has an uncomfortable relationship to America. It was never, for her, the Promised Land, but rather 'the great disappointer' (159). She acknowledges an inner resistance to the country, but emigrates there to follow her husband, Kiyan. Theirs was an arranged marriage, and Kiyan becomes the embodiment of Maryam's relationship to the US. When they meet accidentally one day in Iran, she sees him as 'very American, all at once; very *other*' (158) and this is attractive to her. Yet once she follows him to the US, she recognises that her early views of him had been somewhat false: 'It began to dawn on her that Kiyan was not as acclimated to American life as she had once supposed. He dressed more formally than his colleagues, and he didn't always get their jokes, and his knowledge of colloquial English was surprisingly scanty' (160). It is not accidental that he is simply a memory by the time the novel opens, nor that the idealised construction of him is later unpicked by his daughter-in-law.

Maryam's complicated relationship to the US is manifested in her alternate resistance to and embracing of her foreignness, as well as her desire to make Americans the other (as opposed to being othered herself). All of Maryam's closest friends are non-American born, and talking about Americans is one of their favourite pastimes: 'But almost always the subject of Americans came up, in an amused and marveling tone. They never tired of discussing Americans' (259). Here, the Americans are the foreigners, with incomprehensible ways and bizarre manners. Even Sami partakes in such discussions, claiming that Americans are not as tolerant as they like to believe:

> 'They say they're a culture without restrictions. An unconfined culture, a laissez-faire culture, a do-your-own-thing kind of culture. But all that means is, they keep their restrictions a secret. They wait until you violate one and then they get all faraway and chilly and unreadable, and you have no idea why.' (82)

This is compared to Japan where, Sami argues, ' "at least they tell you the rules. At least they admit they *have* rules" ' (82, italics in original). Listing the unspoken prohibitions against particular kinds of questions in the US, Sami demonstrates his incomprehension: ' "You can't ask how much someone's dress cost. You can't ask the price of their houses. You don't know *what* to ask!" ' (82, italics in original).

It is the one-to-one conversations that are the hardest to navigate, from both sides. After Maryam rejects Dave's proposal of marriage, he latches onto her occasional language issues as a reason for their essential incompatibility. Noting the fact that she often forgets to incorporate a definite or indefinite article in her speech, Dave suggests:

> 'I guess that's understandable, when you've grown up speaking a language that doesn't use "a" or "the," but it implies some, I don't know, resistance. Some reluctance to leave her own culture. I suspect that's what went wrong between the two of us. The language was a symptom, and I should have paid more attention to it.' (227)

Yet it isn't just language that acts as a barrier. Maryam, despite her own resistance to Americans and Americanisms, finds Sami's discussion of his fellow countrymen as something of a betrayal: ' "You with your Baltimore accent," she said. "American born, American raised; never been anywhere else: how can you say these things? You're

American yourself. You're poking fun at your own people!" ' (82). Of course, what makes this claim particularly ironic is Maryam's own delight at talking about the Americans, as well as the fact that she is American herself. Moreover, on more than one occasion, she uses her language as a defence. As Ziba notes, Maryam's language becomes more stilted and accented than normal, when she wants to 'prove that she herself was not American in the least – that she was the opposite of American' (212). Moreover, Maryam and her friends use their foreignness as a convenient excuse to avoid connection. Maryam's Turkish friend Kari, when asked out by lonely widowers, says, ' "I tell them my culture forbids it" ' (152), and Maryam marvels at this technique, wondering if it was better than her own attempts at assimilation.

In one of the most striking presentations of the term 'foreigner', Tyler explores the contested meanings of it as represented on a tee-shirt that Susan wears. Whilst foreignness is alternately assigned to the American and non-American characters, it is never, except tangentially as here, related to the adopted children, and this erasure is significant. In the passage in question, the tee-shirt is so big that it acts as a dress on the child: clearly, then, the term does not fit her. But there is also a humorous side to this image, since the tee-shirt acts as promotional merchandise for the band. Dave, in looking at the child in the oversized shirt, becomes confused, and Maryam has to interpret the scene for him: 'She laughed. "It's not the singing group," she told him. "It's just the word. Sami had that shirt printed for me as a joke when I got my citizenship. I was so sad to become American, you see" ' (168). As a self-label, foreignness is humorous, even if no longer legally applicable, and *Digging to America* explores the way in which legal naturalisation (through choice and adoption) does not ensure that the behaviour of those who are naturalised will be seen as natural.

If, in *Digging to America*, being labelled foreign is complicated and uncomfortable, so, too, is being American. In a significant passage, Dave protests:

'It's harder than you realize, being American,' he told [Maryam]. 'Don't suppose we aren't aware how we appear to the rest of the world. Times I used to travel abroad, I'd see those tour groups of my countrymen and flinch, even though I knew I looked pretty much the same. That's the hell of it: we're all lumped in together. We're all on this same big ship, so to speak, and wherever the ship goes I have to go, even if it's behaving like some . . . grade-school bully. It's not as if I can just jump overboard, you know!' (179, ellipsis in original)

Whilst the reader may be momentarily convinced by Dave's argument, and perhaps even recognise the situation he outlines, Tyler deftly undercuts the protest: ' "Whereas we Iranians, on the other hand," Maryam said wryly, "are invariably perceived as our unique and separate selves" ' (179). In this negotiation and encounter, neither side finds it comfortable to be assigned an identity, particularly from the outside.

Whilst foreignness is the most explicitly addressed identity marker in *Digging to America*, it is also clear that age and gender are also factors that create barriers to understanding, and they cannot be spliced apart from ethnicity or nationality. The Iranian-Americans bemoan their offspring's lack of attention to tradition, and yet in their very lament, they acknowledge the reason for the problems they see:

'They're losing their culture, the young ones. I see this everywhere. They pay their traditional New Year's visits but they're not sure what they're supposed to be doing once they get there. They go through the motions but they keep looking at everyone else to see if they've got it right. They *try* to join in but they don't know how.' (269, italics in original)

The younger generation have difficulties performing their ethnicity, both for their parents' sake, and for others. However, what is also the case is that being asked to perform ethnicity, at whatever age, offers both challenges and secret pleasures. Maryam dislikes her cousin Farah's husband William for the emphasis he places on his wife's exoticism – ' "It seems she's not really Farah at all; she's Madam Iran" ' (154) – momentarily forgetting that Farah delights in such extravagant displays of ethnicity. Maryam even considers Dave's interest in her suspect, whilst Ziba wonders if the relationship is a 'cultural expedition born of Dave's curiosity' (184).

Yet the cultural conflicts that ensue could just as easily be explained by a number of other factors apart from ethnicity. In initially resisting a relationship with Dave, Maryam claims that their different national backgrounds make such a relationship problematic:

'He's so American,' Maryam said, and she hugged herself as if she felt cold. 'He takes up so much space. He seems to be unable to let a room stay as it is; always he has to alter it, to turn on the fan or raise the thermostat or play a record or open the curtains. He has cluttered my life with cell phones and answering machines and a fancy-shmancy teapot that makes my tea taste like metal.'

　　'But Mari-june,' Ziba dared to say. 'That's not American; it's just . . . male.' (212, ellipsis in original)

Indeed, at several strategic points, the female characters suggest that men and women occupy different spaces, and Maryam goes as far as asking, 'Wasn't the real culture clash the one between the two sexes?' (264). Coming from an author who has been accused of ignoring gender politics, such a statement resonates deeply. Engaging with world politics (discussions of the Shah and of 9/11 pepper the text), *Digging to America* assumes no easy answers for cultural clashes, nor any fixed and set response to foreignness.

　　In the over twenty years between *The Accidental Tourist* and *Digging to America*, Tyler's exploration of foreignness has become more nuanced, more complicated. In the former novel, foreignness relates less to ethnicity than to life choices (indeed, Macon's own mother is portrayed as 'foreign' by her children); in the latter novel, foreignness is much more closely linked to differences in ethnicities, but this does not mark a facile equation between the two. Rather, Tyler explores how foreignness is adopted, assumed, projected, misread and even misremembered. In this more complicated version, transatlantic and transpacific crossovers offer opportunities to explore what Americanness is, as well as what foreignness is – however that is defined.

NOTES

1. Charles Vandersee, 'Intertextual, International, Industrial Strength', *American Literary History* 6 (3) (1994): 419.
2. Anne Tyler, *The Accidental Tourist* (New York: Berkley, 1986). Originally published in 1985. Anne Tyler, *Digging to America* (London: Chatto and Windus, 2006). All references to these texts will be cited parenthetically.
3. Charlotte Templin, 'Tyler's Literary Reputation', in Dale Salwak (ed.), *Anne Tyler as Novelist* (Iowa City, IA: University of Iowa Press, 1994), p. 194.
4. C. Wright Mills, *White Collar: The American Middle Classes* (New York: Oxford University Press, 1951), p. 328.
5. Paul Bail, *Anne Tyler: A Critical Companion* (Westport, CT: Greenwood, 1998), p. 10.

6. Donna Gerstenberger, 'Everybody Speaks', in Dale Salwak (ed.), *Anne Tyler as Novelist* (Iowa City, IA: University of Iowa Press, 1994), p. 138.

7. Judith Caesar, 'The Foreigners in Anne Tyler's *Saint Maybe*', *Critique* 37.1 (1995): 71.

8. Templin, 'Tyler's Literary Reputation', p. 179.

9. Paul Giles, *Virtual Americas: Transnational Fictions and the Transatlantic Imaginary* (Durham, NC: Duke University Press, 2002), p. 6.

10. Priscilla Wald, 'Minefields and Meeting Grounds: Transnational Analyses and American Studies', *American Literary History* 10 (1) (1998): 216.

11. Barry Curtis, and Claire Pajaczkowska, ' "Getting There": Travel, Time and Narrative', in George Robertson et al. (eds), *Travellers' Tales: Narratives of Home and Displacement* (London: Routledge, 1994), p. 207.

12. Roland Barthes, 'The Blue Guide', in *Mythologies*, trans. Annette Lavers (London: Cape, 1972), p. 76.

13. Curtis and Pajaczkowska, ' "Getting There" ', p. 209.

14. Heather Henderson, 'The Travel Writer and the Text: "My Giant Goes with Me Wherever I Go" ', in Michael Kowalewski (ed.), *Temperamental Journeys: Essays on the Modern Literature of Travel* (Athens, GA: University of Georgia Press, 1992), p. 247.

15. Caesar, 'Foreigners', p. 73.

16. Patricia Rowe Willrich, 'Watching through Windows: A Perspective on Anne Tyler', *The Virginia Quarterly Review* 68 (1992): 509.

17. Mary F. Robertson, 'Anne Tyler: Medusa Points and Contact Points', in Catherine Rainwater and William J. Scheick (eds), *Contemporary American Women Writers: Narrative Strategies* (Lexington, KY: University Press of Kentucky, 1985), p. 131.

18. Ibid. p. 122.

19. Janis P. Stout, *Through the Window, Out the Door: Women's Narratives of Departure, from Austin and Cather to Tyler, Morrison and Didion* (Tuscaloosa, AL: University of Alabama Press, 1998), p. 137.

20. It is significant that no such party marks the arrival of the Donaldsons' second adopted child, Xiu-Mei. Although the extended family gathers to meet the Chinese baby, and the Yazdans are included in this performance, Dave notes, 'Like most life-altering moments, it was disappointingly lacking in drama' (173). Later, the only ceremony attached to Xiu-Mei is a flawed one. In an effort to wean Xiu-Mei off her reliance on dummies, Bitsy invents the 'Binky Fairy' who will take away the child's dummies, but the ceremony is ruined by inclement weather, and Xiu-Mei manages to retain her dummies

despite her mother's efforts to tie them to helium balloons and whisk them away.

21. Later, this fantasy of Americana is played out for the children, too: Maryam relates the tale of Susan feeling that Christmas isn't real for the Yazdans. When Dave suggests a small tree, some presents, perhaps some carolling, Maryam notes that, in fact, the family had not only allowed, but encouraged such displays, though this was not enough for Susan to perceive their Christmas as 'real'. Dave's response is to laugh: ' "Oh, for goodness' sake," he said. "You're talking about every child in this country! . . . The kid's one hundred percent American" ' (180).

CHAPTER 6

CROSS-DRESSING AND TRANSNATIONAL SPACE: ISABEL ALLENDE'S *DAUGHTER OF FORTUNE*

Isabel Allende's novel *Daughter of Fortune* (1999) engages with a range of journeys across and between continents, leading at least one critic to argue that the novel relates more closely to the emerging field of Inter-American Studies than any other interdisciplinary field;[1] in this argument, the text's focus on the journeys from South to North America take precedence over both the transatlantic and the transpacific journeys that individual characters undertake (or are forced to undergo). As if to back up this point, the Flamingo paperback version of the novel comes complete with a map showing the routes taken by commercial ships, but only those which circumnavigate the Americas.[2] The map focuses on the 'cartography of the characters' travels',[3] but only those that acknowledge ties to the Americas; the transpacific and transatlantic routes are invisible in this rendering.

Whilst I accept that the principal hemispheric journey, and the peripatetic nature of the main heroine within North America both suggest that this arena is the locus of the text, the reality is that the novel is as much defined by the initial transatlantic movements and later transpacific ones as it is by inter-American ones, and that all of these journeys collectively have lasting repercussions for identity shifts. Thus the novel breaks out of the boundaries of a transatlantic narrative to encompass other narratives of movement. This may therefore make it seem an odd text on which to conclude a study of transatlantic literature. However, I would argue that its very joining together of these disparate, clearly global concerns, offers a chance to explore how transatlantic literature opens out into other fields and does not remain static or identified solely through one spatial relationship.

In his article, 'Literary History on the Road: Transatlantic Crossings and Transpacific Crossovers', Takayuki Tatsumi traces transatlantic (and transpacific) lineages and imaginations through a range of literary texts. His aim is to deconstruct any false 'binary opposition between imperialism and postcolonialism',[4] but it intrigues me that in the title of his essay, he contrasts transatlantic 'crossings' with transpacific 'crossovers', subtly suggesting that different ocean spaces offer different points of contestation. In exploring how both the transpacific and transatlantic movements offer identity shifts, *Daughter of Fortune* appears to engage in this very debate, as English entrepreneurs move to Chile for prosperity and to engage in trade, and as Chinese men are shanghaied onto English and Dutch ships that sail for Chile and California. Their different fates in each of these 'new' worlds is carefully delineated in the novel, and crossing itself takes on a variety of meanings.

In addition to its exploration of different oceanic journeys, the novel's clear concern with *gendered* travel and its re-imagination of a nineteenth-century female picaro marks it as one that requires further exploration in a book on transatlantic women's literature. Karen Lawrence argues that 'in the multiple paradigms of the journey plot – adventure, pilgrimage, exile, for example – women are generally excluded, their absence establishing the world of the journey as a realm in which man confronts the "foreign." '[5] In Allende's novel, the 'foreign' is confronted and reconfronted in every delineated space: in Chile, on board ship, and in the rambling American West, and, though she has to cross-dress to achieve it, the female encounters adventure and undertakes a pilgrimage. Her pilgrimage is, to be sure, initially set up as a pilgrimage for love, but the resolution of the text sees a different narrative fate from the one that this family saga appears to set up.

The in-between space of the Atlantic, made powerful in the imagination through the interactions that traverse it, retains a central narrative thrust in *Daughter of Fortune* and changes all that occurs as the narrative unfolds. Allende's novel examines the ways in which transatlantic and transpacific encounters are alternately restricting and transformative, investigating how racialised and gendered identities become blurred in the process of crossing the ocean. Exploring borders and boundaries, as well as the desire to elide fixity, the novel taps into Allende's well-known penchant for exploring magic realism (or magical feminism, as Patricia Hart calls it),[6] but also expands beyond this designation. Rooted in family saga and political intrigue,

Allende's novel attends to both the so-called smaller canvas of domesticity and the larger canvas of world politics. In doing so, she expands the definition of domesticity as her main heroine engages in identity shifts, extensive movement across continents (and within them), cross-dressing and a sloughing off of inherited culture. If, by her upbringing, Eliza Sommers is destined to remain fixed and rooted, by her (contested) birth, she is signalled as aligned with change and movement. Throughout the book, Allende reconfigures the ocean as the origin of a fairy tale adventure for her female picaro and as such, the ocean becomes almost a character in the novel.

Allende argues that by living as writer outside of one's home country, 'You can stand unsheltered by the system and look at it from a certain distance. You appreciate all the ironies; you are always surprised by reality.'[7] In *Daughter of Fortune*, the majority of the characters eventually stand outside their home countries, reflecting on previous homes and inhabiting new ones. Allende suggests that her own feeling of being in exile led her to write nostalgically, fed by 'the desire to recover the world that I had lost'.[8] Yet loss also offers opportunity, and in particular, Allende argues that literature requires 'distance and ambiguity',[9] something that her exilic position affords her.

Gabrielle Foreman argues that Allende is 'animated by the desire to preserve pasts too often trivialized, built over, or erased, and to pass them on'.[10] This is certainly the case through the ways in which she weaves folklore, narratives of love and loss and the daily lives of women into the text. Central to the narrative is Eliza Sommers, a foundling adopted by a wealthy British family in Chile. Eliza's origins recapitulate the fairy tale – her guardian Miss Rose tells Eliza that she was discovered in a basket of the 'finest wicker and lined in batiste', clothed in lace and mink, and accompanied by a silk handkerchief with six gold coins (4). Figuratively, this implied wealth signals Eliza's 'English blood'. However, her long dark tresses suggest an alternative conception. Indeed, the family's servant Mama Fresia tells the girl, ' "You have Indian hair, like mine" ' (4), thus disputing Rose's claim to Eliza's 'racial superiority'; another character eventually suggests that Eliza has Oriental blood.

As befits the complicated narrative, later revelations attest to her partial 'Englishness' (she is indeed related to the Sommers, as the illegitimate daughter of her guardian's brother John, a sea captain who makes only infrequent appearances in the novel). Allende's central character is thus created through and by the transatlantic space; and in varying degrees, those around her inhabit spaces within spaces that seek either to extend or deny the 'contact zone' that Mary Louise Pratt defines in *Imperial Eyes*.

Pratt's definition of the 'contact zone' includes 'social spaces where disparate cultures meet, clash, and grapple with each other, often in highly asymmetrical relations of domination and subordination'.[11] Specifically, Pratt references 'the space of colonial encounters, the space in which peoples geographically and historically separated come into contact with each other and establish ongoing relations, usually involving conditions of coercion, radical inequality, and intractable conflict'.[12] In Allende's text, the site of conflict is at first Chile, then California, and in both places, this conflict is racially and ethnically marked, and gender becomes an entrapping facet of identity. Moreover, these encounters are damaging, if not equally so. For example, the European travellers bring disease to Chile, including a 'fierce epidemic of African measles carried to Valparaíso by a Greek sailor' (10); none of the illnesses that the Europeans suffer matches the virulence of this imported disease, signalling the unfortunate if not in some cases deadly consequences of travel and migration for the host country and its inhabitants.

In Chile, transplanted British characters mark their detached positions in the architecture of their homes, their adherence to British norms, their refusal to acknowledge the weather or seasons of Chile in their dress or manner and their language, which is 'the lingo invented by Britons to communicate with servants' (17). The Sommers in particular maintain what they believe to be a dignified Britishness that admits to no contamination from the geography outside their estate and which retains an aura of respectability. Their soirees preserve a European flavour, and they resist influence from outsiders. Allende suggests that such characters 'formed a small nation within the country' (15), thereby physically and metaphorically embodying the distinction between country and nation. Yet Allende's narrator takes an almost approving stance towards this separatist activity, suggesting that the British 'did it with such refined manners that, far from arousing suspicion, they were considered an example of civility' (15). This message of civility is, however, undercut elsewhere in the text, and the narrator's apparently approving tone is thereby rendered suspect.

In one of the most flagrant early examples in the text of British arrogance in Chile, a charming but fraudulent Protestant missionary, Jacob Todd, aims to tout bibles to the local Indian population despite knowing next to nothing about them, a factor that does not deter him for long. Like many missionaries before him, he has gone to Chile with no knowledge either of Spanish or the Indian tongues, and Allende's geographical metaphor of their behaviour speaks volumes: '[T]hey traveled south to where terra firma broke up into islands like a string of beads' (14). The image of beads, so connected to narratives of conquest and exchange, is ironically appropriate, because the exchange envisioned never happens. The Indians remain resolutely connected to their own religions or have already been converted to a form of Catholicism, the faith of most of the other Chileans. Todd, however, at least tries (at first) to connect, despite the fact that he is really a bible salesman and not a missionary after all; his aim is profit, and he travels to Chile on a bet, first availing himself of information from the British Museum and later of information in Chile itself:

> He set himself the task of learning something about the Patagonian Indians, but after a few half-hearted sweeps through some heavy tomes in the library, he understood that it made little matter what he knew or didn't know, since ignorance on the subject was universal. (37)

That he initially tries to understand his 'customers' through (presumably European) interpretations of their behaviour and mores is itself telling, and the fact that he abandons this search for knowledge more so. The 'universal' ignorance of the Patagonian Indians is quite culturally specific, a fact that Todd fails to recognise. His ignorance also extends to Chile itself; having imagined it a warm and tropical place, he is poorly equipped to deal with its winter when he arrives. Nevertheless, he pronounces on the fate of 'saved' Tierra del Fuego Indians, 'rescued' by English missionaries, brought to England and taught to foreswear their cannibalistic ways. Todd's stories recapitulate paternalistic fantasies of rescue and elevation; they are undercut by the narrator's interrupting intervention, 'he said,' after the revelation of cannibalism. 'He said' implies a reason to disbelieve, a suggestion that the story is simply that: a story, with no significant facts behind it. More significantly, the 'truth' of this narrative is twice called into question, first by the fact that the reader already knows that Todd lacks basic knowledge of the area and its inhabitants, and then by a later revelation that, repatriated, the individuals whom he praises 'returned to their old ways, as if they had never been touched by England' (39).

This fraudulent missionary eventually becomes a fraudulent US reporter, inventing stories about Mexican bandits in order to titillate his reading public and amass his own stash of California gold without ever having to raise a pickaxe. He is thus a recurrent example of transatlantic misunderstanding and miscommunication, his ability to 'read' the locals in the US no more precise than his ability to read the Chilean Indians.

In California, other characters are dislocated, only to be relocated in ways that transgress gender and racial lines. Several of the primary characters explore the limits of national identity, and reconstruct transnational spaces in marginal, liminal sites of, for example, a trav-elling whorehouse, itinerate workers' camps, and ships that take indi-viduals from the old to the new worlds (and indeed, even this construction is taken apart, particularly in the journey from Chile – figuratively both old and new world – to California). Throughout, Allende envisions 'crossings': of ships, of genders and of racial identi-ties, and her text explores how such crossings act as metaphors for the (metaphorically unchartable) transnational space. What follows will explore these various mappings of identity and misunderstanding.

At Sea

From the first page of the text, ships and crossings are invoked, and the narrative adopts a to-ing and fro-ing motion that is maintained throughout. Indeed, in its unusual and liberal use of the flash-forward, Allende's novel continually projects the reader into future spaces, only to draw back again to the novel's present, situated in the historical past of Great Britain, Chile and the US of the 1800s. In one such example, the central character, Eliza, recalls her life:

> if not in precise detail, at least with an astrologer's poetic vagueness. The things we forget may as well never have happened, but she had many memories, both real and illusory, and that was like living twice. She used to tell her faithful friend, the sage Tao Chi'en, that her memory was like the hold of the ship where they had come to know each other: vast and somber, bursting with boxes, barrels, and sacks in which all the events of her life were jammed. (3)

Thus in the very opening pages of the book, Allende signals the impor-tance of ocean crossings, the future of her unusual heroine and the sense that facts are less important than how a story ends up being told. The flash-forward technique does not result in a clear narrative trajectory, despite nodding to the future, because it is impossible to discover from these moments just what path takes the characters there. 'She used to tell' is situated in the future, yet placed in the past, in a jumble of narrative modes that refuse to coalesce. In another early reference to the sea, Allende writes: 'Eliza convinced herself that she was the child of a shipwreck . . . As time passed she concluded that this story wasn't bad at all: there is a certain poetry and mystery about what the sea washes up' (6). Eliza's origins – deliberately obscured – reflect her later fate, which is also bound up with a ship, this time taking her to another 'new world': California.

Eliza is both ward and relative of the Sommers, who are them- selves not a couple but siblings living abroad. Eliza's in-between posi- tion is the cause of social anxiety and disruption for them; indeed, she is almost impossible to commodify, a fact that preoccupies her guardian Jeremy Sommers as he sees into the future and her need for a suitable match. He is unable to determine what kind of match that might be. He is as determined *not* to treat Eliza like a lady as his sister Rose is determined that she should be. Indeed, Rose schools Eliza in all the accomplishments of an English lady, including playing the piano (a skill she will later make use of in a travelling brothel, a fate her guardian could not have imagined whilst insisting on these lessons). Rose also ensures that Eliza's education includes French lessons because 'no well-educated girl could be ignorant of that lan- guage' (51), even as the Sommers themselves are ignorant of Spanish or the other tongues of Chile. Even here, then, an assumed European environment takes precedence over the current South American one. Eliza's environment is contradictory, both including and excluding the foreign (and offering a hierarchy of acceptable and unacceptable foreignness). She grows up in a house which 'was meant to imitate a style then in vogue in London, but the exigencies of landscape, climate, and life in Chile had forced substantial changes and the result was an unfortunate hodgepodge' (6). Such bricolage is a defining feature of transnational texts, as place bleeds into structures and as the remembered past (here, stylish London) becomes reinvented in another space, and also almost inevitably misremembered.

Eliza is kept apart from local children, living in:

the closed world of her benefactors' home, in the eternal illusion of being in England rather than Valparaíso. Jeremy Sommers ordered everything from a catalogue, from soap to shoes, and wore light clothing in the winter and an overcoat in the summer because he followed the calendar of the Northern Hemisphere. (44)

This exclusion from children her own age almost inevitably leads Eliza to mix with the 'Indian' servants, learning their ways of cooking and healing and therefore incorporating quite literally far more of the 'foreign' than her guardians realise. Indeed, the narrative's magically real moments focus on Eliza's preternatural cooking skills. At the young age of 7, she is able to 'skin a beef tongue, dress a hen, make twenty empanadas without drawing a breath, and spend hours on end shelling beans while she listened openmouthed to Mama Fresia's cruel Indian legends and her colourful versions of the lives of the saints' (12). Again, the question of the 'contact zone' is implicit here. As Pratt suggests: 'While subjugated peoples cannot readily control what emanates from the dominant culture, they do determine to varying extents what they absorb into their own, and what they use it for.'[13] Mama Fresia uses these stories to control and captivate the child, undermining the Sommers' attempts to make her into a lady. Thus, Eliza takes into her imagination the jumbled, imported stories of Catholic saints which are already combined with native legends to formulate her own narratives of adventure.

Moreover, her own skills are set up as if in a fairy tale narrative, and indeed, much later in the text, her skills with food offer her a way of supporting herself. Thus what is set up in one context as a fairy tale skill changes into a necessary art for survival, suggesting again the option or idea of transformation, though in this case, from magical to practical skills. In relation to *House of Spirits* but still relevant here, Foreman argues that in Allende's work, 'the stronger the historical moment, the more distant the magical – as if to counter the threat of history's becoming "merely" enchanted and so subsumed.'[14] This does indeed seem to be the case for *Daughter of Fortune* as well, given that Allende's historical focus becomes sharper once the heroine stows away to California. Indeed, woven throughout that part of the narrative are stories of the Quakers' connections to the underground railroad, and the series of catastrophic fires in San Francisco in 1849. The rise of San Francisco in relation to the Gold Rush and the Chinese immigration to the Golden City are also foregrounded, as well as the unseemly history of prostitution, avarice and lawlessness in the American West. Yet the air of magic potions and miraculous cures remains; Eliza later saves her friends from dysentery by remembering the practices and potions of Mama Fresia, perhaps indicating the two-way nature of the contact zone.

When Eliza nears marriageable age, she 'solves' the issue of how to address the question of her in-between status by falling in love with an apparent social inferior and political activist, Joaquín Andieta. This fact triggers the peripatetic nature of the rest of the text. When Joaquín (never an ideal lover except in Eliza's fertile imagination) steals from the Sommers and vanishes to California, Eliza impulsively follows him, stowing away on a ship with the help of a Chinese cook, Tao Chi'en (himself a former herbal doctor). Swearing undying love and promising never to marry another except this first love (a promise she seems to keep in the space of the text),[15] Eliza is again caught in a fairy tale narrative that later becomes the narrative of a picaro, minus the sexual adventures. Thus Eliza abandons the carefully constructed Britishness of her home environment for an encounter with a variety of other identities in flux.

At times, to be sure, the book seems to offer little more than a stereotypical love plot and family saga, but Allende is careful to disrupt her readers' expectations, not least by undercutting the romantic moments between Eliza and Joaquín, revealing that their passion is neither equally felt nor the stuff of which fairy tales are made. Anne Cranny-Francis argues that 'romantic fiction is the most difficult genre to subvert because it encodes the most coherent inflection of the discourses of gender, class and race constitutive of the contemporary social order; it encodes the bourgeois fairy-tale.'[16] However, Allende's text does successfully subvert the romance, precisely through foregrounding its conventions. Set alongside the continual pressure of the romance narrative on the heroine (and her own obsession with the fairy tale as an appropriate myth of origin) is a gradual revelation of the lies that perpetuate the genre. At one level, Eliza recognises the inadequacies of her lover, and the reality that her view of him is a fantasy one (even when they are together, their relationship is based on infatuation and invention; she prefers his written notes to his sullen companionship), and indeed, as the narrative relates, 'Eliza gave herself to the task of idealizing her lover until he became an obsession' (115). The manufactured nature of this 'obsession' suggests its genesis in tales of romantic love rather than fact. At the same time, Eliza does swear undying love to him, a fact that surprises her eventual companion, Tao Chi'en, to the extent that, on one of their first meetings, he 'stared, openmouthed, because he had never seen a woman capable of such extremes in real life, only in classic novels in which the heroines always died at the end' (147). Allende thus self-consciously references the metafictional nature of her text, and her heroine, and sets up, through flash-forwards, the reader's expectation of eventual resolution or punishment.

Eliza is, at this point, both pregnant and abandoned. She is thus a character who, by sleeping with her lover before marriage, has threatened her own reputation and thus her (already tenuous) position, and this is enough to suggest that she is in line for a specific fate. A stereotypical romance would see her punished for her transgressions, either temporarily (before being saved by a man of greater social standing, who would redeem and elevate her) or permanently, through a tragic, but ultimately expected death. Allende undercuts these potential fates by providing Eliza with the escape route of the sea. An oceanic space defined her birth, and now another ocean journey defines her movement towards adulthood. It is ironic and appropriate that she cannot legally go to the US, since 'she had no identification papers, and no chance at all of obtaining a passport, because the United States legation in Chile had been closed due to a frustrated love affair between some North American diplomat and a Chilean lady' (143–4). Thus intercontinental relations at both a micro and a macro level are strained in this text, and Eliza is forced to find alternative ways of escape. Stowing away on ship, she effects this escape through a semi-permanent cross-dressing that comes to define her character more closely than her girlish pledge of everlasting love.[17]

Crossing Over: Dressing and Undressing

If, as Karen Lawrence argues, 'The topos of travel furnishes a testing ground for [a] relational notion of identity, exaggerating the politics of location which infuses all identity formation,'[18] then to combine travel with the motif of gender passing further complicates the issue. Moving outside the position of abandoned, fallen woman in her movement between continents, Eliza refuses the label 'woman' at all. Allende herself explores the ways in which in her own life narrative, the fact of being a woman initially seemed limiting. In an interview with Elyse Crystall, Jill Kuhnheim and Mary Layoun that predates *Daughter of Fortune*, Allende recounts the fact that for the first forty years of her life, she had wanted to be a man.[19] The desire to switch genders is clearly invoked in this later cross-dressing narrative, as Eliza finds strength and passion through pretending she has the freedom and rights that are embodied in the men of the time.

Marjorie Garber argues that, amongst other things, cross-dressing may be linked to 'the anxiety of economic or cultural dislocation, the anticipation or recognition of "otherness" as loss'.[20] It is therefore formally appropriate that Eliza's cross-dressing should begin at sea, and that it should coincide with a period of disorientation and actual loss. Whilst on board the ship, Eliza miscarries her child, with the result that her entire impetus for travel quite literally ebbs away. With no physical reason left to pursue her quest, Eliza nevertheless continues forward, though it is perhaps not surprising that illness disorientates her for a large part of the journey. At this point, there is a strong sense that she will succumb to the fate of a nineteenth-century heroine. Yet she recovers, and, as Allende makes clear, Eliza's crossdressing initiates a period of freedom as well as regret:

> As the articles of a young English lady's clothing piled up on the floor one by one, she was losing contact with known reality and irreversibly entering the strange illusion that would be her life in the months to come. She had the clear sensation of beginning a new story in which she was both protagonist and narrator. (152)

Allende's frequent evocation of story and tale remain apparent here, revealing both the constructed nature of Eliza's narrative and the constructed nature of her previous position.[21] This passage also indicates Eliza's newfound voice (though, ironically, she plays a deaf-mute boy in order to avoid detection at first). Able finally to claim agency, rather than wait for her fate to arrive, Eliza begins to revel in her options, and she becomes, in this account, a wandering picaro, able to have adventures through the invention of maleness. As Elizabeth Young argues, following Cathy N. Davidson:

> early nineteenth-century American versions of the picaresque both excluded and invited women. The genre was so inseparable from the figure of the male adventurer that women could enter it only by masquerade; yet once they did so, they had extraordinary mobility. In a subgenre of 'female picaresques,' women enjoyed a precarious but extravagant life of freedom by cross-dressing.[22]

By setting her novel in the context of the mid-nineteenth century, Allende figuratively recalls these earlier fictional female picaros, whose escape from traditional patterns of gendered behaviour is possible only by disrupting the visible signs of (female) gender. The American picaresque, which derives from its Spanish antecedent, is therefore an interesting transatlantic hybrid that Allende infuses with South American magical realism. Although Allende dismisses the magic realism tag, asserting instead that her novels are just 'realistic

literature' and that the tag is used about her work only because of the
country of her birth,[23] it is clear that in both Eliza's gifts for cooking
and to some extent healing and in Tao Chi'en's own medicinal gifts,
Allende is invoking a sense of release from a Western realist framework. In offering licence to invoke fairy tale skills, Allende enriches
this transatlantic and hemispheric narrative, where odd combinations
co-exist. This again recalls the contact zone, which Pratt suggests
allows for 'copresence, interaction, interlocking understandings and
practices'. As Pratt further argues, 'A "contact" perspective empha-
sizes how subjects are constituted in and by their relations to each
other.'[24]

This relational sense of identity is central to the reader's understanding of Eliza's position. It should not be forgotten that the femi-
nised version of the adventurer – the *adventuress* – explicitly encodes
sexual exploits[25] and is thus connotatively tainted and unusable.
Furthermore, after disembarking from the liminal space of the ship,
Eliza lands in California, glossed in the text as 'no place for women,
only bandits' (147). Her choice is stark, particularly as the women
who do reside in the region are primarily there to service male sexual
needs. Thus her desire to don the dress of a man (or a boy) is a prag-
matic one. If the women on board the ship change from the drab
clothes of their voyage to that of 'full battle dress' (219) or 'sporting
attire' (221) complete with peacock feathers to signify their occupa-
tions once on land, Eliza's deliberate dressing down and across cultures signifies a different road to be taken in this land of bandits.

Unsurprisingly, perhaps, Garber links cross-dressing historically
to prostitution as 'alternative social strategies for social and economic
survival',[26] and it is no coincidence that Eliza is essentially confronted
with her other potential fate when she is first assisted by a prostitute
whilst on board ship, when she encounters enslaved Chinese 'sing-
song' girls sold by poor families into sexual slavery, and when she
travels for a time with a gang of itinerant whores. Her position has
always been an in-between position: in between classes, in between
races; she is now in between genders as well.

Eliza's cross-dressing is a cross-dressing of convenience rather than
a statement about her sexuality, but as Garber notes, exploring representations of cross-dressing along the spectrum of identity formation allows for a more accurate depiction of the activity: '[T]o restrict
cross-dressing to the context of an emerging gay and lesbian identity
is to risk ignoring, or setting aside, elements and incidents that seem
to belong to quite different lexicons of self-definition and political and

cultural display.'[27] Indeed, for Eliza, her cross-dressing is less a display than a disguise, less a consciously assumed pose and more a series of identities that become more natural the more she performs them. Eliza is particularly entranced by how the unfamiliar clothes themselves make her feel: '[T]he man's clothing gave her an unfamiliar freedom; she had never felt so invisible' (222). If to be an English lady in Chile is to be seen (if also kept apart), to be a cross-dressing Chinese boy is to be significantly less visible and more free, despite the low regard in which the Chinese are held in California. Moreover, upon arrival in California, Tao Chi'en ensures her safety not only by disguising her as a boy, but also by insisting that she is deaf-mute, and a little slow, and therefore unable to communicate. Although this may seem a disabling gesture, again it gives her freedom to explore a new cultural arena, both California and Little Canton, without the threat of unmasking.

Indeed, as they walk together through the streets of San Francisco, they encounter a multitude of nationalities – from Americans to Mexicans to Peruvians, amongst others – identified by the narrator as 'Argonauts' in search not of the golden fleece, but of gold itself (223). These men are initially identified less by their country or region of birth than by what connects them: lust for riches and a false sense of the ease with which they would make their profits. Yet though they 'flowed together in the muddy alleyways of San Francisco' (223), suggesting a stereotypical melting pot, they are also distinguished by their dress, so that Australians stand out from Russians, and Chileans from Peruvians. That said, it is also clear that in their dress, they already experience the flow of the contact zone, with 'Oregonians and Russians dressed in deerskin, like Indians' (223), for example, though their barrios are indeed culturally distinct.

California, though not yet a US state, is called a 'land of opportunity' by Eliza (232), as she confuses her new dress with wider freedoms and a narrative of progress so familiar to students of American history and literature. Yet this idealistic account of opportunity obscures the fact that there is no equal opportunity for all: for (apparently) all women and some (particularly Chinese) men, California is a place of danger. Thus Eliza is not entirely safe even in this disguise, and she soon sheds it for another: Chilean boy, so that she moves from a double passing gesture to a single one, that of gender only.

Efrat Tseëlon contends that 'masquerade unsettles and disrupts the fantasy of coherent, unitary, stable, mutually exclusive divisions.'[28] Certainly in her first disguise as a mute Chinese boy, Eliza disrupts every position she has previously occupied. As a stowaway and now an illegal immigrant, she disrupts both class and gender; after she leaves Tao Chi'en, she takes on the persona of Elías Andieta, a Chilean boy, and travels with miners hoping to find gold. Continually seeking her lover, and calling herself his brother in the hopes that he will recognise her pursuit, Eliza maintains her idealised view of Joaquín. She assumes that, since he has no brothers, he will associate the name Elías with Eliza. But he is not the perfect, all-powerful lover, and if he hears that Elías/Eliza is following him, there is never any clue that he reacts in the way that she would like. Their implied eventual encounter is endlessly deferred in the novel.

To fund her journey, Eliza supports herself by writing letters for money, cooking food and playing the piano, thus calling on the skills she learned as the child of British patrons. In one memorable incident, she even plays a man playing a woman in a group of travelling actors, a performance she has to give up because ' "the confusion was driving [her] crazy. [She] didn't know whether [she] was a woman dressed as a man, a man dressed as a woman, or an aberration of nature" ' (274). The gender double-cross amazes her newfound friends, but she has to abandon the troupe of actors in order to restore her own, clearer sense of duplicity.

Eventually, Eliza settles down – if the phrase is accurate – with a caravan of 'soiled doves' – itinerant prostitutes, led by the indomitable Joe Bonecrusher, herself a transvestite, and Babalú the Bad, who performs the role of bodyguard and menacing protector. More importantly, Babalú takes on the role of making a man out of the boy Elías, whom he suspects of being homosexual: '[H]e watched Elías closely, quick to correct him when he sat with his legs crossed or shook back his short mane with a very unmanly gesture' (297). The need to learn manliness as a guard against inappropriate sexual behaviour is ironically appropriate here, for Eliza as a lone woman would be at risk in this environment, but as a boy she is much less so.

This acknowledgement that gender is a set of learned behaviours accords with Judith Butler's theoretical stance on performance. Butler argues that 'repetition is at once a reenactment and a reexperiencing of a set of meanings already socially established; and it is the mundane and ritualized form of their legitimation.'[29] It is thus appropriate that Babalú's lessons meet with eventual success – though at a clear cost to the group's coherent identity. Visited by a Mexican outlaw who offers the false name of 'Jack' when questioned, the group is coerced into offering medical aid. It becomes clear that the man's badly frostbitten fingers require amputation, but Babalú the Bad finds that he is not able to perform the task. Berated by Joe Bonecrusher, Babalú confesses to the invention of his sobriquet and thus his fearful reputation, an episode that culminates in an unmanly display of tears. It is here that Eliza intervenes and performs the minor surgery, after which Babalú comments deferentially, ' "You're a real man, Chile Boy" ' (308). Eliza's learned behaviour is almost excessively offered here, her realness elevated above Babalú's own.

This episode changes the comfortable identities of the travelling group, and Eliza finds herself looking for alternatives, eventually returning to San Francisco with Tao Chi'en and becoming his assistant. This time, she retains her male appearance, but decides against returning to her earlier role of deaf-mute Chinese, preferring to be considered part of an odd companionship between a Chinese man and a Spanish boy. The sexual tension of this choice and how it might manifest itself to others is not overtly addressed. However, it is clear that passing remains both gendered and racialised for Eliza. Increasingly attracted to each other, but unable to acknowledge their cultural differences, Tao and Eliza carefully negotiate their desire: ' "You look like a pretty Chinese girl," Tao had said in an unguarded moment. "You have the face of a handsome Chilean," she had immediately answered' (363). This masking of each other's identifiable racial identities (even as it acknowledges Eliza's hidden sex) is emblematic of their identity conflicts. By this point, Tao is dressed in Western clothes, a costume that initially disappoints Eliza, because it points out his strangeness to her; she cannot read him properly. Each, therefore, is represented as cross-dressing, but Tao's is a racial cross-dressing whilst Eliza's is now entirely gender focused. Both of them are displaced in the US, Tao transpacifically and Eliza hemispherically, but both discover an odd affinity for their new world.

Garber suggests that, for the cross-dresser who is ' "compelled" by social and economic forces to disguise himself or herself', one result is that 'heterosexual desire is for a time apparently thwarted by the cross-dresser's assumed identity.'[30] Passing, Eliza cannot cross the boundary of sexual desire. *Daughter of Fortune* attends to this phenomenon by offering it as a reason for Eliza's decision to reinhabit her cast-off feminine attire (though, significantly, she decides never again to wear a corset). This decision is metaphorically appropriate, given Mary Morris's argument, noted in the Introduction, that the term 'stays' – the binding element of corsets – indicates a lack of movement.[31]

Anne McClintock suggests that cross-dressing, though disruptive of social identities, 'does not guarantee the subversion of gender, race or class power',[32] and indeed it seems that Eliza's choice signals a return to the status quo, one in which subversion is abandoned and normality is reinstated. Given that, throughout the text, Eliza has revelled in the freedom and invisibility that cross-dressing affords her, her return to feminine dress in the closing pages of the novel – a return that surprises and delights Tao Chi'en – is thus perhaps a disappointment for the reader. It seems to signal an acceptance of a lesser role, a circumscription of movement despite her renunciation of the corset. Certainly it could be read as one way to ensure the restoration of a heterosexual norm and the normative behaviour that is expected to attend such relations. What is clear, though, is that despite her resumption of female dress, Eliza is unwilling to become a stereotypical angel in the house. Indeed, in reflecting on her earlier desire to submit, and to become her lover's 'slave', she now recognises that she could not 'give up those new wings beginning to sprout on her shoulders' (276). These metaphorical wings are ones of movement and change, and this recognition coincides with Eliza's acknowledgement of her former lover's real place in the narrative of her life: a catalyst for change, not the end in itself.

Thus, Eliza's return to a 'gender-normal' dress perhaps indicates something more complex than simple compliance. If, as Garber argues, 'The transvestite is a sign of the category crisis of the immigrant, between nations, forced out of one role that no longer fits . . . and into another role, that of a stranger in a strange land,'[33] then Eliza's movement out of the role may indicate her *resolution* of crisis, and her acceptance of space. After all, according to Eliza, '[T]his land is a blank page; here I can start life anew and become the person I want . . . no one knows my past, I can be born again' (280).

If her first birth is aligned with a fairy tale narrative of shipwreck, it is appropriate that her second birth is aligned with a similarly suspect but frequent evoked narrative of *tabula rasa*. Allende's overt manipulation of narrative (here, a narrative of national origin) signals her self-conscious and metafictional positioning of Eliza as heroine. María Claudia André contends that 'Allende's revisionism of foundational narratives from a subaltern perspective presents a different angle generally overlooked.' Thus, according to André, the novel

> document[s] the significant participation that minorities and women
> exercised in the socio-political development of newfound territories in

North and South America [and stresses] how the transgression of either racial, geographical, social and sexual boundaries became a frequent practice of the times and, most likely, the only legitimate practice to exercise mobility and agency.[34]

It is precisely by performing a series of crossings that Eliza comes to represent the new nation. As such, she is the perfect metaphor for transnationalism, which, as Paul Giles argues, 'positions itself at a point of intersection . . . where the coercive aspects of imagined communities are turned back on themselves, reversed or mirrored, so that their covert presuppositions and ideological inflections become apparent'.[35] Giles further argues that 'identity emerges in various forms of paradoxical displacement and nostalgic misremembrance.'[36] Though he is, of course, speaking of the construction of national literatures and the emergence of specific area studies and not individual subjects, his words can easily be applied to this text, and to its heroine who, as we have seen, remembered her life 'if not in precise detail, at least with . . . poetic vagueness' (3). This poetic vagueness allows her to construct an identity which incorporates the foreign and which, criss-crossing time and space, allows for flux, flow, change – all aspects that constitute the transatlantic narrative which incorporates views from the other side.

NOTES

1. See Earl Fitz, 'Inter-American Studies as an Emerging Field: The Future of a Discipline', *Vanderbilt e-Journal of Luso-Hispanic Studies* 1 (2004), http://ejournals.library.vanderbilt.edu/lusohispanic/viewarticle.php?id=20, accessed 26 January 2008.
2. Isabel Allende, *Daughter of Fortune* (London: Flamingo, 2000). Originally published in 1999. All references to this text will be cited parenthetically.
3. María Claudia André, 'Breaking through the Maze: Feminist Configurations of the Heroic Quest in Isabel Allende's "Daughter of Fortune" and "Portrait in Sepia"', *Latin American Literary Review Special Issue 1972–2002, Isabel Allende Today* 30 (60) (2002): 74.
4. Takayuki Tatsumi, 'Literary History on the Road: Transatlantic Crossings and Transpacific Crossovers', *PMLA* 119 (1) (2004): 94.
5. Karen R. Lawrence, *Penelope Voyages: Women and Travel in the British Literary Tradition* (Ithaca, NY: Cornell University Press, 1994), p. 1.
6. See Patricia Hart, *Narrative Magic in the Fiction of Isabel Allende* (Rutherford, NJ: Associated University Presses, 1989).

7. Elyse Crystall, Jill Kuhnheim and Mary Layoun, 'An Interview with Isabel Allende', *Contemporary Literature* 33 (4) (1992): 593.
8. Ibid. p. 588.
9. David Montenegro, *Points of Departure: International Writers on Writing and Politics* (Ann Arbor, MI: University of Michigan Press, 1991), p. 112.
10. Gabrielle P. Foreman, 'Past-on Stories: History and the Magically Read, Morrison and Allende on Call', *Feminist Studies* 18 (2) (1992): 369.
11. Mary Louise Pratt, *Imperial Eyes: Travel Writing and Transculturation* (London: Routledge, 2000), p. 5. Originally published in 1992.
12. Ibid. p. 6.
13. Ibid.
14. Foreman, 'Past-on', p. 379.
15. In the sequel to *Daughter of Fortune*, *A Portrait in Sepia*, it is clear that Eliza eventually marries her companion Tao Chi'en.
16. Anne Cranny-Francis, *Feminist Fiction: Feminist Uses of Generic Fiction* (New York: St Martin's Press, 1990), p. 192.
17. I wish to record my thanks to my former student Sarah Dickinson for her insights into the role of cross-dressing in *Daughter of Fortune*. Our many long discussions about the text have helped me formulate my own views on the role and significance of Eliza's gender passing.
18. Lawrence, *Penelope*, p. xii.
19. Crystall, Kuhnheim, and Layoun, 'An Interview', p. 588.
20. Marjorie Garber, *Vested Interests: Cross-Dressing and Cultural Anxiety* (London: Penguin, 1993), p. 390. Originally published in 1992.
21. Similarly, Allende disrupts the narrative trajectory of Chinese literature, too. Although Tao Chi'en reveals, 'It was not for nothing that the most celebrated heroines of Chinese literature always died at the precise moment of their greatest charm' (p. 171), both Tao and Eliza live long enough to reflect on their immature love and thus outlive the circumscribed fates of 'fictional' lovers.
22. Elizabeth Young, *Disarming the Nation: Women's Writing and the American Civil War* (Chicago, IL: University of Chicago Press, 1999), pp. 160–1.
23. See http://www.isabelallende.com/curious_frame.htm, accessed 26 January 2008, where Allende claims, 'It's strange that my work has been classified as magic realism because I see my novels as just being realistic literature. They say that if Kafka had been born in Mexico, he would have been a realistic writer. So much depends on where you were born.'
24. Pratt, *Imperial*, p. 7.
25. Heidi Slettedahl Macpherson, *Women's Movement: Escape as Transgression in North American Feminist Fiction* (Amsterdam: Rodopi, 2000), p. 88.
26. Garber, *Vested*, p. 3.

27. Ibid. pp. 4–5.
28. Efrat Tseëlon, 'Introduction: Masquerade and Identities', in Efrat Tseëlon (ed.), *Masquerade and Identities: Essays on Gender, Sexuality and Marginality* (London: Routledge, 2001), p. 3.
29. Judith Butler, *Gender Trouble: Feminism and the Subversion of Identity* (New York: Routledge, 1999), p. 178. Originally published in 1990.
30. Garber, *Vested*, p. 70.
31. Mary Morris, 'Women and Journeys: Inner and Outer', in Michael Kowalewski (ed.), *Temperamental Journeys: Essays on the Modern Literature of Travel* (Athens, GA: University of Georgia Press, 1992), p. 25.
32. Anne McClintock, *Imperial Leather: Race, Gender and Sexuality in the Colonial Contest* (New York: Routledge, 1995), p. 67.
33. Garber, *Vested*, p. 79.
34. André, 'Breaking', p. 76.
35. Paul Giles, *Virtual Americas: Transnational Fictions and the Transatlantic Imaginary* (Durham, NC: Duke University Press, 2002), p. 17.
36. Ibid. p. 21.

CONCLUSION

Karen Lawrence maintains that 'the trope of travel – whether in its incarnations as exile or adventure, tourism or exploration – provides a particularly fertile imaginative field for narrative representations of women's historical and personal agency.'[1] As noted in the Introduction, it is precisely for this reason that women's narratives of transatlantic travel are such rich sources for explorations of identity and representation. Fictional travel narratives, like their factual counterparts, provide accounts of *difference* by exploring the politics of location while simultaneously examining localities. As cultural outsiders, travellers comment upon the society from which they spring and the societies to which they now belong (if, in some cases, only temporarily).

This book is one example of the way in which literary studies have been transformed by transnational critiques, which look beyond a single space or area to explore connections across and between such spaces, connections that are complicated, uneven and sometimes fraught. The dynamic interactions suggested by terms such as transatlanticity have been carefully explored within the novels and memoirs that feature in the preceding chapters. The transatlantic space is 'perpetually in motion, perpetually assembling, disassembling, and reassembling itself',[2] and Transatlantic Studies necessarily engages with issues of flux and change. Transatlantic Studies must also, I argue, confront and grapple with issues of identity and gender.

What all of the travel narratives explored in *Transatlantic Women's Literature* have in common is a sense that gender is a condition which impinges upon – even determines – the travel experience.

Each displays a sense that identity is a performance that is fluid, not fixed. This is, of course, intimately bound up in travel itself. The individual texts analysed here contribute to the evolving definitions of transatlantic literature, with important implications for the continued development of Transatlantic Studies as a theorised space.

Salman Rushdie argues that writers with allegiances to more than one space have conflicting experiences of this position:

> Sometimes we feel that we straddle two cultures; at other times, that we fall between two stools. But however ambiguous and shifting this group may be, it is not an infertile territory for a writer to occupy. If literature is in part the business of finding new angles at which to enter reality, then once again our distance, our long geographical perspective, may provide us with such angles.[3]

Rushdie's poetic exploration of what it feels like to be an exiled writer is beautifully rendered, but hides within it a surprising resistance to thinking outside of his own gendered cultural space. It begs the question: How does a travelling woman straddle cultures? Does the fact that, historically, she was supposed to be ladylike and keep her legs together have an effect? Is it too facile to suggest that a lady does not straddle anything? (Indeed, like Isabella Bird, she rides side-saddle to avoid doing so?) Certainly a female adventurer who stands with her legs wide apart is more likely to be seen as an adventuress, with all of the sexual connotations of the term. This construction, of course, also elides ethnic differences as well as historical ones, and is a salient reminder that, as James Clifford argues, 'there is no politically innocent methodology for intercultural interpretation.'[4]

What I have not attempted to do in this book is to suggest that all women's travelling experiences conform to an expected trajectory, that all women experience the same things, or that there is an overarching sense of womanhood that supersedes all differences between individual women. Rather, what I have attempted to argue is that in varying ways, and with varying degrees of resistance and acquiescence, women experience their travelling identities in relation to gendered receptions that highlight and foreground their femaleness. Moreover, I have argued that awareness of gender is key to the expansion of Transatlantic Studies.

Iain Chambers suggests that 'to travel critically means to journey not like Ulysses, on the way home, but like Abraham, cast out of the previous house of knowledge and destined never to return.'[5] But this contrast – between the fates of two men linked to significant cultural texts – offers no other way forward. What about travelling like Lot's wife, looking back? Or like Ruth and Naomi, together rather than separate? Or, in relation to this book, like Jasmine or Helga, Eliza or Muriel, to name but a few of the women travellers who populate this book? In the twenty-first century, it is imperative that women's stories of travel and displacement are seen to be as complex as the travels of the men who have gone before in literary history. Takayuki Tatsumi suggests that 'literary history travels over time, transforming itself and weaving its own road narrative,'[6] and one hopeful consequence of this moving narrative is an understanding and re-evaluating of the place of women in this literary history.

The three sections of this book, focusing on exoticism and ethnicity, memoirs and travel, and home and foreignness, also reveal how these categorisations bleed into each other, with language, desire and identity as key features that recur throughout. If assimilation is a focus of the work of Mukherjee, so it is also a focus for Allende and Tyler; if language constructs meaning for Hoffman, so too does it for Larsen; if Diski offers a Baudrillardian reading of space, so does Tyler engage with notions of hyperreality, though in an inverse construction that seeks Americanisation as a sort of panacea to stave off fear of the 'other'. In exploring both well-known transatlantic texts and those with significantly less critical appreciation, I have attempted to address how women's narratives – in their various ways – address the mythical space of the transatlantic, where narratives of otherness are read and misread.

Isabella Bird, a representative lady traveller of the nineteenth century, both conformed to and confounded notions of the limitations of her sex, and in doing so, she offered up a narrative that, at times, skated on the edge of suggesting that her strength was augmented by her travel, and that women were not as delicate as sometimes supposed. Indeed, at one point she notes: 'All women work in this region, so there is no fuss about my working, or saying, "Oh, you mustn't do that," or "Oh, let me do that." '[7] Though she sometimes regrets this lack of deference to her gender, she more often benefits from it, and inevitably, she contrasts homemaking in England and the Western US:

> I *really* need nothing more than this log-cabin offers. But elsewhere one must have a house and servants, and burdens and worries – not that one may be hospitable and comfortable, but for the 'thick clay' in the shape of 'things' which one has accumulated. My log house takes about five

minutes to 'do,' and you could eat off the floor, and it needs no lock, as it contains nothing worth stealing.[8]

Bird here is clearly offering up the less 'civilised', simpler existence as one to be admired, though by the end of the book she expresses a clear longing for the more complex and hierarchal home that she has (temporarily) left behind. A woman of her time, she expected the world to be organised hierarchically, and as an English woman, to be near the top of that hierarchy. She claims, when faced with adversity, to sit down and knit, thereby reinforcing her femininity, while at the same time delighting in her ability to undertake masculine chores such as driving cattle. Evelyn Bach suggests, in relation to Bird's *Unbeaten Tracks in Japan* but equally applicable here, that this alternation offers 'an ongoing literary cross-dressing and re-dressing' whereby 'the narrative escapes a fixed gender category as Bird contrives to carve out an unsteady niche for herself as that contradiction in terms, the female traveller/writer.'[9]

The metaphor of literary cross-dressing resonates beyond Bird's text: Helga in *Quicksand* is dressed for exoticism, whilst Mukherjee's eponymous heroine Jasmine is trained to dress as an American. Tyler explores the range of responses to otherness and foreignness, with dress accentuating or hiding difference; Hoffman learns what being a girl in Canada means through dressing appropriately. Allende offers the clearest fictional example of cross-dressing, as Eliza dresses across genders as well as ethnicities. Of the authors explored here, only Diski refrains from a sustained focus on costume, though she, too, finds herself affected by appearance when confronted with Amish travellers whose clothes outline their difference. Thus the choice to begin with Bird is one that allows for a variety of issues to be addressed that also relate to and are explored by twentieth- and twenty-first-century women writers.

Nella Larsen's *Quicksand* offers a bridge between Bird's nineteenth-century text and the later twentieth-century texts that are the main focus of this book. In it, Larsen raises issues to do with propriety, dress, behaviour and circumscription, though her short novel offers the additional focus on racial and ethnic difference that Bird's merely slides over through her assumption of hierarchical importance. Yet it is clear from the argument so far put forward that a simple focus on chronology does not offer the best measure of understanding women's engagement with gendered travel. Thus *Quicksand* was paired with *Jasmine* to offer up contrasts and comparisons in the exploration of exoticism, despite the gap of more than sixty years between the publications of these texts. In contrast, there are only thirteen years between Hoffman's first memoir and Diski's second travel text; and Allende's novel, published in 1999, neatly falls between Tyler's two novels, published in 1985 and 2006. There has been no attempt to discuss these texts by publication date because to do so would suggest a false trajectory and a one-way movement forward; if anything, Transatlantic Studies must suggest that, like the ocean itself, many directions are possible at once.

At the same time, the fact that the majority of the books explored here were published in the last twenty years or so is not accidental; this focus suggests that some of the issues raised by travel writers and novelists in the nineteenth century and the early twentieth remain resonant throughout the last century. Of course, there are important differences as well. Christopher Mulvey, in a chapter of *Transatlantic Manners* entitled 'American Woman', suggests that nineteenth-century travel literature 'offered the spectacle of the English and the Americans engaged in mutual social affront'.[10] Whilst of course there is some continuity expressed here, the idea of social affront is one that obtains much less significance in the late twentieth century and early twenty-first than it had at the last fin de siècle. Certainly it is the case that mutual incomprehension continues to be a staple for travel literature; Bill Bryson's humorous forays into Anglo-American relations would not be complete without the delineation of such instances.

But what is particularly striking about late twentieth-century texts, and the reason for my focus upon them, is the ways in which they engage with the changing face of feminism. Even when it is not being explicitly named, feminism has created the potential to explore and expand our understanding of gender and its implications. As gender takes on an increasingly important focus in politics and for critical texts, writers are more able to acknowledge and investigate explicitly issues to do with it. Although gender is only one marker of identity, it is nevertheless an important one that determines to a large extent how individuals are read; within the space of the transatlantic, this offers an important avenue into the texts being analysed here.

It has been equally important to explore issues of mobility and travel in a transatlantic and transnational framework. In this context, Clifford argues that it is necessary 'to rethink cultures as sites of dwelling *and* travel, to take travel knowledges seriously'.[11] Thus, places offer more than one meaning simultaneously, and this links in with other critical perspectives, such as those of Inderpal Grewal and others. Grewal looks at 'linkages between and specificities of cultures rather than at similarities',[12] a perspective that acknowledges the power differentials between places and does not attempt to smooth over those important differences. Rather than suggesting a homogenising equality between spaces and times, attending to linkages offers the opportunity to explore the *effects* of differences, whether that means, for Mukherjee, the way that Indian ghettoes arise in New York, or, for Allende, how Englishness is preserved in a hierarchical framework in South America, linkages with a historical past and a present-day reality. Moreover, in delineating an illegal entry into US territory, both Mukherjee and Allende implicitly set up, for their readers, linkages between these fictional worlds and the political climate that obtains now. As John Rodden argues: 'Allende challenges her readers to ponder the complexities of temporal as well as geographic borders: the countless parallels between the lives of young Latinas in the nineteenth and twenty-first centuries.'[13] If this is an approving view of Allende's work, critics are decidedly more critical of Mukherjee's apparently assimilationist perspective.

Authors with less clear political engagement than Allende also explore the ramifications of global connections. Although Tyler does not explicitly foreground the question of why rich or even moderately well-off Westerners seek to adopt Korean or Chinese babies and import them into the US in *Digging to America*, it is an important underlying issue that addresses gendered behaviour (the need to become a mother or the requirement to give up being one) and political connections and power across space. In choosing to focus not only on a European-American woman's experience of this global trade, but also on an Iranian-American woman's engagement with it, Tyler points out that even within the same geographical space, gendered behaviour may have different meanings, depending on ethnic contexts. Indeed, these very ethnic contexts become a battle over which meaning is contested, from Bitsy's frequent apologies to the Yazdans for her 'First Worldness'[14] to Maryam's increasing reluctance to include the Donaldsons in their celebrations for fear they are merely visiting Iranian culture: 'Why should they have to put on these ethnic demonstrations? Let the Donaldsons go to the Smithsonian for that! she thought peevishly. Let them read *National Geographic*!'[15] Moreover, the central image of digging to America is an inverse of the American child's fantasy of digging to China, and through this very title, Tyler explores what it means to see from another perspective.

Martin Lewis suggests that:

> The conventional present-day schema of global geography, encompassing continental and oceanic constructs alike, is rooted in a specifically European world view. During the colonial era, Western ideas about the division of the globe were forced on, and often eagerly borrowed by, other societies the world over, thereby largely extinguishing competing geographies.[16]

The way that geography is thus implicated in and a by-product of political power is just one manifestation of why it is necessary to adopt a transnational or Transatlantic Studies approach that teases out the effects of these apparent realities (and fantasies, too). As Hoffman reminds us:

> [T]here is no one geographic center pulling the world together and glowing with the allure of the real thing; there are, instead, scattered nodules competing for our attention. New York, Warsaw, Tehran, Tokyo, Kabul – they all make claims on our imaginations, all remind us that in a decentered world we are always simultaneously in the center and on the periphery, that every competing center makes us marginal.[17]

Such a recognition of simultaneous centredness and marginality works well within transatlantic literature, which self-consciously explores issues to do with here and there, connection and disconnection, map-making and cultural geography. From Isabella Bird's nineteenth-century letters home, a text which envisages a static female reader, to Diski's twenty-first century memoir of travels around the US, which does not, transatlantic women's literature addresses the multiple meanings of travel and home, exoticism and ordinariness, the foreign and the familiar. In doing so, and in placing gender firmly in the centre of these narratives, women's transatlantic texts create new ways of exploring space, identity and, most importantly, views from the other side.

NOTES

1. Karen R. Lawrence, *Penelope Voyages: Women and Travel in the British Literary Tradition* (Ithaca, NY: Cornell University Press, 1994), p. 20.
2. Ian Baucom, 'Hydrographies', *The Geographical Review* 89 (2) (1999): 313.

3. Salman Rushdie, *Imaginary Homelands: Essays and Criticism 1981–1991* (London: Granta, 1992), p. 15.

4. James Clifford, *Routes: Travel and Translation in the Late Twentieth Century* (Cambridge, MA: Harvard University Press, 1999), p. 19. Originally published in 1997.

5. Iain Chambers, *Migrancy, Culture, Identity* (London: Routledge, 1994), p. 70.

6. Takayuki Tatsumi, 'Literary History on the Road: Transatlantic Crossings and Transpacific Crossovers', *PMLA* 119 (1) (2004): 94.

7. Isabella Bird, *A Lady's Life in the Rocky Mountains* (London: Penguin, 1997), p. 194. Originally published in 1873, the text that Penguin uses is the 1879 version.

8. Ibid. p. 112, italics in original.

9. Evelyn Bach, 'A Traveller in Skirts: Quest and Conquest in the Travel Narratives of Isabella Bird', *Canadian Review of Comparative Literature/Revue Canadienne de litterature comparee* 22 (3–4) (1995): 593.

10. Christopher Mulvey, *Transatlantic Manners: Social Patterns in Nineteenth-Century Anglo-American Travel Literature* (Cambridge: Cambridge University Press, 1990), p. 66.

11. Clifford, *Routes*, p. 31, italics in original.

12. Inderpal Grewal, *Home and Harem: Nation, Gender, Empire, and the Cultures of Travel* (London: Leicester University Press, 1996), p. 18.

13. John Rodden, 'Isabel Allende, Fortune's Daughter', *Hopscotch: A Cultural Review* 2 (4) (2001): 37.

14. Anne Tyler, *Digging to America* (London: Chatto and Windus, 2006), p. 189.

15. Ibid. p. 36.

16. Martin W. Lewis, 'Dividing the Ocean Sea', *The Geographical Review* 89 (2) (1999): 189–90.

17. Eva Hoffman, *Lost in Translation* (London: Minerva, 1991), p. 275. Originally published in 1989.

BIBLIOGRAPHY

Primary Texts

Allende, Isabel [1999] (2000), *Daughter of Fortune*, London: Flamingo.

Bird, Isabella [1879] (1997), *A Lady's Life in the Rocky Mountains*, London: Penguin.

Diski, Jenny [1997] (1998), *Skating to Antarctica*, London: Granta.

Diski, Jenny [2002] (2004), *Stranger on a Train: Daydreaming and Smoking around America with Interruptions*, London: Virago.

Hoffman, Eva [1989] (1991), *Lost in Translation: A Life in a New Language*, London: Minerva.

Kincaid, Jamaica [1988] (1997), *A Small Place*, London: Vintage.

Larsen, Nella [1928] (1995), *Quicksand and Passing*, London: Serpent's Tail.

Marshall, Paule [1983] (1989), *Praisesong for the Widow*, London: Virago.

Mukherjee, Bharati [1989] (1990), *Jasmine*, London: Virago.

Tyler, Anne [1985] (1986), *The Accidental Tourist*, New York: Berkley.

Tyler, Anne (2006), *Digging to America*, London: Chatto and Windus.

Secondary Texts

Anderson, Benedict [1983] (1991), *Imagined Communities: Reflections on the Origin and Spread of Nationalism*, London: Verso.

André, María Claudia (2002), 'Breaking through the Maze: Feminist Configurations of the Heroic Quest in Isabel Allende's "Daughter of Fortune" and "Portrait in Sepia"', *Latin American Literary Review Special Issue 1972–2002, Isabel Allende Today* 30 (60): 74–91.

Aneja, Anu (1993), ' "Jasmine," the Sweet Scent of Exile', *Pacific Coast Philology* 28 (1): 72–80.

Atwood, Margaret [1981] (1991), *Bodily Harm*, London: Virago.

Bach, Evelyn (1995), 'A Traveller in Skirts: Quest and Conquest in the Travel Narratives of Isabella Bird', *Canadian Review of Comparative Literature/Revue Canadienne de Littérature Comparée* 22 (3–4): 587–600.

Bail, Paul (1998), *Anne Tyler: A Critical Companion*, Westport, CT: Greenwood.

Bannerjee, Debjani (1993), ' "In the Presence of History": The Representation of Past and Present Indias in Bharati Mukherjee's Fiction', in Emmanuel S. Nelson (ed.), *Bharati Mukherjee: Critical Perspectives*, New York: Garland, pp. 161–80.

Barnett, Pamela E. (1995), ' "My Picture of You Is, After All, the True Helga Crane": Portraiture and Identity in Nella Larsen's *Quicksand*', *Signs: Journal of Women in Culture and Society* 20 (3) (Spring): 575–600.

Barthes, Roland (1972), 'The Blue Guide', in *Mythologies*, trans. Annette Lavers, London: Cape, pp. 74–7.

Baucom, Ian (1999), 'Hydrographies', *The Geographical Review* 89 (2) 2: 301–13.

Baudrillard, Jean (1998), *America*, trans. Chris Turner, London: Verso.

Bell, Morag and Cheryl McEwan (1996), 'The Admission of Women Fellows to the Royal Geographical Society, 1892–1914; the Controversy and the Outcome', *The Geographical Journal* 162 (3): 295–312.

Besemeres, Mary (1998), 'Language and Self in Cross-Cultural Autobiography: Eva Hoffman's *Lost in Translation*', *Canadian Slavonic Papers* 40 (3–4): 327–44.

Bhabha, Homi K. [1994] (2006), *The Location of Culture*, London: Routledge.

Blackmer, Corinne E. (1993), 'African Masks and the Art of Passing in Gertrude Stein's "Melanctha" and Nella Larsen's "Passing" ', *Journal of the History of Sexuality* 4 (2): 230–63.

Brickhouse, Anna (2001), 'Nella Larsen and the Intertextual Geography of Quicksand', *African American Review* 35 (4): 533–60.

Brickhouse, Anna (2004), *Transamerican Literary Relations and the Nineteenth-Century Public Sphere*, Cambridge: Cambridge University Press.

Brody, Jennifer DeVere (1992), 'Clare Kendry's "True" Colors: Race and Class Conflict in Nella Larsen's *Passing*', *Callaloo* 15 (4): 1053–65.

Bromley, Roger (1996), 'A Concluding Essay: Narratives for a New Belonging-Writing in the Borderlands', in John C. Hawley (ed.), *Cross-Addressing: Resistance Literature and Cultural Borders*, Albany, NY: State University of New York Press, pp. 275–99.

Butler, Judith [1990] (1999), *Gender Trouble: Feminism and the Subversion of Identity*, New York: Routledge.

Butor, Michel (1992), 'Travel and Writing', in Michael Kowalewski (ed.), *Temperamental Journeys: Essays on the Modern Literature of Travel*, Athens, GA: University of Georgia Press, pp. 53–70.

Caesar, Judith (1995), 'The Foreigners in Anne Tyler's *Saint Maybe*', *Critique* 37 (1): 71–9.

Carchidi, Victoria (1995), ' "Orbiting": Bharati Mukherjee's KaleidoscopeVision', *MELUS* 20 (4): 91–101.

Carter-Sanborn, Kristin (1994), ' "We Murder Who We Were": *Jasmine* and the Violence of Identity', *American Literature* 66 (3): 573–93.

Chambers, Iain (1994), *Migrancy, Culture, Identity*, London: Routledge.

Clemmen, Yves. W. A (1997), 'Nella Larsen's *Quicksand*: A Narrative of Difference', *CLA Journal* 40 (4): 458–66.

Clifford, James [1997] (1999), *Routes: Travel and Translation in the Late Twentieth Century*, Cambridge, MA: Harvard University Press.

Cranny-Francis, Anne (1990), *Feminist Fiction: Feminist Uses of Generic Fiction*, New York: St Martin's Press.

Couser, G. Thomas (1996), 'Personal and Collective Memory in Paule Marshall's *Praisesong for the Widow* and Leslie Marmion Silko's *Ceremony*', in Amritjit Singh et al. (eds), *Memory and Cultural Politics: New Approaches to American Ethnic Literatures* (Boston, MA: Northeastern University Press, pp. 106–20.

Cresswell, Tim (1999), 'Embodiment, Power and the Politics of Mobility: The Case of Female Tramps and Hobos', *Transactions of the Institute of British Geographers* 24 (2): 175–92.

Crystall, Elyse, Jill Kuhnheim and Mary Layoun (1992), 'An Interview with Isabel Allende', *Contemporary Literature* 33 (4): 585–600.

Curtis, Barry and Claire Pajaczkowska (1994), ' "Getting There": Travel, Time and Narrative', in George Robertson et al. (eds), *Travellers' Tales: Narratives of Home and Displacement*, London: Routledge, pp. 199–215.

Davidson, Cathy N. (1987), *Revolution and the Word: The Rise of the Novel in America*, New York: Oxford University Press.

Davies, Carole Boyce (1987), 'Black Woman's Journey into Self: A Womanist Reading of Paule Marshall's *Praisesong for the Widow*', *Matatu: Journal for African Culture and Society* 1 (1): 19–34.

Davis, Thadious M. (1996), *Nella Larsen: Novelist of the Harlem Renaissance: A Woman's Life Unveiled*, Baton Rouge, LA: Louisiana State University Press.

Dayal, Samir (1993), 'Creating, Preserving, Destroying: Violence in Bharati Mukherjee's *Jasmine*', in Emmanuel S. Nelson (ed.), *Bharati Mukherjee: Critical Perspectives*, New York: Garland, pp. 65–88.

de Botton, Alain (2002), *The Art of Travel*, London: Hamish Hamilton.

de Hernandez, Jennifer Browdy (1997), 'On Home Ground: Politics, Location, and the Construction of Identity in Four American Women's Autobiographies', *MELUS* 22 (4): 21–38.

Dimock, Wai Chee (2006), 'Scales of Aggregration: Prenational, Subnational, Transnational', *American Literary History* 18 (2): 219–28.

Dittmar, Linda (1991), 'When Privilege is No Protection: The Woman Artist in *Quicksand* and *The House of Mirth*', in Suzanne W. Jones (ed.), *Writing the Woman Artist: Essays on Poetics, Politics and Portraiture*, Philadelphia, PA: University of Pennsylvania Press, pp. 133–54.

Domosh, Mona (1991), 'Toward a Feminist Historiography of Geography', *Transactions of the Institute of British Geographers* 16 (1): 95–104.

Donnell, Alison (1996), 'Writing for Resistance: Nationalism and Narratives of Liberation', in Joan Anim-Addo (ed.), *Framing the Word: Gender and Genre in Caribbean Women's Writing*, London: Whiting and Birch, 1996, pp. 28–36.

Drake, Jennifer (1999), 'Looting American Culture: Bharati Mukherjee's Immigrant Narratives', *Contemporary Literature* 40 (1) (1999): 60–84.

Durczak, Jerzy (1992), 'Multicultural Autobiography and Language: Richard Rodriguez and Eva Hoffman', in Jadwiga Maszewska (ed.), *Crossing Borders: American Literature and Other Artistic Media*, Lodz: Wydawnictwo Naukowe PWN, pp. 19–30.

Fachinger, Petra (2001), 'Lost in Nostalgia: The Autobiographies of Eva Hoffman and Richard Rodriguez', *MELUS* 265 (2): 111–27.

Fanetti, Susan (2005), 'Translating Self into Liminal Space: Eva Hoffman's Acculturation in/to a Postmodern World', *Women's Studies* 34: 405–19.

Fitz, Earl (2004), 'Inter-American Studies as an Emerging Field: The Future of a Discipline', *Vanderbilt e-Journal of Luso-Hispanic Studies* 1, http://ejournals.library.vanderbilt.edu/lusohispanic/viewarticle.php?id=20.

Fjellestad, Danuta Zadworna (1995), ' "The Insertion of the Self into the Space of Borderless Possibility": Eva Hoffman's Exiled Body', *MELUS* 20 (2): 133–47.

Foreman, P. Gabrielle (1992), 'Past-on Stories: History and the Magically Read, Morrison and Allende on Call', *Feminist Studies* 18 (2): 369–88.

Freeman, Carla (2001), 'Is Local: Global as Feminine: Masculine? Rethinking the Gender of Globalizations', *Signs* 26 (4): 1007–37.

Friedrich, Marianne M. (1999), 'Reconstructing Paradise: Eva Hoffman's *Lost in Translation*', *Yiddish* 11 (3–4): 159–65.

Frye, Northrop (1971), *The Bush Garden: Essays on the Canadian Imagination*, Toronto: Anansi.

Fussell, Paul [1980] (1982), *Abroad*, Oxford: Oxford University Press.

Garber, Marjorie [1992] (1993), *Vested Interests: Cross-Dressing and Cultural Anxiety*, London: Penguin.

Gerstenberger, Donna (1994), 'Everybody Speaks', in Dale Salwak (ed.), *Anne Tyler as Novelist*, Iowa City, IA: University of Iowa Press, pp. 138–46.

Giles, Paul (2001), *Transatlantic Insurrections: British Culture and the Formation of American Literature, 1730–1860*, Philadelphia, PA: University of Pennsylvania.

Giles, Paul (2002), *Virtual Americas: Transnational Fictions and the Transatlantic Imaginary*, Durham, NC: Duke University Press.

Giles, Paul (2006), *Atlantic Republic: The American Tradition in English Literature*, Oxford: Oxford University Press.

Gillman, Susan, Kirsten Silva Greusz and Rob Wilson (2004), 'Worlding American Studies', *Comparative American Studies* 2 (3): 259–70.

Gilroy, Paul (1993), *The Black Atlantic: Modernity and Double Consciousness*, London: Verso.

Gitenstein, R. Barbara (1997), 'Eva Hoffman: Conflicts and Continuities of Self', in Thomas S. Gladsky and Rita Holmes Gladsky (eds), *Something of My Very Own to Say: American Women Writers of Polish Descent*, New York: Eastern European Monographs/Columbia University Press, pp. 261–76.

Gough, Elizabeth (2004), 'Vision and Division: Voyeurism in the Works of Isabel Allende', *Journal of Modern Literature* 27 (4): 93–120.

Gray, Jeffrey (1994), 'Essence and the Mulatto Traveler: Europe as Embodiment in Nella Larsen's "Quicksand" ', *Novel: A Forum on Fiction* 27 (3): 257–70.

Gray, Rockwell (1992), 'Travel', in Michael Kowalewski (ed.), *Temperamental Journeys: Essays on the Modern Literature of Travel*, Athens, GA: University of Georgia Press, pp. 33–50.

Grewal, Inderpal (1996), *Home and Harem: Nation, Gender, Empire, and the Cultures of Travel*, London: Leicester University Press.

Grewal, Inderpal (2005), *Transnational America: Feminisms, Disaporas, Neoliberalisms*, Durham, NC: Duke University Press.

Grewal, Inderpal and Caren Kaplan (eds) (1994), *Scattered Hegemonies: Postmodernity and Transnational Feminist Practices*, Minneapolis, MN: University of Minnesota Press.

Grice, Helena (2003), 'Who Speaks for US? Bharati Mukherjee's Fictions and the Politics of Immigration', *Comparative American Studies* 1 (1): 81–96.

Halliwell, Martin (2005), *Transatlantic Modernism: Moral Dilemmas in Modern Fiction*, Edinburgh: Edinburgh University Press.

Hannerz, Ulf (1996), *Transnational Connections: Culture, People, Places*, London: Routledge.

Hart, Patricia (1989), *Narrative Magic in the Fiction of Isabel Allende*, Rutherford, NJ: Associated University Presses.

Hassan, Ihab (1990), *Selves at Risk: Patterns of Quest in Contemporary American Letters*, Madison, WI: University of Wisconsin Press.

Hemingway, Ernest [1960] (2000), *A Moveable Feast*, London: Vintage.

Henderson, Heather (1992), 'The Travel Writer and the Text: "My Giant Goes with Me Wherever I Go"', in Michael Kowalewski (ed.), *Temperamental Journeys: Essays on the Modern Literature of Travel*, Athens, GA: University of Georgia Press, pp. 230–48.

Hirsch, Marianne (1994), 'Pictures of a Displaced Girlhood', in Angelika Bammer (ed.), *Displacements: Cultural Identities in Question*, Bloomington, IN: Indiana University Press, pp. 71–89.

Hoffman, Eva (1999a), 'The New Nomads', in André Aciman (ed.), *Letters of Transit: Reflections on Exile, Identity, Language, and Loss*, New York: The New Press, pp. 35–63.

Hoffman, Eva [1993] (1999b), *Exit Into History: A Journey through the New Eastern Europe*, London: Vintage.

Hoffman, Eva [1998] (1999c), *Shtetl: The History of a Small Town and an Extinguished World*, London: Vintage.

Hoffman, Eva [2004] (2005), *After Such Knowledge: A Meditation on the Aftermath of the Holocaust*, London: Vintage.

Hones, Sheila and Julia Leyda (2004), 'Towards a Critical Geography of American Studies', *Comparative American Studies* 2 (2): 185–203.

Hoppe, John K. (1999), 'The Technological Hybrid as Post-American: Cross-Cultural Genetics in *Jasmine*', *MELUS* 24 (4): 137–56.

Hostetler, Ann E. (1990), 'The Aesthetics of Race and Gender in Nella Larsen's *Quicksand*', *PMLA* 105 (1): 35–46.

Huggan, Graham (2000), 'Counter-Travel Writing and Post-Coloniality', in Liselotte Glage (ed.), *Being/s in Transit: Travelling, Migration, Dislocation*, Amsterdam: Rodopi, pp. 37–59.

Hughes, Langston [1956] (1998), *I Wonder as I Wander*, in Alasdair Pettinger (ed.), *Always Elsewhere: Travels of the Black Atlantic*, London: Cassell, 1998.

Hutchinson, George (1997), 'Nella Larsen and the Veil of Race', *American Literary History* 9 (2) (1997): 329–49.

Ingram, Susan (1996), 'When Memory is Cross-Cultural Translation: Eva Hoffman's Schizophrenic Autobiography', *Tradition, Terminology, Redaction* 9 (1): 259–76.

Kanaganayakam, Chelva (1996), 'Exiles and Expatriates', in Bruce King (ed.), *New National and Post-Colonial Literatures*, Oxford: Oxford University Press, pp. 201–13.

Kanhai, Rosanne (1996), ' "Sensing Designs in History's Muddles": Global Feminism and the Postcolonial Novel', *Modern Language Studies* 26 (4): 119–30.

Kaplan, Caren (1994), 'The Politics of Location as Transnational Feminist Critical Practice', in Inderpal Grewal and Caren Kaplan (eds), *Scattered Hegemonies: Postmodernity and Transnational Feminist Practices*, Minneapolis, MN: University of Minnesota Press, pp. 137–52.

Kaplan, Caren (1995), ' "A World Without Boundaries:" The Body Shop's Trans/National Geographics', *Social Text* 43: 45–66.

Kaplan, Caren (1996), *Questions of Travel: Postmodern Discourses of Displacement*, Durham, NC: Duke University Press.

Karpinski, Eva C. (1996), 'Negotiating the Self: Eva Hoffman's *Lost in Translation* and the Question of Immigrant Autobiography', *Canadian Ethnic Studies* 28 (1): 127–35.

Kaufman, Will and Heidi Slettedahl Macpherson (eds) (2000), *Transatlantic Studies*, Lanham, MD: University Press of America.

Kellman, Steven G. (1998), 'Lost in the Promised Land: Eva Hoffman Revises Mary Antin', *Proof Texts: A Journal of Jewish Literary History* 18 (2): 149–59.

King, Russell, Paul White and John Connell (eds) (1995), *Writing across Worlds: Literature and Migration*, London: Routledge.

Kirby, Kathleen M. (1993), 'Thinking through the Boundary: The Politics of Location, Subjects, and Space', *Boundary II* 20 (2): 173–89.

Koshy, Susan (1994), 'The Geography of Female Subjectivity: Ethnicity, Gender, and Diaspora', *Diaspora* 3 (1): 69–84.

Kowaleski, Michael (ed.) (1992a), *Temperamental Journeys: Essays on the Modern Literature of Travel*, Athens, GA: University of Georgia Press.

Kowalewski, Michael (1992b), 'Introduction: The Modern Literature of Travel', in Michael Kowalewski (ed.), *Temperamental Journeys: Essays on the Modern Literature of Travel*, Athens, GA: University of Georgia Press, pp. 1–16.

Kristeva, Julia (1991), *Strangers to Ourselves*, London: Harvester Wheatsheaf.

Kroetsch, Robert (1989), *The Lovely Treachery of Words: Essays Selected and New*, Toronto: Oxford University Press.

Krupnick, Mark (1993), 'Assimilation in Recent American Jewish Autobiographies', *Contemporary Literature* 34 (3): 451–74.

Larson, Charles (1992), *An Intimation of Things Distant: The Collected Fiction of Nella Larsen*, New York: Anchor.

Larson, Charles R. (1993), *Invisible Darkness: Jean Toomer and Nella Larsen*, Iowa City, IA: University of Iowa.

Lawrence, Karen R. (1994), *Penelope Voyages: Women and Travel in the British Literary Tradition*, Ithaca, NY: Cornell University Press.

Layoun, Mary (1994), 'The Female Body and "Transnational" Reproduction; or, Rape by Any Other Name?', in Inderpal Grewal and Caren Kaplan (eds), *Scattered Hegemonies: Postmodernity and Transnational Feminist Practices*, Minneapolis, MN: University of Minnesota Press, pp. 63–75.

Lazarus, Emma (1903), 'The New Colossus', http://www.legallanguage.com/poems/statuelibertypoem.html

Lehmann, Sophia (1998), 'In Search of a Mother Tongue: Locating Home in Diaspora', *MELUS* 23 (4): 101–18.

Levine, Philippa (2004), *Gender and Empire*, Oxford University Press.

Lewis Martin W. (1999), 'Dividing the Ocean Sea', *The Geographical Review* 89 (2): 188–214.

Lewis, Martin W. and Karen Wigen (1999), 'A Maritime Response to the Crisis in Area Studies', *The Geographical Review* 89 (2): 161–8.

Linebaugh, Peter and Marcus Rediker (2000), *The Many Headed Hydra: Sailors, Slaves, Commoners, and the History of the Revolutionary Atlantic*, Boston, MA: Beacon Press.

MacCannell, Dean [1976] (1999), *The Tourist: A New Theory of the Leisure Class*, Berkeley, CA: University of California Press.

McClintock, Anne (1995), *Imperial Leather: Race, Gender and Sexuality in the Colonial Contest*, Routledge: New York.

McDowell, Deborah E. (1995), *'The Changing Same': Black Women's Literature, Criticism, and Theory*, Bloomington, IN: Indiana University Press.

Macpherson, Heidi Slettedahl (2000), *Women's Movement: Escape as Transgression in North American Feminist Fiction*, Amsterdam: Rodopi.

Macpherson, Heidi Slettedahl (2004), 'Women's Travel Narratives and the Politics of Location: Somewhere in Between', in Kristi Siegel (ed.), *Gender, Genre and Identity in Women's Travel Writing*, New York: Peter Lang, pp. 193–208.

Macpherson, Heidi Slettedahl and Will Kaufman (eds) (2002), *New Perspectives in Transatlantic Studies*, Lanham, MD: University Press of America.

Mills, C. Wright (1951), *White Collar: The American Middle Classes*, New York: Oxford University Press.

Mills, Sara [1991] (1993), *Discourses of Difference: An Analysis of Women's Travel Writing and Colonialism*, London: Routledge.

Minh-ha, Trinh T. (1994), 'Other Than Myself/My Other Self', in George Robertson et al. (eds), *Travellers' Tales: Narratives of Home and Displacement*, London: Routledge, pp. 9–26.

Monda, Kimberly (1997), 'Self-Delusion and Self-Sacrifice in Nella Larsen's Quicksand', *African American Review* 31 (1): 23–39.

Montenegro, David (1991), *Points of Departure: International Writers on Writing and Politics*, Ann Arbor, MI: University of Michigan Press.

Morris, Mary (1992), 'Women and Journeys: Inner and Outer', in Michael Kowalewski (ed.), *Temperamental Journeys: Essays on the Modern Literature of Travel*, Athens, GA: University of Georgia Press, pp. 25–32.

Morrison, Toni [1987] (1988), *Beloved*, London: Picador.

Mukherjee, Bharati (1997), 'American Dreamer', *Mother Jones*, www.motherjones.com/commentary/columns/1992/01/mukherjee.html

Mulvey, Christopher (1990), *Transatlantic Manners: Social Patterns in Nineteenth-Century Anglo-American Travel Literature*, Cambridge: Cambridge University Press.

Muthyala, John (2003), ' "America" in Transit', *Comparative American Studies* 1 (4): 395–420.

Muthyala, John (2006), *Reworlding America: Myth, History, and Narrative*, Athens, OH: Ohio University Press.

Nelson, Emmanuel S. (ed.) (1993), *Bharati Mukherjee: Critical Perspectives*, New York: Garland.

Nethersole, Reingard (2001), 'Models of Globalization', *PMLA* 116 (3): 638–49.

Newman, Lance, Joel Pace and Chris Koenig-Woodyard (eds) (2006), *Transatlantic Romanticism: An Anthology of British, American, and Canadian Literature, 1767–1867*, New York: Longman.

'Obituary Note' (1905), *Journal of the Royal African Society* 4 (14): 261.

Oster, Judith (1998), 'See(k)ing the Self: Mirrors and Mirroring in Bicultural Texts', *MELUS* 23 (4): 59–83.

Pettinger, Alasdair (1998), 'Introduction', in *Always Elsewhere: Travels of the Black Atlantic*, London: Cassell.

Pratt, Mary Louise [1992] (2000), *Imperial Eyes: Travel Writing and Transculturation*, London: Routledge.

Proefriedt, William A. (1989–90), 'The Immigrant or "Outsider" Experience as Metaphor for becoming an Educated Person in the Modern World: Mary Antin, Richard Wright and Eva Hoffman', *MELUS* 16 (2): 77–89.

Quiello, Rose (1994), 'Breakdowns and Breakthroughs: The Hysterical Use of Language', in Dale Salwak (ed.), *Anne Tyler as Novelist*, Iowa City, IA: University of Iowa Press, pp. 50–64.

Radhakrishnan, R. (2001), 'Globalization, Desire, and the Politics of Representation', *Comparative Literature* 53 (4): 315–32.

Rediker, Marcus (1987), *Between the Devil and the Deep Blue Sea*, Cambridge: Cambridge University Press.

Rhodes, Chip (1994), 'Writing of the New Negro: The Construction of Consumer Desire in the Twenties', *Journal of American Studies* 28 (2): 191–207.

Roach, Joseph (1996), *Cities of the Dead*, New York: Columbia University Press.

Roberts, Kimberley (1997), 'The Clothes Make the Woman: The Symbolics of Prostitution in Nella Larsen's *Quicksand* and Claude McKay's *Home to Harlem*', *Tulsa Studies in Women's Literature* 16 (1): 107–30.

Robertson, George (1994), 'As the World Turns', in George Robertson et al. (eds), *Travellers' Tales: Narratives of Home and Displacement*, London: Routledge, pp. 1–6.

Robertson, George, Melinda Mash, Lisa Tickner, Jon Bird, Barry Curtis and Tim Putnam (eds) (1994), *Travellers' Tales: Narratives of Home and Displacement*, London: Routledge.

Robertson, Mary F. (1985), 'Anne Tyler: Medusa Points and Contact Points', in Catherine Rainwater and William J. Scheick (eds), *Contemporary American Women Writers: Narrative Strategies*, Lexington, KY: University Press of Kentucky, pp. 119–42.

Rodden, John (2001), 'Isabel Allende, Fortune's Daughter', *Hopscotch: A Cultural Review* 2 (4): 32–9.

Roy, Anindyo (1993), 'The Aesthetics of an (Un)willing Immigrant: Bharati Mukherjee's *Days and Nights in Calcutta* and *Jasmine*', in Emmanuel S. Nelson (ed.), *Bharati Mukherjee: Critical Perspectives*, New York: Garland, pp. 127–41.

Rubenstein, Roberta (2004), *Home Matters: Longing and Belonging, Nostalgia and Mourning in Women's Fiction*, Houndmills: Palgrave.

Rushdie, Salman (1992), *Imaginary Homelands: Essays and Criticism 1981–1991*, London: Granta.

Said, Edward (2000), *Reflections on Exile and Other Literary and Cultural Essays*, London: Granta.

Salwak, Dale (ed.) (1994), *Anne Tyler as Novelist*, Iowa City, IA: University of Iowa Press.

Sarup, Madan (1994), 'Home and Identity' in George Robertson et al. (eds), *Travellers' Tales: Narratives of Home and Displacement*, London: Routledge, pp. 93–104.

Savin, Ada (1994), 'Passage to America or When East Meets West – Eva Hoffman's *Lost in Translation: A Life in a New Language*', *Caliban* 31: 57–63.

Sieber, Harry (1977), *The Picaresque*, London: Methuen.

Silverman, Debra B. (1993), 'Nella Larsen's *Quicksand*: Untangling the Webs of Exoticism', *African American Review* 27 (4) (1993): 599–614.

Skvorecky, Josef [1977] (1986), *The Engineer of Human Souls*, London: Picador.

Spivak, Gayatri Chakravorty (1985), 'Three Women's Texts and a Critique of Imperialism', *Critical Inquiry* 12: 243–61.

Stamm, Ulrike (2000), 'The Role of Nature in Two Women's Travel Accounts: Appropriate and Escape', in Liselotte Glage (ed.), *Being/s in Transit: Travelling, Migration, Dislocation*, Amsterdam: Rodopi, pp. 155–72.

Stoddart, David R. (1991), 'Do We Need a Feminist Historiography of Geography, And If We Do, What Should It Be?', *Transactions of the Institute of British Geographers* 16 (4): 484–7.

Stout, Janis P. (1998), *Through the Window, Out the Door: Women's Narratives of Departure, from Austin and Cather to Tyler, Morrison and Didion*, Tuscaloosa, AL: University of Alabama Press.

Street, Sarah (2002), *Transatlantic Crossings: British Feature Films in the United States*, London: Continuum.

Sweeney, Fionnghuala (2006), 'The Black Atlantic, American Studies and the Politics of the Postcolonial', *Comparative American Studies* 4 (2): 115–33.

Tate, Claudia (1995), 'Desire and Death in *Quicksand*, by Nella Larsen', *American Literary History* 7 (2): 234–60.

Tatsumi, Takayuki (2004), 'Literary History on the Road: Transatlantic Crossings and Transpacific Crossovers', *PMLA* 119 (1): 91–102.

Templin, Charlotte (1994), 'Tyler's Literary Reputation', in Dale Salwak (ed.), *Anne Tyler as Novelist*, Iowa City, IA: University of Iowa Press, pp. 175–96.

Thadious M. Davis (1994), *Nella Larsen: Novelists of the Harlem Renaissance: A Women's Life Unveiled*, Baton Rouge, LA: Louisiana University Press.

The United States Passport: Past, Present, and Future (1976), Washington, DC: US Government Printing Office.

Thelen, David (1999), 'The Nation and Beyond: Transnational Perspectives on United States History', *The Journal of American History* 86 (3): 965–75.

Tseëlon, Efrat (2001), 'Introduction: Masquerade and Identities', in Efrat Tseëlon (ed.), *Masquerade and Identities: Essays on Gender, Sexuality and Marginality*, London: Routledge, pp. 1–17.

Tucker, Lindsey (1994), *Textual Escap(e)ades: Mobility, Maternity, and Textuality in Contemporary Fiction by Women*, Westport, CT: Greenwood.

Urry, John [1990] (2002), *The Tourist Gaze*, London: Sage.

Vandersee, Charles (1994), 'Intertextual, International, Industrial Strength', *American Literary History* 6 (3): 409–33.

Wald, Priscilla (1998), 'Minefields and Meeting Grounds: Transnational Analyses and American Studies', *American Literary History* 10 (1): 199–218.

Wall, Cheryl A. (1986), 'Passing for What? Aspects of Identity in Nella Larsen's Novels', *Black American Literature Forum* 20 (1–2): 99–111.

Wall, Cheryl A. (1995), *Women of the Harlem Renaissance*, Bloomington, IN: Indiana University Press.

White, Paul (1995), 'Geography, Literature and Migration', in Russell King et al. (eds), *Writing across Worlds: Literature and Migration*, London: Routledge, pp. 1–19.

Wickramagamage, Carmen (1992), 'Relocation as Positive Act: The Immigrant Experience in Bharati Mukherjee's Novels', *Diaspora: A Journal of Transnational Studies* 2 (2): 171–200.

Willrich, Patricia Rowe (1992), 'Watching through Windows: A Perspective on Anne Tyler', *The Virginia Quarterly Review* 68: 497–516.

Wilson, Rob and Wimal Dissanayake (1996), 'Introduction: Tracking the Global/Local', in Rob Wilson and Wimal Dissanayake (eds),

Global/Local: Cultural Production and the Transnational Imaginary, Durham, NC: Duke University Press, pp. 1–20.

Young, Elizabeth (1999), *Disarming the Nation: Women's Writing and the American Civil War*, Chicago, IL: University of Chicago Press.

Young, Robert J. C. (1995), *Colonial Desire: Hybridity in Theory, Culture, and Race*, London: Routledge.

INDEX